The EVERYTHING

Learning Spanish Book

Second Edition

Dear Reader,

I know learning a new language isn't easy—I, too, have had to start from the beginning and learn a language that I now call my own. It took a lot of effort on my part, but it was also a great deal of fun. It took me places that I never expected.

Whatever your reason for learning Spanish, I'm glad you're getting started. Today, Spanish is one of the most widely spoken languages in the world. Just think—Spanish-language speakers are everywhere, from Argentina to Puerto Rico to Spain to the United States. By learning just one language, you can tap into so many cultures!

But before you can go off and explore on your own, you need to sit down and do some studying. Don't get discouraged—keep chipping away at memorizing vocabulary words and practicing Spanish grammar. And try your best to find ways to practice what you're learning. It's the only way to really be able to hold on to it.

Good luck!

Julie Gutin

The EVERYTHING® Series

Editorial

Publisher	Gary M. Krebs
Director of Product Development	Paula Munier
Managing Editor	Laura M. Daly
Associate Copy Chief	Sheila Zwiebel
Acquisitions Editor	Lisa Laing
Development Editor	Katie McDonough
Associate Production Editor	Casey Ebert
Technical Review:	Strictly Spanish, LLC

Production

Director of Manufacturing	Susan Beale
Associate Director of Production	Michelle Roy Kelly
Prepress	Erick DaCosta
	Matt LeBlanc
Design and Layout	Heather Barrett
	Brewster Brownville
	Colleen Cunningham
	Jennifer Oliveira
Series Cover Artist	Barry Littmann

Visit the entire Everything® Series at *www.everything.com*

THE

EVERYTHING®

LEARNING SPANISH BOOK

Second Edition

Speak, write, and understand
basic Spanish in no time

Julie Gutin

Adams Media
Avon, Massachusetts

To my family

An Everything® Series Book.
Everything® and everything.com® are registered trademarks of F+W Publications, Inc.
Published by Adams Media, an F+W Publications Company
57 Littlefield Street, Avon, MA 02322 U.S.A.
www.adamsmedia.com

ISBN 10: 1-59869-173-2
ISBN 13: 978-1-59869-173-3

Printed in the United States of America.

J   I   H   G   F   E   D   C   B

Library of Congress Cataloging-in-Publication Data
is available from the publisher.

This publication is designed to provide accurate and authoritative information with regard to the subject matter covered. It is sold with the understanding that the publisher is not engaged in rendering legal, accounting, or other professional advice. If legal advice or other expert assistance is required, the services of a competent professional person should be sought.

—From a *Declaration of Principles* jointly adopted by a Committee of the American Bar Association and a Committee of Publishers and Associations

Many of the designations used by manufacturers and sellers to distinguish their products are claimed as trademarks. Where those designations appear in this book and Adams Media was aware of a trademark claim, the designations have been printed with initial capital letters.

This book is available at quantity discounts for bulk purchases.
For information, please call 1-800-289-0963.

Contents

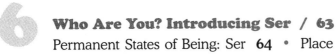

Introduction

▶ WELCOME TO THE second edition of *The Everything® Learning Spanish Book* and the exciting and diverse world of Spanish! Perhaps you chose this book because you want to be able to communicate with some of your coworkers, neighbors, or clients. Perhaps you want to feel more comfortable traveling in countries where Spanish is the national language. Maybe you enjoy listening to Latin jazz and would like to understand the lyrics to some of your favorite songs. Whatever your reasons for learning this popular language, you've come to the right place.

Don't be surprised when at some point in your mastery of Spanish you find yourself rewarded in ways you had not even considered. When you find yourself in Mexico City and need to ask for directions, imagine the sense of accomplishment you will feel as you approach the first person you see and say confidently, *"¡Perdón! ¿Dónde está la calle San José?"* (Excuse me, where is San Jose Street?) Imagine your feelings when the person answers in Spanish and you are able to understand the directions!

Learning Spanish will expand your intellectual horizons. You will be in a position to learn about Hispanic cultures from the inside—by listening to Latin music, reading books in Spanish, and conversing with native speakers. You will have more personal opportunities to witness how other people live day by day in your own neighborhood, on their own terms. Not only will you be able to listen to their opinions on family, life, work, and society in general, but you will be able to come to mutual understanding by sharing your own.

Knowing Spanish might even get you a promotion! Given the trend toward globalization, you will be able to take advantage of many opportunities that already exist, but that you currently know nothing about. The business opportunities are obvious—a larger market for you to sell to or find employment in.

To be sure, learning a new language is a difficult undertaking, but if you persevere, the results will be worth your effort. And there's more good news—Spanish isn't as foreign a language as you might think. Take a quick look at the chapters of this book. I'm sure you'll recognize a few words or phrases here and there. If you ever studied Spanish or another Romance language, something did stick, even if you don't realize it. Even if you've never studied a foreign language before, you'll discover that you already know a few things. Don't feel like you are starting from scratch. You'll see that even those years of studying English grammar will be helpful.

You are about to embark on a very exhilarating and at times frustrating journey that will lead you to look at your own life differently and will reward you with experiences as yet unimagined. Whatever your interests are in learning Spanish, this book will help you achieve the goals that you have set for yourself. *Buena suerte* (good luck) in your endeavor!

This project couldn't have happened without Frank Zambrano, who wrote the first edition of this book, and Lisa Laing, my acquisitions editor, who worked with me every step of the way.

A lot of credit for this book also goes to the rest of the Adams team—Gary Krebs, Laura Daly, Katie McDonough, and Casey Ebert.

I would like to acknowledge all of my Spanish teachers—your hard work made this book possible. I couldn't have done it without you!

As always, a big thanks to my family for all their love and support. And to ShihYan—thanks for everything.

Chapter 1

Starting with the Basics

This chapter will introduce you to the Spanish language and start you off on the right track with advice on how to study. Remember, to be rewarding, learning a new language should always be enjoyable, but you must dedicate attention and time for this endeavor in order for you to make progress.

Developing Basic Study Skills

If you are full of enthusiasm to sit down and learn *español* (Spanish) at one go—*¡relájate!*—stop and relax. Learning a language is not like crash dieting; it's a gradual process that requires planning and concentration. Here is what you should know as you incorporate learning Spanish into your everyday life.

Things to Remember

Avoid negative thinking—that you can never master a foreign language, or that it's impossible for you to pronounce certain words correctly. Relax, and concentrate on what you do know and *can* do, and then keep adding on to that. If you can't think of a particular word, choose another one to help you explain yourself. If you can't understand what someone is saying to you, ask him to repeat.

The expressive potential of a sentence is often more than the sum of its parts. Don't just concentrate on memorizing words—you also need to know how to put these words together to make meaningful statements. Learning whole phrases will help you make your point quicker.

ALERT!

The glossaries in this book are for quick reference only. To really have Spanish vocabulary available to you at your fingertips, invest in an English-to-Spanish and Spanish-to-English dictionary. Choose the one that best suits you, the one you will have completely dog-eared within a month.

Use new phrases as soon as you have learned them and as many times as possible. Don't wait until you have everything down perfectly before you begin using Spanish in conversation. When it comes to languages, perfect fluency and pronunciation are myths. Your goal should be to get out there and start talking as soon as possible.

Get online. You're just a click of a mouse away from finding free instruction, opportunities to practice, reference materials, and cultural information, as well as paid online Spanish courses. For those who have yet to master the World Wide Web, the library can be a good source of additional information.

Immerse yourself in the world of Spanish. Eat at Spanish and Latin American restaurants. Listen to Latin music: *boleros, cumbias, flamenco, merengue, pasillos, pasodoble, salsas, sevillanas, el son, tango, rancheras,* and *rock.* Go out to Latin dance clubs. Seek out movies in Spanish playing at international film festivals, and rent Spanish films on video or DVD—most will offer subtitles or dubbed tracks in Spanish. Read bilingual books and magazines (check to see if your area has a local *Extra Bilingual Newspaper*). Try watching Spanish television—at first you won't understand it, but it might be fun to guess what is happening.

FACT

There are at least four major Spanish-language networks available in the United States: *Galavisión* (cable), *TeleFutura, Telemundo,* and *Univision.* Check your local listings for these and other offerings.

Combine your hobbies and interests with the study of Spanish. If you love playing tennis, learn how to say everything you know about the game in Spanish. Religion, politics, work, and recreation all have their Spanish vocabulary.

What You Shouldn't Do

Don't force yourself to spend hours at a time learning Spanish—you don't want to make studying a chore. Instead, set up study periods of about fifteen to twenty minutes a day, five days a week, and take the time to review instead of rushing on to learn new material.

Most importantly, don't panic. Take your time to learn new material, find somebody to answer your questions, look up words in the dictionary, and don't allow yourself to be intimidated by anything. Make mistakes and learn from them. When you goof up, you can either look mortified or just laugh about it—the choice is up to you.

Making the Most of the Spanish Environment

Focus your attention on all things Spanish that you find in your daily life. Put yourself in situations where you have no choice but to use your Spanish. Begin to think in Spanish.

When you are in the thick of things, listen for key words. Try to identify the verb. Are there any pronouns you can hook some meaning to? Does the word vaguely remind you of a word in English? Forget about trying to decode every single word—getting the main ideas first will help you fill in the details.

Listen for familiar intonation patterns and pay attention to the speaker's gestures. When you speak, don't be afraid to gesture as well. Nod your head and smile when you understand or agree. Twist your flat horizontal palm back and forth for "so-so." Use your thumb and forefinger to indicate "a little bit." Cover your nose when something smells awful. Some gestures seem universal; others are tied to the language, culture, or region. Be observant and proactive in investigating what common gestures are appropriate in any region you visit. You should be aware that some gestures might be misinterpreted—be especially careful with the "okay" hand sign.

To ask someone to clarify or repeat something, use the following phrases:

Perdón. ¿Cómo? **Excuse me. What?**
¿Me lo repite más despacio, **Can you repeat it [what you said]**
por favor? **for me more slowly, please?**

Remember to relax and smile. Your audience is having as much trouble understanding you as you are having speaking. They want you to succeed. Take a deep breath and have a sense of humor about your mistakes. A smile goes a long way.

What You Already Know

In many places around the United States, Spanish is encountered at every turn—on street signs, on buses, at banks, and at restaurants. As soon as people begin learning Spanish, they discover that they know more Spanish than they had originally thought. In fact, Spanish is all over the world. Given the number of countries where Spanish is the official language, it most certainly ranks as one of the most widely spoken languages.

Recognizing Spanish-Sounding Words

To prove that you know more Spanish than you think you do, take a little quiz. Take a look at the following list, and see how many words you can understand.

accidente	cruel	motor
actor	doctor	musical
adorable	elefante	natural
animal	error	plan
asistir	famoso	popular
atractivo	favor	potente
auto	fútbol	presidente
autor	honorable	radio
catedral	hospital	respetable
central	hotel	simple
cereal	humor	taxi
ciclista	idea	teléfono
color	importante	usual
conductor	información	visible
convertible	inventor	
criminal	local	

Although you might not yet know how to pronounce these words in Spanish, you should be able to figure out what they mean, because all of these words are cognates. Cognates are words in different languages that share a similar meaning and spelling because they originated from the same word. True cognates share the same meaning. Pure cognates are spelled identically in both languages. False cognates share a common origin and spelling, but have completely different meanings.

Words such as *actor, animal, central, error, hospital, idea, natural, radio,* and *taxi* are true pure cognates. (Note that even though these words are spelled the same way in English and in Spanish, the pronunciations are different. You'll learn pronunciation guidelines and accents in the next chapter.) Words like *accidente, autor, elefante, presidente,* and *teléfono* are true cognates—they share similar but not exactly identical spelling.

But some cognates are false—although the pairs may look similar, they carry different meanings in different languages. Here's why: Many cognates between English and Spanish originated from Latin—hence the words "Latino" and "Latin America." Over time, these words gained new meanings in each language, and ended up evolving in completely different ways:

- *asistir:* "to attend" (not "to assist")
- *anciano:* "elderly man" (not "ancient")
- *carta:* "letter," when referring to a form of written correspondence (not "cart" or "card")
- *chanza:* "joke" (not "chance")
- *constipado:* "congested," as when suffering from a cold (not "constipated")
- *delito:* "crime" (not "delight")
- *embarazada:* "pregnant" (not "embarrassed"—though misusing this word could certainly lead to embarrassment!)
- *fútbol:* "soccer" (not "football")
- *recordar:* "to remember" (not "to record")

Learning the Common Suffixes

From the true pure cognates, you may notice a one-to-one correspondence in Spanish and English of the following suffixes: *–al*, *–ble*, and *–or.*

–al (pertaining or related to; an extension of; a place)		
criminal	pertaining to crime	*crimen* (crime)
hospital	place for hospice and treatment	*hospedar* (to receive the needy)
usual	an extension of use, usual	*usar* (to use)
–ble (having the ability or aptitude to or capacity of; this suffix transforms verbs into adjectives)		
adorable	adorable, capable of being adored	*adorar* (to adore)
convertible	convertible, capable of being converted	*convertir* (to convert)

-or (agents th...

	vents	*inventar* (to invent)
		amar (to love)

...nings of the words that use them. A
...r lengthy. Here are a few:

...d –or

		–or
		auditor
		compositor
		destructor
		detector
		editor
		inferior
		inspector
		–or
		instructor
		mentor
f...		*pastor*
ir...		*profesor*
la...	*...tral*	*protector*
mi...le	*oficial*	*reflector*
negociable	*original*	*rumor*
organizable	*parcial*	*seductor*
ostensible	*racional*	*superior*
presentable	*tradicional*	*valor*
preferible	*universal*	*vigor*

From the other cognates, you see various suffixes that are familiar, but just a little off:

–aje (pertaining to, particularly broadened to a collection; similar to English "–age")

bagaje	military baggage	
equipaje	baggage	*equipo* (equipment)

–ano/–ana (pertaining to origin, location; relating to beliefs and affiliations; similar to English "–an")

americano, americana	American (male, female)
anciano, anciana	an elderly man, woman

–ante/–ente (related to an event, the nature of, or an agent; similar to "–ant" and "–ing" in English)

accidente	an unexpected event	*accidentar* (to produce an unexpected event)
importante	something of great effect	*importar* (to import or to cause to matter)
potente	of powerful nature	*poder* (to be able to do; power)
presidente	one who presides	*presidir* (to hold a group's most important post)

–ción/–sión (abstraction of an act or state of being; similar to the English "–tion" and "–sion")

atención	attention	*atender* (to pay attention)
información	information	*informar* (to inform)

–ico/–ica (relating to; being similar to; similar to the English "–ic" and "–al")

físico	physical, physicist	*física* (physics)
idéntico	identical	*identidad* (identity)

–ista (pertaining to one who does; similar to English "–ist")

ciclista	one who rides a bicycle	*bicicleta* (bicycle)
periodista	reporter, one who writes for a newspaper	*periódico* (newspaper)

–ivo/–iva (relating to an action; expresses tendency, disposition, or function; similar to English "–ive")

atractivo	attractive	*atraer* (to attract)
extensivo	extensive	*extender* (to extend)

–oso/–osa (relating to possession or characteristic; similar to English "–ous," "–ful," and "–y")		
asqueroso	disgusting	asco (disgust)
famoso	famous	fama (fame)

–ura (abstraction of an act or state of being; similar to English "–ture," "–ure," and "–ness")		
criatura	baby, small child	criar (to breed and rear)
cultura	culture	culto (cultured)

Other suffixes to remember include those in the following tables:

–ario/–aria (pertaining to the subject; relating to an act or thing; similar to English "–ary")		
millonario	millionaire	millón (million)
voluntario	voluntary	voluntad (free will)

–ncia (relating to an act or state; result of an action; abstraction; similar to English "–nce" and "–ncy")		
abstinencia	abstinence	abstener (abstain)
elegancia	elegance	elegante (elegant)
insistencia	insistence	insistir (to insist)

–dad (relating to an abstraction and a state of being; similar to English "–ty," "–ness," and "–hood")		
brevedad	brevity	breve (brief)
claridad	clarity	claro (clear, light)
enfermedad	sickness, disease	enfermo (sick)

–ismo (pertaining to an action or practice; state or condition; principles similar to "–ism")		
atletismo	athleticism	atleta (athlete)
idealismo	idealism	idea (idea)

–mente (pertaining to the manner, the timing, and the place of an action; similar to "–ly")		
afortunadamente	fortunately	fortuna (fortune)
relativamente	relatively	relacionar (to relate)

You already know so much Spanish! Take a look at all the words you know again. Look up the words you're not sure of. There will be times when you find words that are so obviously close to the English, that you wonder why you didn't figure it out on your own. Take heart. When that happens, you probably will never have to look that word up again.

Chapter 2

Pronunciation I: The Alphabet and Vowels

Now that you're convinced that you already know a lot of Spanish words, the issue comes down to injecting that certain Spanish flavor, that secret salsa, into them. In this chapter you will learn the Spanish alphabet and then take a look at the Spanish vowels. Then, after a break, go on to the next chapter, to work on your consonants.

Sounding Native

What does sounding like a native really mean? In Spain, a number of people learn Aragonese, Asturo-Leonese, Basque, Catalan, or Gallego, as well as the country's official language, castellano (Castilian Spanish). Many within the populations of Latin America are bilingual speakers of Spanish and another, indigenous, language—Spanish serves them as a means of communicating with people outside of their group or region, often for the purposes of commerce.

FACT

Español (ehs-pah-NYOL) means "Spaniard" (from Spain, Spanish), and *castellano* (kahs-teh-YAH-noh) means "Castilian," the language you call "Spanish"—the official language of Spain.

Because Spanish is spoken in so many countries, sounding native is hard to define. If you were asked to teach someone to sound like a native speaker of English, which native speaker would you choose—an American professor of English at Harvard or a police officer working on the south side of Chicago? A Londoner who speaks with a cockney accent, or an Aussie from Melbourne?

Whether you speak a particular Spanish dialect or not, if you were not born within the boundaries of Spain or a Latin American country, you will always be a *gringo* (GREEN-goh). In most places, "foreigner" is all that it means, so, for example, a person born in Vermont to a Chilean couple is still a *gringo*. His Chilean family, however, may actually use the term *gringuito* (green-GEE-toh) to demonstrate affection.

Clarifying Your Goals

What are your pronunciation goals? Do you want to impress your friends with the effortless trilling of your *r*s when ordering *arroz con lentejas* (rice with lentils) at your local Ecuadorean eatery? Do you want to adopt a particular dialect of Spanish to sound just like a Mexican, or a Puerto Rican, or a Salvadoran? Or do you simply want to achieve a fluency that would allow you to make yourself understood? By putting in the effort to study Spanish and by attempting to speak to your audience in its "native" tongue, you are well on your way to accomplishing the latter.

Your fluency will be achieved only through relaxation, practice, patience, and more practice. With a few exceptions, like the trilled *r*, Spanish and English share the same sounds and letters. There are a few rules that are unique to Spanish, but there are far fewer of them to memorize than in English.

Learning the Alphabet

In Spanish, the alphabet is called *el abecedario* (ehl ah-beh-seh-DAH-ryoh). When you take a look at the alphabet, you will see how similar it is to the one we use in English. For the most part, the Spanish letters are the same graphically as those employed in English. What's nice about them is that, unlike their American English counterparts, their pronunciation is consistent (most of the time!), which makes learning to read in Spanish a whole lot easier.

El Abecedario (The Spanish Alphabet)

Letter	Spanish Pronunciation	Letter	Spanish Pronunciation
a	ah	n	EH-neh
b	beh	ñ	EH-nyeh
c	seh	o	oh
ch	cheh	p	peh
d	deh	q	koo
e	eh	r	EH-reh
f	EH-feh	s	EH-seh
g	hheh	t	teh
h	AH-cheh	u	oo
i	ee	v	veh
j	HHOH-tah	w	DOH-bleh veh
k	kah	x	EH-kees
l	EH-leh	y	ee GRYEH-gah
ll	EHL-yeh, EH-yeh	z	SEH-tah, ZEH-tah
m	EH-meh		

FACT

There used to be another letter in the alphabet, *rr*, but it was officially dropped by the Royal Academy of Spain in the nineties. It was rumored that other double letters, *ch* and *ll*, would be dropped as well, but such hasn't been the case.

TRACK 1

Quick Pronunciation Guide

Letter	Pronunciation	Example
a	"a" in "father"	*mano* (MAH-noh), hand
b	"b" in "box"	*bella* (BEH-yah), pretty
c	"c" in "call"	*caja* (KAH-hhah), box
	"c" in "city"	*cine* (S̄IH-neh), movies
ch	"ch" in "change"	*chicle* (CHIH-kleh), gum
d	"d" in "deck"	*día* (DIH-ah), day
e	"e" in "pen"	*pera* (PEH-rah), pear
f	"f" in "fine"	*fe* (feh), faith
g	"g" in "go"	*ganar* (gah-NAHR), to win
	a hard "h"	*gemelo* (hheh-MEH-loh), twin
h	silent	*hola* (OH-lah), hello
i	"ee" in "seen"	*listo* (LIH-stoh), ready
j	a hard "h"	*justo* (HHOOS-toh), just
k	"k" in "karma"	*kiosco* (KYOH-skoh), kiosk
l	"l" in "lick"	*lado* (LAH-doh), side
ll	"y" in "yay" or "j" in "déjà vu"	*llanto* (YAHN-toh, ZHAHN-toh), crying
m	"m" in "more"	*mayo* (MAH-yoh), May
n	"n" in "nickel"	*nada* (NAH-dah), nothing
ñ	similar to "ni" in "onion"	*niño* (NIH-nyoh), baby
o	"o" in "more"	*mosca* (MOHS-kah), fly

Letter	Pronunciation	Example
p	"p" in "open"	*país* (pah-EES), country
q	"q" in "quiet"	*queso* (KEH-soh), cheese
r	a hard "r" sound, like "tt" in "matter"	*oro* (OH-roh), gold
s	"s" in "smart"	*sonar* (soh-NAHR), to ring
t	"t" in "stay"	*tocar* (toh-KAHR), to touch
u	"oo" in "boot"	*tuyo* (TOOH-yoh), yours
v	between "v" and "b"	*vencer* (vehn-SEHR, behn-SEHR), to overcome
w	"w" in "way"	*waterpolo* (wah-tehr-POH-loh), waterpolo
x	"x" in "taxes"	*exilio* (eh-KSIH-lyoh), exile
y	"y" in "yellow" or "j" in "déjà vu"	*yo* (yoh, zhoh), I
z	"s" in "smart" or "z" in zebra	*zapato* (sah-PAH-toh, zah-PAH-toh), shoe

Introducing the Vowels

Vowels, or *vocales* (voh-CAH-lehs), are letters representing sounds that are generated in the vocal chords and can, on their own, form a syllable, or *sílaba* (SEE-lah-bah). Spanish vowels, when not accompanied by another vowel, have only one characteristic pronunciation, whereas their English counterparts have in excess of three. If you've mastered the fifteen-plus vowel sounds in English, you'll have no trouble with the five vowel sounds in Spanish.

Each of the five vowels may be placed in one of two categories: *abierta* (ah-BYEHR-tah, "open") or *cerrada* (seh-RRAH-dah, "closed"). The "openness" or "closedness" of a vowel is determined by the extent to which you must open your mouth: *a, e,* and *o* are considered *vocales abiertas,* whereas *i* and *u* are described as *vocales cerradas.* A *vocal abierta* may also be described as *fuerte* (FWEHR-teh, "strong") and a *vocal cerrada* as *débil* (DEH-beel, "weak").

QUESTION?

What is a diphthong?
A diphthong is a complex vowel formed by two vowels that essentially become one sound, because both are pronounced within the same syllable.

The Vowel A

The first *letra* (letter) of *el abecedario* is a *vocal abierta*. When saying it, your mouth is widely open and the distance between the palate and the tongue is at its greatest. You use the sound of *a* every day: What do you say when after a long day's work you can finally sit down and put up your feet? Or when you go to the doctor and he asks you to open your mouth as he peers inside? Exactly! You say "ahhhhhhh." Now just skip the six extra h's and you have the Spanish letter *a*.

TRACK 2

Practice Pronunciation of Vowel A

Spanish	English
ajo	garlic
altar	altar
América	America
árbol	tree
clavo	nail
fruta	fruit

True to its *abierta* vowel category, *a* does not combine to form diphthongs with its sister letters *e* and *o*, but it does combine with *las vocales cerradas*. That is, when *a* is immediately in front of an unaccented *i* or a *u*, the sound that is produced is neither a pure *a*, the dominant vowel in this case, nor a pure *i or u*, the subordinate vowels within the combination. As a result, the *ai* sound is not "ah-ee" but rather "i" as in "tie." The *au* resembles the "ahw" combination in "ouch."

What happens if the unaccented *i* or *u* precedes the *a*? Listen to Track 3 and try repeating the words you hear.

Practice Pronunciation of Diphthongs AI and AU

Spanish	English
ausente	absent
aire	air
audaz	bold
auto	automobile
baile	dance
traicionero	traitor

You've just seen how the *i* and the *u* kowtow to the stronger *a,* but what if another *vocal fuerte* challenges *a*? Well nothing, really. Each vowel keeps its own sound and is pronounced.

Practice Pronunciation of Vowel Combinations AE and AO

Spanish	English
aéreo	aerial
atraer	to attract
caer	to fall
caos	chaos
maestro	teacher
paella	Spanish rice dish

The Vowel E

E is the fifth letter of the alphabet, also a *vocal fuerte*. Pronounce it between the palate and the tongue by opening your mouth halfway. The letter *e* alone has the sound "eh" as in "get," and does not sound at all like the "ay" in "say," or "e" in "hyphen," "gene," "been," or "terse."

Practice Pronunciation of Vowel E

Spanish	English
crecer	to grow
estar	to be (located)
hacer	to do
joven	young
nacer	to be born
necesito	I need

As a *vocal fuerte*, *e* keeps its own sound when combining with other *vocales fuertes*. Practice pronouncing words with *ea*, *ee*, and *eo* as you listen to Track 6.

TRACK 6

Practice Pronunciation of Combinations EA, EE, and EO

Spanish	English
crear	to create
creer	to believe
deseo	desire, wish
peaje	toll
peor	worse
reaccionar	to react
reanudar	to renew

TRACK 7

Practice Pronunciation of Words That Begin with Es–

Spanish	English
esbelto	proportioned
esbozo	first draft
escala	scale
escultura	sculpture
especial	special
estilo	style

Remember, a *vocal fuerte* forms diphthongs only with *vocales débiles*. When *e* is immediately followed by an unaccented *i* or *u*, the sound produced is a blend—the *ei* sound becomes "ey" as in "haystack"; the *eu* generally resembles "ehw" (unless the *u* is accented or naturally stressed within the word). To practice diphthongs *eu* and *ei*, review the following table and listen to Track 8.

TRACK 8

Practice Pronunciation of Diphthongs EU and EI

Spanish	English
afeitar	to shave
euforia	euphoria
europeo	European
neumático	tire
reino	kingdom
treinta	thirty

When the positions are reversed, that is, when an unaccented *i* or *u* is immediately followed by an *e*, the sounds that are produced are both expected and surprising. As with the letter *a*, the *i* takes on a sound similar to "y" within the *ie* combination, like in the English word "yet." The *ue* combination is a little trickier to get right away because it can have two possible, mutually exclusive pronunciations. In many words, *ue* will have the "weh" sound as in the English word "wet." To practice *ie* and *ue*, listen to Track 9.

TRACK 9

Practice Pronunciation of Combinations IE and UE

Spanish	English
cuento	story
duelo	sorrow
mientras	while
muebles	furniture
pueblo	town, village

Spanish	English
riesgo	risk
sediento	thirsty
siempre	always

In some cases, the *u* in the *ue* combination is *muda* (mute), and the diphthong is pronounced as *e*. The *u* becomes silent when *ue* is preceded by a *g* or a *q*.

TRACK 10

Practice Pronunciation of Vowels UE Preceded by G or Q

Spanish	English
descargue	an unloading
guedeja	lion's mane
guerra	war
pagué	I paid
parque	a park
quemar	to burn
queso	cheese
relampagueo	lightning flash

The Vowel I

The *i* is a *vocal cerrada* and is spoken through the smallest opening between the palate and the tongue. When unaccompanied by other vowels, *i* most resembles the "ee" sound in the word "machine." It is never pronounced as the English letter "i" in "mint," "edible," or "site."

TRACK 11

Practice Pronunciation of Vowel I

Spanish	English
avenida	avenue
bistec	(beef) steak

Spanish	English
cita	appointment
fácil	easy
gentil	courteous
marido	husband

Remember that when followed by other vowels, the *i* is usually a weak part of the diphthong, and is not sounded out. To practice the combinations *ia, ie, io,* and *iu,* listen to and repeat after Track 12.

Practice Pronunciation of IA, IE, IO, and IU

TRACK 12

Spanish	English
ciego	blind
cielo	sky
desperdiciar	to waste
hierro	iron
idioma	language
pie	foot
piedad	pity, mercy
viuda	widow

However, if the *i* is accented (*í*), it is pronounced as "ee" even though it may precede or follow another vowel.

Practice Pronunciation of Í with Another Vowel

TRACK 13

Spanish	English
caída	fall
día	day
freír	to fry
frío	cold

Spanish	English
lío	mess
maíz	corn
oír	to hear
país	country
panadería	bakery
reír	to laugh

In *ui* combinations, as in the *ue* combinations, the *u* is silent when it is preceded by a *g* or a *q*. That is, the *ui* combination sounds like *i*.

Practice Pronunciation of UI Preceded by G or Q

TRACK 14

Spanish	English
Arequipa	a city in Peru
guiñar	to wink
guisado	stew
guitarra	guitar
quiero	I want
quitar	to take away
siguiente	following
siquiera	at least

The Vowel O

The last of the *vocales fuertes* is *o,* a vowel spoken through a medium-sized opening between the palate and the tongue. *O* has the sound "oh," similar to but actually shorter than the "o" in the English word "toll."

Practice Pronunciation of Vowel O

TRACK 15

Spanish	English
olor	smell
olvidar	to forget

Spanish	English
oreja	exterior ear
oro	gold
operar	to operate
ojo	eye
oler	to smell
golpe	blow, hit
mozo	waiter
mortal	fatal

ALERT!

In English, the letter "o" may be pronounced in four different ways: as in "cod," "bone," "lemon," or "now." In Spanish, however, it retains the same pronunciation—as long as it is not joined with another vowel.

Combinations with *o* follow the same rules as other *vocales abiertas* and *vocales cerradas* with an accent, with the one exception being the *ou* combination.

Practice Pronunciation of Vowel O with Other Vowels

TRACK 16

Spanish	English
alcohol	alcohol
cohibir	to inhibit
coincidir	to coincide
oasis	oasis
oigo	I hear
poema	poem
roedor	rodent
toalla	towel
zoológico	zoo

The Vowel U

The last of the Spanish vowel is a *vocal débil* and is spoken through a small-to-medium opening between the palate and the tongue. The *u* often adopts the "oo" sound as in "too."

TRACK 17

Practice Pronunciation of Vowel U

Spanish	English
blusa	blouse
curso	course
dulce	sweet
luna	moon
menú	menu
nube	cloud
unir	to unite
uña	fingernail
usar	to use
útil	useful

You've already seen many different *u* combinations. In general, an unaccented *u* in combination with other *vocales* takes on a *sonido* (sound) similar to the English "w."

One exception to the rule is that *u* is mute in the following combinations: *gue, gui, que,* and *qui.* However, there are a few words where the *u* in the diphthong is NOT mute. To indicate that the *u* should be pronounced, a *diéresis* (¨) is added over it (*ü*). Listen to Track 18 to compare pronunciations of *gue* and *gui* with *güe* and *güi.* Note that *qüe* and *qüi* do not exist in Spanish.

TRACK 18

Practice Pronunciation of CU, GU, GÜ, HU, and QU

Spanish	English
antiguo	old
averiguar	to inquire
cigüeña	stork

Spanish	English
cuidar	to care for
huevo	egg
desagüe	drain
huir	to flee
máquina	machine
quedar	to stay
bilingüe	bilingual
quien	who
pingüino	penguin

Similarly, if naturally stressed or accented within a word, *u* keeps its "oo" sound.

TRACK 19

Practice Pronunciation of Accented Vowel U

Spanish	English
ataúd	coffin
baúl	chest or trunk
grúa	crane
laúd	lute

Congratulations! You've just finished the vowels. If you're feeling a little overwhelmed, don't worry. Just take a break and remind yourself that learning a language takes time. You'll begin to feel more comfortable as you continue.

Pronunciation II: Consonants and Accent Marks

3

Spanish consonants are a little tougher than Spanish vowels—Spanish has a few more consonants than English, and when combined with other letters, some consonants take on different pronunciations. Take your time; if you feel that this chapter has a lot of information to learn at one sitting, take breaks and go back occasionally to review what you've learned.

Introducing the Consonants

Las consonantes (the consonants) are sounds that can only be pronounced with the help of vowels, and letters representing these sounds make up the rest of the Spanish alphabet. Most Spanish consonants are very similar to their English counterparts. This chapter will examine the Spanish consonants by breaking them down into smaller groups.

The Consonants B and V

There's some disagreement about the Spanish pronunciation of consonants *b* and *v*. Some Spanish guides will tell you these two letters represent the same sound, while others maintain there's a subtle (or not so subtle) difference in pronunciation. For the purposes of this book, it will be assumed that there is a difference.

B is a *consonante labial* (labial consonant, or consonant formed by the lips). It is formed at the union of one's upper and lower lips and is a clipped version of the American English "b." (*M* and *p* also belong to the same category.) *V*, on the other hand, is a *consonante dentolabial* (a dentolabial consonant, formed by the lips and the teeth). It is formed at the union of one's upper front teeth and lower lip and is similar to though softer than the American English "v." (*F* also belongs to the dentolabial category.) Track 20 gives examples of pronunciations for both *b* and *v*.

TRACK 20

Practice Pronunciation of Consonants B and V

Spanish	English
barón	baron
baso	I base
miembro	member
embarazada	pregnant
tubo	tube
tuvo	(s)he had
vaca	cow
varón	male

Spanish	English
vaso	glass
devolver	to return
enviar	to send

In regions where *b* and *v* are equivalent, the letters follow additional rules. At the beginning of a word or following the letters *m, n,* or *ñ,* the softer *b* sound is employed. However, when located within a word, the *b* sound is harder and closer to the *v* sound.

The Consonants C, K, and Q

C (except in the combinations *ce* and *ci*), *q*, and *k* share the American English "k" sound. For the two *c* exceptions, read on to the following section. The letter *ch* is also covered separately.

TRACK 21

Practice Pronunciation of C, Q, and K

Spanish	English
coser	to sew/stitch
blanco	white
acabar	to finish
mecánico	mechanic(al)
placa	license plate
sacar	to draw out
kilo	kilogram
kilómetro	kilometer
kilovatio	kilowatt
quebrar	to break
quedar	to remain
quejarse	to complain
quizás	perhaps

Spanish	English
quijada	jaw
aquel	that (at a distance)

The Consonants C, S, and Z

The Spanish *s* is easy. It sounds the same as the American English "s." How you should pronounce *c* (in combinations *ce* and *ci*) and *z* will vary, depending on the dialect of Spanish you use. In Latin America and Andalusia (a region in southern Spain), they are also pronounced as "s." In most regions of Spain, *c* (when followed by *e* or *i*) and *z* sound like the American English "th" sound in "thin."

FACT

You might have noticed that natives of Latin America who learn English have difficulty with the "th" sounds in words like "thin" or "thought." That's because this sound does not occur in Latin American Spanish.

TRACK 22

Practice Pronunciation of Ce, Ci, S, and Z

Spanish	English
accidente	accident
acecinar	to dry-cure
aceituna	olive
centeno	rye
cerca	near
lucir	to shine
cintura	waist
ciruela	plum
posible	possible
asesinar	to murder
esbozo	outline
salpicar	to sprinkle

Spanish	English
tasa	rate
taza	cup/bowl
omisión	omission

The Combination Ch

Ch (cheh) sounds like the American English "ch" in "church." Dictionaries published before 1994 listed *ch* as a separate letter after *c*. Now words that begin with a *ch* can be found under the letter *c*, between *ce* and *ci*. Use the following table to practice words with *ch*.

TRACK 23

Practice Pronunciation of Ch

Spanish	English
charla	conversation
chuleta	chop (like a pork chop)
chanclas	slippers
cuchillo	knife
chicle	chewing gum
chocolate	chocolate
poncho	poncho, cape
ancho	wide, broad
colchón	mattress
echar	to throw out
hecho	fact, deed

The Consonants D and F

The Spanish *D* is a dentolingual consonant. As such, it is pronounced a little more like "th" in the English words "the," "this," or "that," than like the "d" in "dad" (with clenched teeth). Try to practice saying the Spanish *d* by placing the very tip of your tongue between your teeth and saying English words that begin with "d."

However, if you can't hear any difference between the Spanish *d* and the English one, don't worry too much about it. It's not crucial—you will be understood if you don't pronounce it exactly the right way, though of course your *gringo* accent will be unmistakable.

Practice Pronunciation of Consonant D

TRACK 24

Spanish	English
debajo	under(neath)
suceder	to happen
madrina	godmother
madrugar	to rise early
pedazo	piece
sudar	to sweat
tenedor	fork
redondo	round
perder	to lose

Another dentolabial consonant is the *f,* pronounced just like the English "f" in "food." In English, this same sound may be spelled out with the combination "ph," but in Spanish, equivalent words are modified in spelling. For example, the English word "telephone" becomes *teléfono* in Spanish.

Practice Pronunciation of Consonant F

TRACK 25

Spanish	English
fácil	easy
ferocidad	fierceness
fijar	to fasten
febril	feverish
elefante	elephant
diferente	different
fiar	to trust, lend
difícil	difficult

The Consonants G and J

When *g* is followed by any consonant or *a, o,* or *u,* it sounds like the American English "g" in "golf." In combinations *ge* and *gi,* it carries a sound not found in American English—an overemphasized "hh" that starts at the back of the throat.

Practice Pronunciation of Consonant G

TRACK 26

Spanish	English
gordo	fat
bolígrafo	pen
rogar	to plead
vergüenza	shame, shyness
gusto	pleasure
guardar	to store
gusano	worm, caterpillar
gozar	to enjoy
grueso	thick, stout
escoger	to choose
genial	pleasant
exigir	to demand, require
lógico	logical

The letter *j* represents the same "hh" sound as the one you'd just heard in combinations *ge* and *gi.* Note that the sound combination of "j" in "Jack" does not occur in Spanish.

Practice Pronunciation of Consonant J

TRACK 27

Spanish	English
ejemplo	example
joya	jewel
juez	judge
masaje	massage

Spanish	English
paisaje	landscape
reloj	watch
ejército	army

The Consonant H

H in Spanish is a relic—once upon a time, it was used to designate an aspirated sound that no longer exists. Today, it is silent, unless coupled with the letter *c* to denote "ch."

TRACK 28

Practice Pronunciation of Consonant H

Spanish	English
desahogo	emotional relief
exhalar	to exhale
hábil	skillful
hábito	habit
hablar	to speak
rehusar	to refuse
humilde	humble

The Consonants L and LL

The single *l* is among the few letters that consistently has the same exact pronunciation in Spanish as in English. The pronunciation of *ll*, however, varies depending on where the speaker is from. Listen to the *ll* words on Track 29 to hear what the most common pronunciation is.

ESSENTIAL

You might hear the ll combination pronounced like "y" in "yellow," the "ly" sound in "million," the "j" sound in "treasure," or the "sh" sound in "she." All are considered correct, though it will help if you stick with one pronunciation consistently.

TRACK 29

Practice Pronunciation of L and LL

Spanish	English
ladrón	thief
lechuga	lettuce
licencia	license
lodo	mud
lujo	luxury
perla	pearl
sal	salt
caballo	horse
cabello	hair
hallar	to find
millón	million
zambullir	to dive

The Consonants M, N, and Ñ

M and *n* have the same sounds as their respective English counterparts, except for a curious difference: In similar words in English and Spanish, the English "mm" and "nn" is usually dropped in favor of a single "m" or "n," though occasionally the double "n" is kept.

Practice Pronunciation of M and N

TRACK 30

Spanish	English
anual	annual
anunciar	to announce
mojado	wet
comercial	commercial
interesante	interesting
innovar	to innovate
inocente	innocent
recomendar	to recommend

M and *n* are fairly easy to understand—they are very similar to their English counterparts. However, what about that *ñ*? The closest American English approximation to *ñ*, pronounced "EH-nyeh," is the "ni" sound in "onion." Try practicing this sound with the words on Track 31.

Practice Pronunciation of Consonant Ñ

TRACK 31

Spanish	English
acompañar	to accompany
año	year
compañero	companion
niñez	childhood
puño	fist
reñir	to quarrel

The Consonant P

P is very similar to the American English "p," minus the trailing breath. The clipped nature of both *B* and *P* often leads to confusing one with the other. Note that the combination "pp" does not occur in Spanish, so the Spanish version of the verb "appear" is spelled as *aparecer*, with one *p*.

Practice Pronunciation of Consonant P

TRACK 32

Spanish	English
poesía	poetry
aplicar	to apply
papel	paper, role
oprimir	to press, oppress
platicar	to chat
pelea	fight
episodio	episode
hipo	hiccup
oponer	to oppose

The Consonant R and Combination RR

The Spanish *r* is the letter that gives people the most trouble, because it must be trilled. Remember that all *rr*s and the *r*s at the beginning of a word are generally held longer than the rest. Begin practicing your trilled *r*s with the words you hear on Track 33.

Practice Pronunciation of Consonant R

TRACK 33

Spanish	English
bucear	to scuba-dive
Corea	Korea
radiografía	X-ray picture
raíz	root, origin
reto	challenge
sierra	mountain range
terreno	land, field
ferrocarril	railroad

The Consonant T

The Spanish *t* sounds similar to the "t" in "total." *T*, however, is pronounced with a short burst and the tip of the tongue positioned between both sets of teeth. The difference in these sounds is very subtle. Keep in mind, also, that Spanish does not have the "th" or "tt" combinations. As a result, when translating English words that employ these combinations, Spanish simply replaces them with a single *t*.

Practice Pronunciation of Consonant T

TRACK 34

Spanish	English
atención	attention
atraer	to attract
autor	author
catedral	cathedral
tela	fabric

Spanish	English
tinto	tinged, red (wine)
tomar	to take, to drink
tomate	tomato
triste	sad

The Consonants X and Y

The letter *X* has different pronunciations depending on its position within the word. Between vowels, within letter combinations *exce–* and *exci–*, and at the end of the word, it sounds like "ks" or "gs." In some regions, when an *x* begins a word or is situated in between a vowel and a consonant, it has an "s" sound. In some words, it sounds the same as the Spanish *ge* or *j* (that is, like an overemphasized American English "h"). It also takes on a "sh" sound in some words that originate from indigenous Latin American languages. But don't worry about trying to memorize all these rules. Fortunately, you won't encounter the Spanish *x* very often.

TRACK 35

Practice Pronunciation of Consonant X

Spanish	English
examen	exam
excelente	excellent
excitante	exciting
extranjero	foreigner
mexicano	Mexican
texano	Texan
xilófono	xylophone

You might have learned a long time ago that the American English vowels included "a," "e," "i," "o," "u," and sometimes "y." Though not considered *una vocal* in the strictest sense, the Spanish *y* usually acts like the *vocal i* when it sounds like the "y" in "yam." *Ay, ey,* and *oy* share their pronunciations with *ai, ei,* and *oi,* respectively; *uy* sounds like "oo-y." On its own, *y* sounds like "ee." Practice pronouncing *y* with the words you hear on Track 36.

TRACK 36

Practice Pronunciation of Consonant Y

Spanish	English
apoyo	support
hay	there is, there are
hoy	today
muy	very
raya	line
rey	king
suyo	yours
yerno	son-in-law

You've done it! You've just completed the Spanish alphabet! Take this time to pat yourself on the back—you deserve it. If you liked practicing Spanish pronunciations by doing tongue twisters, search for more online—just enter *trabalenguas* into a search engine, and see where it takes you.

Introducing Accent Marks

Now that you know how to read each Spanish letter, you need to learn something else that will help you read words in Spanish—the rules for choosing which syllable in a word should be stressed, and the purpose of accent marks.

In Spanish, there is one accent mark (*el acento agudo,* an acute accent mark), denoted as (´) and placed over the vowel to indicate that the syllable should be stressed. Only the words that do not follow the rules of Spanish actually have accent marks. These rules are:

- If a word ends with an n, an s, or a vowel, the emphasis is generally placed on the second-to-last syllable within that word. These words are known as palabras llanas.
- If a word ends in a consonant other than n or s, the emphasis is generally placed on the last syllable within that word. These words are known as palabras agudas.

If a word is not accented according to these simple rules, the accented syllable is denoted with an accent mark. Every Spanish word is classified in terms of where the word is accented, implicitly or explicitly. In addition to *llanas* and *agudas*, words are also categorized as *esdrújulas* (accented on the third-to-last syllable) and *sobresdrújulas* (accented on the fourth-to-last syllable and beyond). All *esdrújulas* carry an accent mark.

Accents provide you with more than a pronunciation guide. In English, some words require a context to know their pronunciation and meaning. Compare "The project is due tomorrow" and "He wanted to project an air of confidence." In Spanish, accent marks are sometimes used to help distinguish words. Take a look at a few examples that follow. Note that the only difference between these pairs is the accent mark—their pronunciations are exactly the same.

Examples of Using Accent Marks to Distinguish Words

Spanish	English
él	he
el	the (definite article used with male nouns)
qué	what
que	that
sólo	only
solo	alone
quién	who (question word)
quien	who

Chapter 4

Subjects: Who Are You?

As you might remember from grade school, every sentence has at least one subject—the thing or person who performs the action indicated by the verb. This chapter will give you all you need to know about the subject of a Spanish sentence to get you on your way to start putting together complete sentences.

Determining the Gender

Most of the time, the subject of your sentence will be a noun. Nouns work the same way in Spanish as they do in English—with one major exception. In Spanish, all nouns have an assigned gender, whether the noun represents a person, place, or thing. The sex of a noun is either natural, referring to people who do have an established gender, or grammatical, where gender has been arbitrarily assigned to things or concepts.

Natural Gender

Most nouns in this category come in two versions: masculine and feminine. Take a look at the following table.

Natural Gender Nouns

Masculine	Feminine
muchacho (boy)	*muchacha* (girl)
perro (male dog)	*perra* (female dog)
doctor (male doctor)	*doctora* (female doctor)
inglés (Englishman)	*inglesa* (Englishwoman)
hombre (man)	*mujer* (woman)
toro (bull)	*vaca* (cow)
periodista (male journalist)	*periodista* (female journalist)
estudiante (male student)	*estudiante* (female student)

There are four basic rules for dealing with natural gender nouns:

- When a masculine noun ends in *–o*, substitute an *–a* to make it feminine. For example, *muchacho* becomes *muchacha*, and *perro* becomes *perra*.
- When a masculine noun ends in a consonant, add an *–a* at the end to make it feminine. For example, *doctor* becomes *doctora*, and *inglés* becomes *inglesa*.

- Sometimes nouns have only one gender. For example, there is no feminine noun for *hombre*, so use *mujer*; *toro* becomes *vaca*.
- Sometimes the same word may be used for both genders; in these cases, the gender is specified by articles or adjectives. This rule includes (but is not limited to) words that end in *–ista* or *–e*. For example, *el periodista* becomes *la periodista*, *el estudiante* becomes *la estudiante*, and *el modelo* becomes *la modelo*.

Grammatical (Assigned) Gender

Grammatical gender does not follow a logical pattern and must be memorized. You can, however, identify some cases of grammatical gender by looking at the endings.

Masculine Endings

Ending	Example	English	Feminine Exceptions
–aje	*viaje*	journey	n/a
–men	*examen*	exam	n/a
–gen	*origen*	origin	*imagen* (image), *margen* (margin)
–or	*doctor*	male doctor	*labor* (work)
–o	*libro*	book	*mano* (hand)

Feminine Endings

Ending	Example	English	Masculine Exceptions
–ad	*verdad*	truth	n/a
–ud	*salud*	health	*ataúd* (coffin)
–ed	*merced*	mercy	n/a
–ión	*religión*	religion	some concrete nouns like *gorrión* (sparrow)
–umbre	*costumbre*	custom	n/a

Ending	Example	English	Masculine Exceptions
–ie	serie	series	n/a
–sis	síntesis	synthesis	análisis (analysis), énfasis (emphasis), éxtasis (ecstasy)
–a	libra	pound, lb.	mapa (map); some abstract nouns like problema

Some nouns are feminine even though they end with an –o because they are really abbreviations. For example, *foto* (photo) is a feminine noun because it is really *fotografía* (photograph), a noun that ends with an –a.

An "S" for Plural

Making nouns plural is easy, because in most cases the concept is the same as in English—just add an –s or an –es. Well, there are some variations, so take a look at the following rules:

- When the noun ends with an unstressed vowel, just add an –s. For example, *playa* (beach) becomes *playas* in plural.
- When the noun ends with a consonant other than –s, add an –es. For example, *flor* (flower) becomes *flores* in plural.
- When the noun ends with a stressed vowel, add an –es. For example, *iraní* (Iranian) becomes *iraníes*; *inglés* (Englishman) becomes *ingleses* in plural.
- When the noun ends with an unstressed vowel and –s, don't add anything. For example, *crisis* remains *crisis* in the plural.

How Articles Can Help

So far, all these rules may have left you dismayed. Do you really have to keep all those noun endings in mind just to establish the gender? Well, here is where the articles can help. Once you know the article, you can figure out whether the noun is feminine or masculine, singular or plural. Just as in English, Spanish articles come in two categories: definite and indefinite.

Definite Articles

Think of the definite article as one pointing to a concrete noun. In English, we've only got one: "the." In Spanish, you have four forms, depending on the noun's gender and number (one or more than one).

Definite Article ("The")

Number	Masculine	Feminine
Singular	*el*	*la*
Plural	*los*	*las*

With the exception of proper names, Spanish articles are employed liberally with most nouns, even in places where the translation into English would drop them. And please don't forget to keep conjugating (or matching) your articles and your nouns—they must always match in gender and number.

When you learn a new noun, use the following strategy: Rather than making up mnemonic devices or memorizing complicated rules, memorize nouns with *la* or *el* before the singular form—it's the easiest way to keep track of their grammatical gender. For example, just as long as you remember that "the house" is *la casa*, you will know that this noun is feminine.

Exceptions to the Rule

How a word is stressed plays a significant role in determining the article used with it, so the exception rule goes as follows: A masculine article is always used before the singular form of a word beginning with a stressed *a* or *ha*. Take a look at some examples in the following table.

Feminine Nouns That Take On Masculine Article in the Singular

Singular	Plural	English
el agua	las aguas	the water(s)
el águila	las águilas	the eagle(s)
el alma	las almas	the soul(s)
el ave	las aves	the bird(s)

An Aside on Prepositions

Here is another important point to remember—when the definite article follows prepositions *a* or *de*, they form a contraction: *a + el = al; de + el = del*. Try pronouncing *a el* quickly and then switch to *al*; you'll quickly see why Spanish speakers formed this contraction: It's a lot easier and faster to pronounce. And the same goes for the transformation from *de el* to *del*.

A Matter of Meaning

Some nouns have both a masculine form and a feminine one—which means the meaning differs based on what article it travels with. For example, take the word *capital*. Your first guess should be that it's masculine, and it can be: *el capital* means "capital" (as in, a sum of money, an economic term). But—surprise, surprise!—there's also a feminine noun *capital,* with an entirely different meaning. *La capital* is a capital of a country. And the two terms are not interchangeable.

Nouns That Rely on Articles for Meaning

Masculine Noun	English	Feminine Noun	English
el cólera	the cholera	la colera	the anger
el coma	the coma	la coma	the comma
el cometa	the comet	la cometa	the kite
el corte	the cut	la corte	the court
el cura	the priest	la cura	the cure
el frente	the front line in battle	la frente	forehead

Masculine Noun	English	Feminine Noun	English
el guía	the person who guides	*la guía*	the book, booklet or female guide
el orden	the opposite of chaos	*la orden*	the command, request
el pez	the fish	*la pez*	the tar
el policía	the police officer	*la policía*	the police force
el radio	the radius, the physical radio	*la radio*	the radio programming

Indefinite Articles

But don't forget, in addition to the four definite article forms, Spanish also boasts four matching indefinite articles. In English, there's really only one, "a," though it is modified to "an" before any word that begins with a vowel ("a book," but "an apple"), and it is only used with singular nouns (no such thing as "a books," right?). In Spanish, you have *un* or *una* (depending on the gender of the noun) as equivalents to "a" or "an," and the indefinite articles *unos* and *unas* when the nouns are plural—you might think of these articles as meaning "some."

ALERT!

Note that in Spanish, *uno* means "one" (1) and *unos* and *unas* are the masculine and feminine versions of "some." When applying a Spanish "one" to a masculine noun, *uno* loses its final vowel. For example, *un libro* could be translated as "one book" or "a book," depending on context.

Indefinite Articles ("A," "An," or "Some")

Number	Masculine	Feminine
Singular	*un*	*una*
Plural	*unos*	*unas*

For example:

Hay unos carros en el estacionamiento.	**There are some cars in the parking lot.**
Mis amigas son unas chicas bonitas.	**My friends are (some) pretty girls.**
Es una actitud amistosa.	**It's a friendly attitude.**
Allí hay un banco.	**There is a bank over there.**

From Nouns to Pronouns

A subject may be a noun or a pronoun; basically, pronouns are words that are used to substitute for nouns: "you" can replace "the reader," "his" may be used instead of "John Smith's," and "them" might refer to "the students." In English, "I," "we," "you," "he, "she," "it," and "they" are known as subject pronouns. In Spanish, there are just a bit more pronouns to choose from, because there are multiple versions for that humble word "you."

Personal Pronouns in English

Number	Singular	Plural
First Person	I	we
Second Person	you	you (or you all)
Third Person	he, she, it	they

Personal Pronouns in Spanish

Number	Singular	Plural
First Person	*yo*	*nosotros* (m), *nosotras* (f)
Second Person	*tú*	*vosotros* (m), *vosotras* (f)
Third Person	*él* (m), *ella* (f), *ello*	*ellos* (m), *ellas* (f)
Third Person	*usted*	*ustedes*

Subject pronouns in Spanish and English are organized by person (first, second, or third) and number (singular or plural), but when you compare the two tables, you will notice a number of differences.

QUESTION?

What is a grammatical person?
Basically, it's the point of view. First person is from the point of view of the speaker (I did this, we did that). Second person is from the point of view of the person being spoken to (you did that, why don't you . . . ?). Third person is from the point of view of another person, neither the speaker nor the listener (he did this, they did that).

The most obvious difference is the additional third person category. *Usted* and *ustedes* are second-person pronouns because they translate as "you" and deal with the person being spoken to. However, in Spanish they are conjugated as third-person pronouns (more on conjugation later). That's because *usted* is an old contraction of *vuestra merced* (your mercy), a very formal address that was made in third person (just as in English you would say "your mercy wishes," but "you wish").

In the plural, only use *nosotras, vosotras,* or *ellas* when all members of the group are female (or, in the case of *ellas,* all objects represented are feminine-gender nouns). When referring to males or mixed groups, use the masculine versions of the pronouns. For example, *las casas* (the houses) are *ellas,* but *los actores y las actrices* (the actors and actresses) are *ellos.*

"You" and "You" and "You"

Have you noticed that the Spanish pronoun chart lists five forms of "you"—*tú, usted, ustedes, vosotros,* and *vosotras*? That's a lot of options for just one English word. But let's take things one at a time.

First, consider the number: Are you addressing one person or more than one? If one, your options narrow down to *tú* or *usted*. If more than one, you'll be choosing from *ustedes, vosotros,* and *vosotras* (more on the special *vosotros* and *vosotras* forms later).

Next, you have to consider whether to address the person or persons formally or informally. *Tú* and *vosotros/vosotras* are informal forms. *Usted* and *ustedes* are the formal versions ("your mercy" is a pretty exalted way of addressing someone, after all).

In English, we never have to worry about whether you should address people with a formal or informal "you," so this will definitely take some getting used to. And it's not always clear which form to use. A good rule of thumb is this: *tú* and *vosotros/vosotras* should be used to address your friends, or by permission only. In all other case, start out with *usted/ustedes*, until the person or people you're talking to invite you to switch to the informal version. The verb for using the *tú* form is *tutear*. *Me puede tutear* means, "you can use the *tú* form with me."

Formal/Informal "You" Guidelines

Usted, Ustedes (Formal Address)	Tú, Vosotros, Vosotras (Informal Address)
Demonstrates respect.	Demonstrates acceptance.
Used with elders (including your parents).	Used with friends and people your age, as well as with younger people and children.
Used with persons of rank or nobility.	Used with colleagues (informality pre-established).
Used with strangers.	Used with friendly acquaintances.
Used to maintain social distance.	Used to reduce social distance.

It's All About Good Manners

Choosing formal versus informal address is really just a matter of manners. You want to show respect for the person you're speaking to, and you do that by choosing the correct form of address. But how do you guide yourself through this potential social minefield?

First, unless you are attending an event where informality is actually encouraged, remember that any initial meeting should begin with each party's using the formal form of address, *usted*. An exception might be when you are being introduced to a friend's social circle. Try to pick up on social cues as offered by the people you are meeting. If the situation is social and the party you meet treats you informally, try to determine why they are being familiar. Is it because that person wants you to feel relaxed and within an accepting environment (then feel free to respond with *tú*)? Or is it that the person is much older than you are and has the social option of being familiar (in this case, it's best to stick to *usted*)?

If the situation warrants it and you want to break the ice, encourage the person you meet to treat you informally—if this person requests that you do likewise, go ahead. If the person does not reciprocate this request, be straightforward and ask how the person prefers to be treated. Ask if you may address the person informally, and be prepared for any answer. There is nothing wrong with requesting familiarity as long as you do it formally and don't respond negatively to either answer. Here are some examples of what you might say:

¿Me permite tratarlo/tratarla a usted de tú?	**Do you permit me to treat you in the familiar?**
¿Me permite tutearlo/tutearla?	**May I use the familiar form of address with you?**
¿Lo/La puedo tutear?	**Can I use the familiar form of address with you?**

Common Courtesy

Respect or courtesy (*la cortesía*) may be expressed in a variety of ways. In addition to the formality within verbs, you will find courteous titles similar to the ones used *en inglés* (in English).

Formal Titles

señor García	Mr. Garcia
señora Robles	Mrs. Robles
señorita Sánchez	Miss Sanchez

As *en inglés*, Spanish uses *abreviaturas de cortesía*—notice that these abbreviations are capitalized, whereas the full words are capitalized only at the beginning of a sentence.

Formal Title Abbreviated

Sr.	Mr.
Sra.	Mrs.
Srta.	Miss

When addressing a person directly, it is customary to simply say the appropriate title followed by the person's last name:

¿Cómo está (usted), señor Smith?	**How are you, Mr. Smith?**
Buenos días, señorita Salgado.	**Good morning, Miss Salgado.**

However, when speaking about someone or when identifying yourself and others by title, the definite article is used appropriate to the person's gender:

La Sra. Menéndez vive en Lima.	**Mrs. Menendez lives in Lima.**
Yo soy el Sr. Gómez.	**I am Mr. Gomez.**

There are two other forms of address that you may come across: *don* and *doña*. Though once used as a title for nobility and land ownership, in many regions *don* and *doña* have simply replaced *señor* and *señora*. In some regions, the term *doña* has evolved into a criticism of sorts, equivalent to a "gossip" or a "busy-body."

Politeness in Conversation

When you start a polite conversation, you can rely on one of the following greetings, depending on the time of day. You'll find these quite versatile—they may be used in both formal and informal situations.

buenos días	good morning (before noon)
buenas tardes	good afternoon (between noon and dusk)
buenas noches	good night (after dusk)

By its very nature, polite speech is very structured and almost formulaic. In addition to a universal greeting, a typical encounter will likely include the following query and response:

¿Cómo está (usted)?   **How are you?**
Bien, gracias. ¿Y usted?   **(I am) well, thank you. And yourself?**

The following is a simple dialogue to help you practice what you have learned so far. The conversation is taking place at a conference; Linda Rodríguez and Alonso Calderón have never met before.

Linda: *Buenos días, señor.*
             Good morning, sir.

Alonso: *Buenos días. Yo soy el Sr. Calderón, Alfonso Calderón.*
             Good morning. I am Mr. Calderon—Alfonso Calderon.

Linda: *Linda Rodríguez, con mucho gusto. ¿Me permite tutearlo?*
             Linda Rodriguez, nice to meet you. May I address you informally?

Alonso: *Sí. ¿Y yo la puedo tutear también?*
             Yes, and may I address you informally too?

Linda: *Sí. ¿Cómo estás?*
             Yes. How are you?

Alonso: *Muy bien, gracias. ¿Y tú?*
             Very well, thanks. And you?

Linda: *Muy bien.*
             Very well.

In Conjunction

You can string nouns together with conjunctions—those little particles "and," "or," "but," . . . well, you get the point. In Spanish, as in English, conjunctions are the connectors of words, phrases, and complete sentences. They may be divided into two broad forms:

- Those words that relate two or more items of equal function.
- Those words that mark a dependence of one item on another.

The two most basic conjunctions to learn are *y*, which usually translates to "and," and *o*, usually translated as "or" in English. As one-vowel words, these two conjunctions are vulnerable to a particular spelling change that is done to avoid colliding two vowels and losing the sound of *y* and *o*. When *y* precedes a word that begins with *i* or *hi*, it changes to *e*. For example, compare the following two sentences:

Yo soy inteligente y honesto.	**I am intelligent and honest.**
Yo soy honesto e inteligente.	**I am honest and intelligent.**

See, to avoid the "*y inteligente*" collision (if you were to pronounce this phrase correctly, you would have to drop one of the ee's because the *y* and the *i* sound exactly the same), the *y* transforms to *e*, which is pronounced "ey."

A similar spelling and pronunciation change occurs with *o*. When it precedes a word that begins with *o* or *ho*, this conjunction will change to *u*. For example:

Quiero seis o siete chocolates.	**I want six or seven chocolates.**
Quiero siete u ocho chocolates.	**I want seven or eight chocolates.**

Again, to avoid the collision of the two "oh" sounds in *o* and *ocho,* the conjunction *o* changes to *u* (pronounced "oo").

Other conjunctions in Spanish include *pero* (but), *ni . . . ni . . .* (neither . . . nor . . .), *que* (that), and *porque* (because).

Chapter 5

Verbs: What Do You Do?

In this chapter you will continue your development of self-expression by learning about the basic Spanish verbs. Your prior experience will provide you the conceptual tools for successfully completing this material. As with the previous chapters, *relájate*, y *¡adelante!* (relax, and forward!)—at your own pace, of course.

Working with Verbs

El verbo (the verb) is one of the most fundamental building blocks for Spanish expression. With it, you can often describe an action and who is performing that action. The simplest sentence *en inglés* (in English) requires a separate subject and predicate: "I am." *En español* (in Spanish), that sentence becomes simpler still, *Soy*. Because each verb is conjugated according to its subject, its ending will indicate who is doing the action—in this case, the pronoun *yo* (I) is optional, and may be dropped.

QUESTION?

What does "conjugating" mean?
"Conjugating" refers to modifying a verb based on such factors as number (singular or plural), person (first, second, or third), tense (past, present, future, etc.), or mood (indicative, command, or subjunctive). In Spanish, all verbs must be conjugated according to their subjects for number and person, and also according to the tense and mood that they convey. (To find out what is meant by "mood," refer to the next section.)

A Spanish verb is made up of two parts: the base and the ending. Think of the base as the repository that holds the essence and definition of the verb, and the ending as the personal label indicating who owns the action and when it is occurring. For example: *Camino* (I walk) may be divided into *camin–* (base) and *–o* (the ending that indicates a first-person singular subject "I" and that the verb is in the present tense of the indicative mood). Furthermore, verbs are subdivided into regular and irregular. To say a verb is regular is to say that its base is unchanged regardless of the ending employed and that its endings will follow regular patterns. An irregular verb's base might vary according to a specific conjugation and some of its endings might be irregular as well.

The Verb's Mood

The grammatical "mood" isn't about how the verb is feeling—whether it's sad or gloomy or happy or confused. But in a way, it's not all that different. Any complete thought that you can convey possesses mood, also referred to as "voice," whether it is by what you say, how you say it, or under what circumstances you say it. When talking about the mood of an expression, you are focusing on the speaker's motivation in stating something in a particular way. The moods that you will encounter in Spanish fall under three general categories.

Indicative

Also known as the active voice, the indicative is the mood with which you try to express "what is" in an objective manner—by using facts, observations, and narration. You can argue (and many would probably agree) that no observation can be objective. This poses no problem in using the indicative; the use of this mood does not depend on truth so much as it depends on the speaker's motivation to lend authority to his or her statements. In a sense, you can say that it is the truth as he, or she, sees it and/or wishes to convince others to see it.

Imperative

With the imperative, you express action as commands, warnings, and requests. Keep in mind that there are no imperious overtones with respect to a command. Also, *en español*, a command and a request are not opposites but actually equivalent. The same structure underlies both; the difference lies in the situation and the tone of voice that you employ. You've seen a form of this mood in the introduction to this chapter, with the command that asked you to relax.

Subjunctive

By using the subjunctive, you try to express "what might be" or "what ought to be." This mood is contrary to the indicative in that it allows expression that is more apparently subjective. As such, it may express doubt, desire, emotion, impersonal opinion, and uncertainty. Native Spanish speakers employ the subjunctive naturally. So much so that it may become a holy grail of sorts for you to master after you become fairly proficient in the language. You will touch upon the subjunctive in Chapter 16.

The Most Basic Form: Infinitive

The infinitive allows you to speak of a verb without really needing to assign it as an action to anyone or anything. It allows you to speak of an action in the abstract, as a noun. In English, infinitives are verbs preceded by a "to": to be, to go, to stay, and so on. The Spanish infinitives do not have any function words equivalent to the English "to" to precede them, but you can recognize them by one of three possible endings: *–ar*, *–er*, and *–ir*. These three groupings aren't arbitrary—they signal how the verb should be conjugated. For every tense, you'll learn three sets of regular endings, one for each of these groups.

Spanish verbs have tenses that correspond loosely with the English present tense, past tense, future tense, and so on. You will start with the present tense, and then go on to learn about other tenses as you make your way through the book.

There Is Nothing Like the Present

Most language books teach present-tense verbs first, since these are generally most straightforward, and also the most useful. You can employ the present-tense verbs in situations that describe the following:

- **An action that occurs now.** For example: *Camino a la parada de bus.* (I walk/am walking to the bus stop.)
- **An ongoing experience.** For example: *Fumo demasiado.* (I smoke too much.)

- **A future act that will occur soon within a specified time frame.** For example: *Empiezo el trabajo dentro de un mes.* (I [will] start the job within a month.)
- **An act that you wish to convince yourself, or others, will occur.** For example: *Si encuentro un vestido rojo, lo compro.* (If I find a red dress, I will buy it.)

Conjugating Verbs in the Present Tense

First, let's take a look at conjugating regular verbs in the present tense. Remember: In order to conjugate a verb, you must first determine its infinitive form to figure out whether it belongs to the *–ar, –er,* or *–ir* category. Then, simply drop the infinitive ending, and add the appropriate one to indicate correct person and number.

Look at the following table to see how to conjugate the regular verbs *cantar* (to sing), *aprender* (to learn), and *vivir* (to live). You may prefer to memorize the complete verb conjugations rather than just the endings—they'll help you remember how to conjugate other verbs in the present tense.

–Ar Verb Endings

–ar	cantar	to sing (infinitive)
–o	*(yo) canto*	I sing
–as	*(tú) cantas*	you sing (informal, singular)
–a	*(él, ella) canta*	he, she, it sings
	(usted) canta	you sing (formal, singular)
–amos	*(nosotros, nosotras) cantamos*	we sing
–áis	*(vosotros, vosotras) cantáis*	you sing (informal, plural)
–an	*(ellos, ellas) cantan*	they sing
	(ustedes) cantan	you sing (formal, plural)

–Er Verb Endings

–er	aprender	to learn (infinitive)
–o	(yo) aprendo	I learn
–es	(tú) aprendes	you learn (informal, singular)
–e	(él, ella) aprende	he, she, it learns
	(usted) aprende	you learn (formal, singular)
–emos	(nosotros, nosotras) aprendemos	we learn
–éis	(vosotros, vosotras) aprendéis	you learn (informal, plural)
–en	(ellos, ellas) aprenden	they learn
	(ustedes) aprenden	you learn (formal, plural)

–Ir Verb Endings

–ir	vivir	to live (infinitive)
–o	(yo) vivo	I live
–es	(tú) vives	you live (informal, singular)
–e	(él, ella) vive	he, she, it lives
	(usted) vive	you live (formal, singular)
–imos	(nosotros, nosotras) vivimos	we live
–ís	(vosotros, vosotras) vivís	you live (informal, plural)
–en	(ellos, ellas) viven	they live
	(ustedes) viven	you live (formal, plural)

QUESTION?

Does it seem strange that the *usted* and *ustedes* forms take on the verb forms of the third person?

Remember, the explanation is simple: *Usted* is an abbreviation of *vuestra merced* (your mercy), which technically corresponds to "it," a third-person pronoun. Although this phrase was shortened to form the modern pronoun "you," it remained in the third person.

Practicing Conjugations

The only way you can learn conjugating is through practice. Use what you've learned in this chapter to complete some of the following exercises. Fill in the blanks with the correct form of the verb listed in parentheses. Refer to Appendix E for answers.

1. *Yo* _____ *(abrir) la puerta para entrar.* (I open the door to come in.)
2. Nosotros _____ *(deber) estudiar mejor.* (We should study better.)
3. *Sandra y sus amigas* _____ *(caminar) hacia la parada de autobús.* (Sandra and her friends are walking to the bus stop.)
4. *¿Ustedes* _____ *(asistir) a las charlas del profesor Juárez?* (Do you attend the lectures of Professor Juarez?)
5. *Yo* _____ *(estudiar) los fines de semana.* (I study on weekends.)
6. *Carlos, ¿por qué (tú)* _____ *(acudir) a las reuniones?* (Carlos, why do you go to the meetings?)
7. *Juan* _____ *(prometer) hacer sus tareas.* (Juan promises to do his chores.)
8. *Mañana (nosotros)* _____ *(caminar) al trabajo.* (Tomorrow we will walk to work.)
9. *Usted siempre* _____ *(cumplir) con sus promesas.* (You always keep your promises.)
10. *Yo* _____ *(aprender) la lección.* (I am learning the lesson.)
11. *Tú* _____ *(beber) demasiado.* (You drink too much.)
12. *Ellas* _____ *(buscar) la calle Main.* (They are looking for Main Street.)
13. *¿Ustedes* _____ *(trabajar) en la ciudad?* (Do you work in the city?)
14. *Él* _____ *(recibir) cartas cada día.* (He receives letters every day.)
15. *Yo* _____ *(vivir) feliz aquí.* (I live happily here.)

Chapter 6

Who Are You? Introducing Ser

Now that regular verbs are a piece of cake, how about something a little more complex to spice up the mix? The Spanish verbs *ser* and *estar* both translate as "to be," but they cannot be used interchangeably. The next two chapters will show you how to distinguish between these two verbs, and the correct contexts for their usage.

Permanent States of Being: Ser

What if somebody were to ask you: "Who are you?" What would you say? How would you describe yourself?

¿Quién es usted?	**Who are you?**
Yo soy María Fernanda.	**I am Maria Fernanda.**
Soy profesora de matemáticas.	**I am a math teacher.**
Soy alta y rubia.	**I am tall and blond.**
Soy de Chile.	**I am from Chile.**

Maria's description of herself contains permanent facts: her name, her occupation, what she looks like, and where she is from. This is why she used *soy,* the *yo* form of the verb *ser,* to describe herself. *Ser* is an irregular verb, which means you can't just use the regular present-tense endings to conjugate it.

To learn how to conjugate *ser* in the present tense, take a look at the following table and listen to Track 37 to practice saying the conjugated forms out loud.

TRACK 37

Conjugating Ser in the Present Tense

(yo) soy	I am
(tú) eres	you are (informal, singular)
(él, ella, usted) es	he, she, it is; you are (formal, singular)
(nosotros, nosotras) somos	we are
(vosotros, vosotras) sois	you are (informal, plural)
(ellos, ellas, ustedes) son	they are; you are (formal, plural)

Place of Origin

Use *ser* when discussing place of origin and nationality. For example:

¿De dónde es usted?	**Where are you from?**
Soy de Rusia.	**I am from Russia.**

¿Es usted ruso?	**Are you Russian?**
Sí, soy ruso. / Sí, lo soy.	**Yes, I am Russian. / Yes, I am.**
No, no lo soy.	**No, I'm not.**

The following table lists other countries and words for nationality (which can be used as either adjectives or nouns). Please remember to add the right endings to words of nationality, depending upon whether they describe males or females, and whether they refer to one or many. For example, "American" may be *americano, americana, americanos,* or *americanas.* Unless there are irregularities, generally only the male singular form is provided.

Vocabulary: Countries and Their Citizens

País (Country)	Ciudadano (Citizen)
Afganistán	*afgano*
Alemania	*alemán, alemana*
Argentina	*argentino*
Australia	*australiano*
Austria	*austriaco*
Bélgica	*belga* (masculine and feminine)
Brasil	*brasileño*
Canadá	*canadiense* (masculine and feminine)
Chile	*chileno*
China	*chino*
Colombia	*colombiano*
Costa Rica	*costarricense*
Ecuador	*ecuatoriano*
Egipto	*egipcio*
Francia	*francés, francesa*
Gran Bretaña	*británico*
Grecia	*griego*

País (Country)	Ciudadano (Citizen)
Guatemala	guatemalteco
Haití	haitiano
Holanda	holandés, holandesa
India	indio
Inglaterra	inglés, inglesa
Irán	iraní (masculine and feminine)
Iraq	iraquí (masculine and feminine)
Irlanda	irlandés, irlandesa
Israel	israelí (masculine and feminine)
Italia	italiano
Jamaica	jamaicano
Japón	japonés, japonesa
México	mexicano
Nicaragua	nicaragüense
Panamá	panameño
Perú	peruano
Polonia	polaco
Puerto Rico	puertorriqueño
República Checa (Czech Republic)	checo
República de Eslovenia	esloveno
El Salvador	salvadoreño
Sudáfrica (South Africa)	sudafricano
Suecia (Sweden)	sueco
Suiza (Switzerland)	suizo
Tailandia	tailandés, tailandesa
Turquía	turco
Venezuela	venezolano
Yugoslavia	yugoslavo

ALERT!

Notice that in Spanish you don't need to capitalize adjectives of nationality as you would in English, so "American" becomes *americano*, and so on. However, names of countries are capitalized in both languages.

There is no doubt that U.S. citizens are known as "Americans" throughout the world. In many Latin American countries, however, *americanos* are people who live in the western hemisphere. U.S. citizens are termed *estadounidenses*, from the words *Estados Unidos* (United States). More colloquially, Spanish speakers refer to Americans as *norteamericanos, yanquis*, or *gringos*.

Some people who live in Latin America do not identify themselves as *hispanos*.

Being "hispanic" is a political identity that diverse immigrant groups use to participate in the greater society within the United States. As such, it does little to actually describe the white, indigenous, black, Asian, and multiracial people that may comprise the category.

Physical Characteristics

The adjectives appearing in the following describe characteristics that are permanent, and don't change from day to day. They go with the verb *ser*.

Physical-Characteristic Adjectives

alto	tall
anciano	elderly
bajo	short
bello	beautiful
bonito	pretty
calvo	bald

Physical-Characteristic Adjectives

delgado	thin
elegante (masculine and feminine)	elegant
feo	ugly
fuerte (masculine and feminine)	strong
gordo	fat
grande	big, large
grueso	stocky
guapo	handsome
hermoso	beautiful (can be used as "heavy" when referring to people)
joven (masculine and feminine)	young
mayor (masculine and feminine)	older
moreno	dark-haired (can refer to skin)
pelirrojo	redheaded
pobre (masculine and feminine)	poor
rubio	blond(e)
viejo	old

Here are some examples of using a physical-characteristic adjective and the verb *ser:*

Los chicos son muy jóvenes.	**The boys are very young.**
Rosalinda es morena, con ojos oscuros.	**Rosalinda is dark-haired, with dark eyes.**
Vosotros sois unos tipos fuertes.	**You are some strong guys.**
Soy una chica muy guapa.	**I'm a very pretty girl.**

Ser and the Preposition De

You will often find yourself using the preposition *de* when describing personal characteristics with the verb *ser.* First, let's review this preposition and how it is used.

Though *en inglés* you would use two different prepositions, "of" and "from," *en español* you simply use *de*. *De* is often used to express a sense of belonging. In English, you have the construction "'s"—you can say, "Charlie's book," "kids' toys." In Spanish, that's not an option. Instead, you have to remember to flip the phrase around and use *de: el libro de Charlie* (the book of Charlie), *los juguetes de los niños* (the toys of the kids).

Take a look at the following examples of how *de* and the verb *ser* are used in the Spanish sentence.

TRACK 38

La mesa es de madera.	**The table is made of wood.**
Jonathan es de Chicago.	**Jonathan is from Chicago.**
La muñeca de Jenny es de Inglaterra.	**Jenny's doll is from England.**
Yo soy la hija de Luis y Ana Moncayo.	**I am the daughter of Luis and Anna Moncayo.**
El pan es de trigo.	**The bread is made of wheat.**
Yo estoy en clase de dos a tres.	**I am in class from two to three.**
Ella es de Chicago.	**She is from Chicago.**
Soy de estatura mediana.	**I am of medium height.**

Occupation

For the purposes of Spanish grammar, think of occupation as a permanent characteristic that goes with the verb *ser*. For example:

¿Cuál es su profesión? ¿Qué hace usted?	**What is your profession? What do you do?**
Soy actriz.	**I am an actress.**

As you can see, the indefinite article "a/an" isn't used before a person's profession. Now, here is some useful vocabulary to talk about professional occupations in Spanish.

Las Profesiones (Occupations)

actor, actriz	actor, actress
amo,a (de casa)	homemaker
analista de inventario (masculine and feminine)	inventory analyst
arquitecto,a	architect
asistente ejecutivo, asistente ejecutiva	executive assistant
banquero,a	banker
camarero,a	waiter
consejero,a de inversiones	investment advisor
consultor(a) de mercadeo	marketing consultant
contador(a)	accountant
director(a)	director
diseñador(a)	designer
diseñador(a) de software	software developer
estudiante (masculine and feminine)	student
farmacéutico,a	pharmacist
gerente (masculine and feminine)	manager
ingeniero químico	chemical engineer
juez(a)	judge
maestro,a	teacher
médico,a	doctor
mercader(a)	merchant
modista (masculine and feminine)	dressmaker
músico,a	musician
pediatra (masculine and feminine)	pediatrician
periodista (masculine and feminine)	journalist
piloto (masculine and feminine)	pilot
profesor(a) de música	music teacher
repostero,a	pastry maker

sastre (masculine and feminine)	tailor
supervisor(a)	supervisor
tabernero,a	barkeeper
vendedor(a)	salesperson

Personal Relationships

The verb *ser* is used for describing personal relationships for the same reason that it is used to describe occupations—relationship roles are considered to be permanent characteristics. You will always be your parents' daughter or son, and they will always be your parents. While some relationships might not last quite as long, they are still considered permanent in the grammatical sense. Take a look at these sentences as examples and listen to how they're pronounced on Track 39.

TRACK 39

Carolina es la amiga de Estefi.	**Carolina is Estefi's friend.**
Las dos estudiantes son grandes enemigas.	**The two students are great enemies.**
Marco y Juan son socios.	**Marco and Juan are associates.**
Ellos son rivales.	**They are rivals.**
Elena es la hija de Sandra.	**Elena is the daughter of Sandra.**

Note that relationships that go with *ser* need not be family relationships. For the vocabulary on the relationships between family members, see Chapter 14.

Counting on Ser

Ser is also used in the language of numbers and counting. Think about it this way: The fact that two plus two is four is a permanent characteristic, not a temporary state, so you would say *dos más dos son cuatro*. Take a look at the following simple math steps and how to say them in Spanish. (For a complete overview of Spanish numerals, refer to Chapter 9.)

$2 \times 2 = 4$	*dos por dos son cuatro*
$10 + 10 = 20$	*diez más diez son veinte*
$9 - 2 = 7$	*nueve menos dos son siete*
$8 \div 8 = 1$	*ocho dividido por ocho es uno*

The verb *ser* can also be used in discussing prices, where it can substitute *costar* (to cost). For instance, compare the following two sentences:

El kilo(gramo) de manzanas es dos euros. **The kilogram of apples is 2 euros.**

La copa de vino tinto cuesta siete dólares. **The glass of red wine costs seven dollars.**

Figure It Out

It's time to practice trying to decipher meaning from Spanish sentences, even if you haven't yet learned all the words. Try to translate the following sentences, which use the verb *ser*.

1. *Nosotros somos italianos. Vivimos en Roma.*

   _____

2. *Ellos son unos tipos muy interesantes.*

   _____

3. *Tres menos uno son dos.*

   _____

4. *Yo soy diseñadora en una compañía grande.*

   _____

5. *Vosotros sois los padres de Elena.*

   _____

Chapter 7

How Are You? Introducing Estar

Now that you understand the verb *ser* and how it is used in Spanish, you can go on to examine its sister "to be" verb, *estar*. Whereas *ser* is a verb of permanence, *estar* is reserved for more transitory meanings. It will help you discuss such "temporary" points as the weather, your mood, and somebody or something's physical location.

Location and Temporary State

Estar can help you answer the questions "Where are you?" and "How are you?" Use this verb when referring to a person's physical location or temporary state of being. For example:

¿Cómo está usted?	**How are you?**
Estoy muy bien, gracias.	**I'm very well, thanks.**
¿Dónde está usted?	**Where are you (located)?**
Estoy en mi casa.	**I'm at home.**

But before you go on, it's important to learn how the verb *estar* is conjugated in the present tense. As you might have guessed, *estar* is another one of those irregular verbs, though it does not veer off the regular path quite as far as *ser*.

Conjugating Estar in Present Tense

(yo) estoy	I am
(tú) estás	you are (informal, singular)
(él, ella, usted) está	he, she, it is; you are (formal, singular)
(nosotros, nosotras) estamos	we are
(vosotros, vosotras) estáis	you are (informal, plural)
(ellos, ellas, ustedes) están	they are; you are (formal, plural)

Estar is often used when dealing within a time frame—the how, when, where, and who at a particular point in time. *¿Cómo está usted?* is a common social inquiry—part courtesy, part small talk, generally a way to catch up on current physical, mental/emotional, positional, and professional condition.

Physical State

Match the verb *estar* with the adjectives and adverbs in the following table to describe how you feel. Keep in mind that adjectives and adverbs need to agree in person and number with their respective subjects. For example: *Él está cansado. Ella está cansada. Ellos están cansados. Ellas están cansadas.* (He/she/they are tired.)

Vocabulary: Describing How You Feel

así así (masculine and feminine)	so-so
cansado	tired
débil (masculine and feminine)	weak
despierto	awake
dolorido	in pain
dormido	asleep
ebrio	drunk
enfermo	sick
mareado	dizzy
ocupado	busy
sobrio	sober

Usted no está mareado todavía.	**You are still not dizzy.**
Los niños están dormidos.	**The kids are sleeping.**
Yo estoy débil después de tanto trabajo.	**I am (feeling) weak after so much work.**
Ustedes no están sobrios, están ebrios.	**You aren't sober, you're drunk.**

Mental State

In addition to physical conditions, *estar* is also used to describe mental and emotional conditions. The following table contains some vocabulary you will need to help you describe your state of being.

Vocabulary: Mental and Emotional Conditions

aburrido	bored
afectuoso	affectionate
amable (masculine and feminine)	kind, amiable
amistoso	friendly
avergonzado	embarrassed
bondadoso	good, kind
cariñoso	loving
celoso	jealous
cómico	funny
contento	satisfied, happy
enfadado	angry
feliz (masculine and feminine)	happy
molesto	annoyed
preocupado	worried
temeroso	fearful

Yo estoy feliz.	**I am happy.**
Vosotros estáis tranquilos ya.	**You are already (feeling) calm.**
Estás loca con preocupación.	**You are crazy with worry.**
Estamos muy cómicos hoy.	**We are very funny today.**

Point of Location

Estar also expresses a "positional" situation—where you are at a particular time, answering the question *¿Dónde está usted?* (Where are you?) Physical location may include an actual place (country, town, street, building, and so on), or a reference to a place in relation to a person's environment.

¿Dónde está usted? Estoy:

en México	in Mexico
en la calle Sucre	on Sucre Street
en casa	at home
aquí	here
acá	over here (in this general area)

Refer to the following table for a list of prepositions you can use to indicate the location of an object or person:

Prepositions

a mano derecha	on the right side
a la derecha de	to the right of
a mano izquierda	on the left side
a la izquierda de	to the left of
al fondo de	at/in the back of
al lado de	to the side of, next to
abajo	downstairs
arriba	upstairs
adentro	inside
afuera	outside
cerca de	close to
lejos de	far from
debajo de	under
sobre	over, on top of
atrás	in the back
delante de	in front of
detrás de	behind
enfrente	in front (facing)

In English, "where you are" isn't necessarily tied to a physical position, but can also point to a position within a process. This also holds true for Spanish: *¿En qué día está en su dieta?* (In what day are you on your diet?) *Estoy en mi tercer día.* (I am in my third day.)

The following are some examples of sentences with prepositions you have just learned. Listen to them on the CD.

TRACK 40

Los niños están afuera.	**The children are outside.**
Celso está detrás de su amigo en la fila.	**Celso is behind his friend in the line.**
Yo vivo enfrente de una iglesia.	**I live in front of a church.**
La tienda está lejos del banco.	**The store is far from the bank.**
El coche está atrás.	**The car is in the back.**
Las llaves están sobre la mesa.	**The keys are on top of the table.**
César trabaja cerca de su casa.	**Cesar works close to his home.**
El regalo está debajo del árbol.	**The present is beneath the tree.**

Situational Prepositions

The "situational" aspect of *estar* is brought out by the prepositions that frequently follow it immediately. It is this aspect that makes it so flexible and as a result more widely used than *ser*.

Preposition *Con*

The preposition *con* (with) may be used to express physical proximity:

Estoy con el teléfono inalámbrico.	**I am with the wireless phone.**
Estoy con mis padres.	**I am with my parents.**

It may also be used to express religious or ideological proximity:

Está con Dios.	**He is with God.**
Está con los demócratas.	**She is with the Democrats.**

Con is also used to express physical, mental, or emotional experiences (primarily used with nouns that describe a physical state):

Estoy con vergüenza.	**I am embarrassed.**

Preposition *Contra*

The preposition *contra* (against), sometimes used together with *en,* may be used to express physical contact or opposition to ideology or circumstances:

Estoy contra la pared.	**I am leaning against the wall.**
Están en contra de la guerra.	**They are against the war.**
Estamos en contra del socialismo.	**We are in opposition to socialism.**

Preposition *De*

The preposition *de* (of, from) may be used to express physical position, mental position, a change in position, or a momentary condition. Here are some examples with the phrase *estar de:*

Estamos de pie.	**We are standing; literally: on our feet.**
Están de vacaciones.	**They are on vacation.**
Estamos de acuerdo.	**We are in agreement.**

Preposition *Entre*

The preposition *entre* (between) may be used to express physical position or mental or emotional condition (usually idiomatic). For example:

Estás entre amigos.	**You are among friends.**
Están entre la espada y la pared.	**They are trapped; literally: they are between a sword and a wall.**
Estoy entre sí y no.	**I am undecided; literally: between yes and no.**

Preposition *Para*

The preposition *para* in combination with *estar* may be used to express a prepared condition, mood, or inclination to act for someone or something. Take a look at the following examples:

Estoy para llegar a casa.	**I am about to arrive at home.**
Estamos para ir a la tienda.	**We are about to go to the store.**
Está para fiestas.	**He is generally open to parties.**

Preposition *Por*

The preposition *por* (for), in combination with *estar,* may be used to express a reasoned or emotional preference for a person and ideology, or as a reasoned preference or contemplation of an act.

Estamos por los derechos humanos.	**We are for human rights.**
Estoy por ir al cine.	**I am in favor of going to the movies.**
Están por ir a la tienda.	**They are going to go to the store.**

Preposition *Sin*

The preposition *sin* (without) may be used to express a lacking condition:

Estoy sin dinero.	**I am without money.**
Estamos sin dormir.	**We are without sleep.**

Prepositions and Estar

Translate the following sentences to Spanish, using *con, contra, de,* or *sin.* Use your English-to-Spanish and Spanish-to-English dictionary to look up words you don't already know.

1. I am here with a friend.

_____

2. We are returning with Rita.

_____

3. Today I am not having luck.

_____

4. She is cold.

_____

5. I am in a hurry.

_____

Estar and the Present Progressive Tense

Often when translating the present tense of verbs, you will find some reference to the action as it progresses. It's not unusual to see *yo camino* translated as "I am walking." While the Spanish present tense does capture an action in the moment, it is more like a simple snapshot than a video. The present progressive is the tense that allows you to "see" the action as it is occurring.

The present progressive actually combines two different parts of speech, *estar* (conjugated according to the subject) and the present participle of the verb that shows action in progress, to realize a description of an action in movement. Think of the present progressive as the equivalent of the English construction "is –ing." To see at how *cantar* (to sing), *aprender* (to learn), and *vivir* (to live) are conjugated in the present progressives, refer to the following table.

Present Progressive Tense

yo estoy cantando, aprendiendo, viviendo
I am singing, learning, living

tú estás cantando, aprendiendo, viviendo
you are singing, learning, living (informal, singular)

él, ella, usted está cantando, aprendiendo, viviendo
he, she, you are singing, learning, living (formal, singular)

nosotros, nosotras estamos cantando, aprendiendo, viviendo
we are singing, learning, living

vosotros, vosotras estais cantando, aprendiendo, viviendo
you are singing, learning, living (informal, plural)

ellos, ellas, ustedes están cantando, aprendiendo, viviendo
they, you are singing, learning, living (formal, plural)

Here are some examples of how to use the present progressive tense:

Jonathan está corriendo en el parque.	**Jonathan is running at the park.**
¿Estás hablando por teléfono?	**Are you talking on the phone?**
Mis padres están viviendo ahora en Madrid.	**My parents are living in Madrid now.**

As you will learn other verb tenses, you will also discover that the construction of *estar + verbo* that forms the present progressive tense, which you have just learned, also exists in other tenses: *yo estaba cantando* (I used to be singing), *estuve aprendiendo* (I was learning), *he estado viviendo* (I have been living), *yo estaré celebrando* (I will be celebrating).

Which Is Which?

To a native English speaker, it might not always be obvious when to use *ser* and when to use *estar*—in English, we have only one "to be" verb. If you need the most basic guideline, memorize the following rules of thumb:

- *Ser* corresponds to expressions of permanent characteristics.
- *Estar* corresponds to description of situation.

For instance, compare the following pairs:

Ella es de Florida./Ella está en Florida.	**She's from Florida./She is in Florida.**
Ellos son felices./Ellos están felices.	**They are happy people./They are happy (now).**

For a more detailed list of rules on how to choose between *ser* and *estar*, refer to the following table.

Rules for Using Ser and Estar

Use Estar	Use Ser
situación física (a physical situation)	*profesión, oficio, y actividad* (profession, occupation, and activity)
estado físico (physical state)	*parentesco y relaciones* (familial and other relationships)
estado mental (mental state)	*personalidad* (personality)
apariencia temporal (temporary appearance)	*apariencia característica* (characteristic appearance)
los resultados de una acción (results of an action)	*posesión* (possession)
el progreso de una acción (progress of an action)	*acción, con ocurrir o tener lugar* (action, when something occurs or takes place)
materia y origen (essence and origin)	
tiempo, cantidad, precio, y número (time, quantity, price, and number)	
construcciones de impersonalidad (impersonal constructions)	

Ser or Estar?

Translate the following sentences using the appropriate form of *estar* and *ser*. Use the vocabulary words provided in Chapters 6 and 7, and reference your English-to-Spanish and Spanish-to-English dictionary to look up words you don't already know. (Answers are provided in Appendix E.)

1. We are sick.

   _____

2. Miguel's friend is French.

   _____

3. I am very tired.

   _____

4. I am a calm person.

   _____

5. Venezuelans are friendly.

   _____

Chapter 8

As Time Goes By: Other Verb Tenses

So far, the discussion of verbs has been centered on the present. But at any given moment, you might be remembering the past, using what you've learned there, or looking toward the future, making plans. Just as verbs are conjugated according to person and number, they are also conjugated according to their point in time—their tense.

Conjugating Regular Verbs

For most Spanish regular verbs that you come across, their use will be as simple as "plug and play." If you know who is acting and when the action is occurring in relation to you, simply attach the appropriate ending to the verb base and, like magic, you've expressed a complete thought in Spanish.

With respect to regular verbs, the key lies in owning the tenses to the extent that you can decide in a split second what tense to use. As you practice memorizing the tenses and their endings, apply verbs immediately to yourself and your situation and then extend your situation to others. Repetition will help you focus in on, and eventually internalize, the base of a few model verbs. At some point, probably when you least expect it, you'll start "sensing" how the thousands of regular verbs relate to these models, and you will have begun to conquer Spanish.

Preterite Tense

The preterite tense refers to the simple past and often to a single occurrence within one instance or recurring more specific instances. It is important to understand that the action is rooted in the past and physically and psychologically cut off from the present; the past action has terminated and is in effect complete (in grammar, complete tenses are known as "perfect" ones). The action may be tied to the past in terms of any of the following:

- A particular moment or date. For example: *Nací el 12 de junio de 1966.* (I was born on June 12, 1966.)
- Several isolated instances. For example: *Llamé cinco veces.* (I called five times.)
- Duration. For example: En aquel año *trabajé en el Cuerpo de Paz.* (In that year, I worked in the Peace Corps.)

Conjugating Verbs in the Preterite Tense

As you remember, regular verbs may fall into the *–ar, –er,* or *–ir* category. The following table will provide you with the endings you need to learn in order to be able to conjugate verbs in the preterite tense. The regular verbs used as examples are the same as in Chapter 5, where you were first introduced to these verbs: *cantar* (to sing), *aprender* (to learn), and *vivir* (to live). Note that in the preterite, the *–er* and *–ir* verbs share identical endings.

–Ar Verb Endings in the Preterite Tense

–ar	cantar	to sing (infinitive)
–é	(yo) canté	I sang
–aste	(tú) cantaste	you sang (informal, singular)
–ó	(él, ella) cantó	he, she, it sang
	(usted) cantó	you sang (formal, singular)
–amos	(nosotros, nosotras) cantamos	we sang
–asteis	(vosotros, vosotras) cantasteis	you sang (informal, plural)
–aron	(ellos, ellas) cantaron	they sang
	(ustedes) cantaron	you sang (formal, plural)

–Er Verb Endings in the Preterite Tense

–er	aprender	to learn (infinitive)
–í	(yo) aprendí	I learned
–iste	(tú) aprendiste	you learned (informal, singular)
–ó	(él, ella) aprendió	he, she, it learned
	(usted) aprendió	you learned (formal, singular)
–imos	(nosotros, nosotras) aprendimos	we learned
–isteis	(vosotros, vosotras) aprendisteis	you learned (informal, plural)
–eron	(ellos, ellas) aprendieron	they learned
	(ustedes) aprendieron	you learned (formal, plural)

–Ir Verb Endings in the Preterite Tense

–ir	vivir	to live (infinitive)
–í	(yo) viví	I lived
–iste	(tú) viviste	you lived (informal, singular)
–ó	(él, ella) vivió	he, she, it lived
	(usted) vivió	you lived (formal, singular)
–imos	(nosotros, nosotras) vivimos	we lived
–isteis	(vosotros, vosotras) vivisteis	you lived (informal, plural)
–eron	(ellos, ellas) vivieron	they lived
	(ustedes) vivieron	you lived (formal, plural)

Imperfect Tense

The companion to the preterite, the imperfect (or copreterite) tense also refers to the simple past. However, whereas the preterite is enclosed by time, the imperfect is not. An action can have occurred over a span of time with no clear beginning or ending point. There may or may not be a connection with the present; it may or may not still be happening. This vagueness regarding the end to an action, or this developing and lasting quality of past action, is the reason for this tense's being named the "imperfect" tense. The action of the imperfect tense may be tied to the following:

- An unspecified amount of time. For example: *De niño, quería un caballo.* (As a boy, I wanted a horse.)
- An indefinite number of occurrences, such as a habit or custom. For example: *Cada vez que la veía, me sentía feliz.* (Each time I saw her, I felt happy.)

Conjugating Verbs in the Imperfect Tense

The following table includes the verb endings for verbs in the imperfect tense. Notice that the *yo* form and *él, ella, usted* form of these verbs is the same. To avoid confusion, simply add the relevant pronoun to identify the correct person. And as with the preterite tense endings, imperfect *–er* and *–ir* verbs share the same set of endings.

–Ar Verb Endings in the Imperfect Tense

–ar	cantar	to sing (infinitive)
–aba	*(yo) cantaba*	I sang
–abas	*(tú) cantabas*	you sang (informal, singular)
–aba	*(él, ella) cantaba*	he, she, it sang
	(usted) cantaba	you sang (formal, singular)
–ábamos	*(nosotros, nosotras) cantábamos*	we sang
–abais	*(vosotros, vosotras) cantabais*	you sang (informal, plural)
–aban	*(ellos, ellas) cantaban*	they sang
	(ustedes) cantaban	you sang (formal, plural)

–Er Verb Endings in the Imperfect Tense

–er	aprender	to learn (infinitive)
–ía	*(yo) aprendía*	I learned
–ías	*(tú) aprendías*	you learned (informal, singular)
–ía	*(él, ella) aprendía*	he, she, it learned
	(usted) aprendía	you learned (formal, singular)
–íamos	*(nosotros, nosotras) aprendíamos*	we learned
–íais	*(vosotros, vosotras) aprendíais*	you learned (informal, plural)
–ían	*(ellos, ellas) aprendían*	they learned
	(ustedes) aprendían	you learned (formal, plural)

–Ir Verb Endings in the Imperfect Tense

–ir	vivir	to live (infinitive)
–ía	(yo) vivía	I lived
–ías	(tú) vivías	you lived (informal, singular)
–ía	(él, ella) vivía	he, she, it lived
	(usted) vivía	you lived (formal, singular)
–íamos	(nosotros, nosotras) vivíamos	we lived
–íais	(vosotros, vosotras) vivíais	you lived (informal, plural)
–ían	(ellos, ellas) vivían	they lived
	(ustedes) vivían	you lived (formal, plural)

Preterite and Imperfect Together

It's not uncommon to combine the preterite and the imperfect verbs in the same sentence, especially with the words *de* and *cuando*. Take a look at the following examples.

A la vez que hacía la broma, sonrió.	**As he was telling the joke, he smiled.**
Ayer cuando caminaba al trabajo, vio un accidente.	**Yesterday when he was walking to work, he saw an accident.**
Nunca hablaba mal de otros, pero lo hizo hoy.	**He never used to speak badly of others, but today he did.**

For additional vocabulary words that will help you form similar sentences in the imperfect and preterite tense, refer to the following table.

Vocabulary Often Used with the Imperfect and Preterite Tense

a la vez	at the same time
algunas veces	sometimes
a menudo	often
a veces	at times

Vocabulary Often Used with the Imperfect and Preterite Tense

cada día	each day, every day
contadas veces	seldom
de vez en cuando	once in a while
esta vez	this time
frecuentemente	frequently
muchas veces	many times
nunca	never
repetidas veces	repeatedly
siempre	always
tantas veces	so many times
toda la semana	all week long
toda la vida	whole life

Take a look at the following two phrases: *cada mes* (each month) and *cada semana* (each week). Though mes is a masculine noun and *semana* is a feminine noun, the word *cada* does not change its ending. And, of course, it does not exist in the plural—"each" is always a singular idea.

Preterite Versus Imperfect

Non-native English speakers often have trouble differentiating between the preterite and the imperfect. Though verbs in these two tenses may sometimes be translated as the same verb tense in English, differences do exist.

The preterite is a precise and limiting tense. The imperfect, on the other hand, is less restricted; it represents the vagueness of time with respect to the action. For a detailed review of when to use the preterite and the imperfect, refer to the following table.

Preterite Versus Imperfect

Preterite	Imperfect
An act that occurs as a single event.	An act that was customary in the past.
An act limited in the times it is performed.	An act that may be ongoing indefinitely.
An act that is defined within specified time frames.	An act that is defined within broad frames.

The following are some examples to help you differentiate between the imperfect and the preterite.

TRACK 41

Ella fue al cine ayer.
She went to the movies yesterday.

De niña, ella iba al cine cada sábado.
As a young girl, she used to go to the movies every Saturday.

Me gustó la película.
I liked the movie.

A Jonathan le gustaba mucho el programa de televisión de Los Tres Chiflados.
Jonathan liked The Three Stooges television program very much.

La cita comenzó a las diez de la mañana.
The meeting began at ten in the morning.

De niños, comenzaban a llorar cada vez que oían el trueno.
As children they used to begin to cry every time they heard thunder.

Present Perfect Tense

The present perfect tense is constructed by using a form of the auxiliary verb *haber* (to have) with the past participle form of the primary verb. It characterizes a past connected to a now-expanded present. In a nutshell, the present perfect tense is used to describe the following:

- **An immediate past.** For example: *No he comido porque acabo de llegar.* (I've not eaten because I have just arrived.)

- **A past inhabited by the speaker.** For example: *Últimamente he tenido mucho sueño.* (Lately, I have been very sleepy.)
- **Information independent of time.** For example: *No he hablado con María.* (I haven't talked to Maria.)
- **A psychologically or emotionally linked past.** For example: *He perdido a mi abuelita hace diez años.* (I lost my grandmother ten years ago.)

Conjugating Verbs in Present Perfect Tense

Present perfect is a composite tense—that is, the main verb *haber* (in this case the Spanish equivalent of the English verb "to have") is conjugated in the present tense and then matched with a past participle form of another verb. So conjugating verbs in this tense is really easy: All you need to know is how to conjugate *haber* and set the other verb as a past participle.

Let's start with *haber,* which (no surprise!) is an irregular verb. Note that though it translates as "have" in the sense of "I have done . . . ," it is not used in the other sense of "have" (possession, ownership). That verb is *tener* and will be covered in Chapter 10.

Conjugating Haber in the Present Tense

(yo) he	I have
(tú) has	you have (informal, singular)
(él, ella, usted) ha	he, she, it has; you have (formal, singular)
(nosotros, nosotras) hemos	we have
(vosotros, vosotras) habéis	you have (informal, plural)
(ellos, ellas, ustedes) han	they have; you have (formal, plural)

Forming the past participle is even easier: If a verb ends in *–ar,* its corresponding past participle substitutes *–ar* with *–ado.* If it ends with *–er* or *–ir,* its corresponding past participle substitutes *–er* or *–ir* with *–ido.*

Present Participle Conjugations of Cantar, Aprender, and Vivir

Pronoun	Cantar	Aprender	Vivir
yo	he cantado	he aprendido	he vivido
tú	has cantado	has aprendido	has vivido
él, ella, usted	ha cantado	ha aprendido	ha vivido
nosotros, nosotras	hemos cantado	hemos aprendido	hemos vivido
vosotros, vosotras	habéis cantado	habéis aprendido	habéis vivido
ellos, ellas, ustedes	han cantado	han aprendido	han vivido

Future Tense

Finally! A verb tense that is just as easy to learn in Spanish as in English. What the future tense describes is fairly straightforward. The following types of actions are treated in the future tense:

- Actions asserted as certain to occur within a period following the present. For example: *Viajaré a Londres en septiembre.* (I will travel to London in September.)
- A probable action given uncertain but possible circumstances. For example: *Comeré el almuerzo si tengo tiempo.* (I will eat lunch if I have time.)

Conjugating Verbs in the Future Tense

The endings for verbs in the future tense are the same for *–ar, –er,* and *–ir* verbs. However, there's a little trick you'll need to remember: You add the ending to the infinitive form *without* dropping the infinitive ending. The following table lists the conjugation endings, as well as examples.

Conjugating Verbs in Future Tense

Ending	Pronoun(s)	Cantar	Aprender	Vivir
–é	yo	cantaré	aprenderé	viviré
–ás	tú	cantarás	aprenderás	vivirás

Ending	Pronoun(s)	Cantar	Aprender	Vivir
–á	él, ella, usted	cantará	aprenderá	vivirá
–emos	nosotros, nosotras	cantaremos	aprenderemos	viviremos
–éis	vosotros, vosotras	cantaréis	aprenderéis	viviréis
–án	ellos, ellas, ustedes	cantarán	aprenderán	vivirán

Conditional Tense

The conditional tense in Spanish is generally equivalent to the English construction "would + verb." In Spanish, the conditional has five basic uses:

- It roots a future action to the past. For example: *Manuel me dijo que llegaría antes de las tres.* (Manuel told me that he would arrive before three.) *Pensaban que sus hijos no crecerían tan rápido.* (They were thinking that their kids would not grow up so quickly.)
- It allows for the hypothetical—with the implication that the conditional statement is unlikely. For example: *Te compraría un pasaje a Europa, pero perdí todo el dinero en Las Vegas.* (I would buy you a trip to Europe, but I lost all my money in Las Vegas.) *Te ayudaría a mover el sofá, pero desgraciadamente me lesioné la espalda hoy por la mañana.* (I would help you move the sofa, but unfortunately I hurt my back this morning.)
- It gives room for a probability that is more expansive and may include conjecture or approximation. For example: *¿Con quién hablaría Juan a esas horas de la noche?* (With whom would Juan speak at that hour of night?) *Serían las diez cuando la vi.* (It might have been ten when I saw her.)
- It allows for a concession in light of a contrary view or experience introduced by *pero* (but). For example: *Sería tacaño pero nunca me negó su ayuda.* (He might have been stingy but he never refused me his help.) *Ella tendría poca instrucción formal pero es una persona brillante.* (She might have had little formal education but she is a brilliant person.)

- It provides an alternative to the copreterite in expressing a courteous request. For example: *¿Podría decirme donde está la parada de autobús?* (Could you tell me where the bus stop is?) *¿Me dejarías usar tu teléfono?* (Would you allow me to use your phone?)

The underlying idea to remember about the conditional is that the future is not so certain because what it depends on is either unlikely or too expansive to pin down and know readily.

The conditional tense also appears in "if/then" constructions that are posed in the past tense. For instance, in English you would say, "If I had a dog, I would take care of it well." In Spanish, you would use the conditional for the "then" clause: *Si tuviera un perro, lo cuidaría bien.*

Conditional-Tense Conjugations

Conjugating verbs in the conditional tense is very easy, as long as you know the future-tense base. For regular verbs, that's simply the infinitive form, which you will use without dropping the *–ar, –er,* or *–ir* ending. (Irregular verbs will have the same base in the conditional tense as they do in the future tense. You will learn the irregular future conjugations in Chapter 15.)

The conditional endings are the same for all three groups of verbs. For some examples, take a look at the following table:

Conjugating Verbs in Conditional Tense

Ending	Pronoun(s)	Cantar	Aprender	Vivir
–ía	*yo*	*cantaría*	*aprendería*	*viviría*
–ías	*tú*	*cantarías*	*aprenderías*	*vivirías*
–ía	*él, ella, usted*	*cantaría*	*aprendería*	*viviría*
–íamos	*nosotros, nosotras*	*cantaríamos*	*aprenderíamos*	*viviríamos*
–íais	*vosotros, vosotras*	*cantaríais*	*aprenderíais*	*viviríais*
–ían	*ellos, ellas, ustedes*	*cantarían*	*aprenderían*	*vivirían*

Conjugating Ser and Estar

You already know how to conjugate regular verbs, but unfortunately not all Spanish verbs are regular. You have already learned the irregular present-tense verb forms for *ser* and *estar*. Now let's see how these verbs conjugate in preterite, imperfect, present perfect, and future tense (remember, you can use the future-tense base of the irregular verb to conjugate it in the conditional tense).

The Preterite Tense

In the preterite, *ser* is used on "permanent" characteristics that nevertheless had a definite ending point—think of them as life-altering changes. *Estar*'s focus on the situational goes along better in describing a simple past that is at odds with the present. After all, a lot of things do in fact change, particularly situations. The action is still rooted in the past and cut off from the present, but the changes that may occur in the movement toward the present are more easily assigned to a discrete point in time, rather than a continuum as is the case with the imperfect tense.

Fui bajo.	**I was short. (But now I'm tall.)**
Ayer estuve cansado.	**I was tired yesterday. (But I'm not tired anymore.)**

Try to memorize the preterite conjugation forms of *ser* and *estar*.

Ser and Estar in the Preterite Tense

Pronoun(s)	Ser	Estar
yo	*fui*	*estuve*
tú	*fuiste*	*estuviste*
él, ella, usted	*fue*	*estuvo*
nosotros, nosotras	*fuimos*	*estuvimos*
vosotros, vosotras	*fuisteis*	*estuvisteis*
ellos, ellas, ustedes	*fueron*	*estuvieron*

Imperfect Tense

Estar, in the imperfect, describes continuous, habitual, or customary acts of "being" that coincide with the English "I used to be" or "I was (being)." For example:

Estaba en el jardín cuando llegó el sol.	**I was in the garden when the sun came.**

The preterite and the imperfect can actually coincide. That is, the preterite can be contained within a time frame established by the copreterite as in:

Ayer mientras estaba en el trabajo, hablé con Luisa.	**Yesterday while I was at work, I talked to Luisa.**

With regard to *ser,* the imperfect tense may describe habitual or customary acts of "being" that coincide with the English "used to be" during a fairly vague period of time. It is often employed to complete the phrase "When I was . . ."

Cuando era niño, era travieso.	**When I was a boy, I was mischievous.**
Cuando era adolescente, era buena estudiante.	**When she was an adolescent, she was a good student.**

Notice that these time frames are common to everyone. You've also been a child and an adolescent at one time or another. Because the imperfect makes no reference to something having ended, it is often used to render descriptions of personal characteristics by relying on the preposition *de.* You can say:

De joven, era audaz.	**When I was young, I was an audacious kid.**
De soltera, era demasiado seria.	**When I was single, I was too serious.**
De casado, era tranquilo.	**When I was married, I was calm.**

For conjugated forms of *ser* and *estar* in the imperfect, refer to the following table.

Ser and Estar in the Imperfect Tense

Pronoun(s)	Ser	Estar
yo	era	estaba
tú	eras	estabas
él, ella, usted	era	estaba
nosotros, nosotras	éramos	estábamos
vosotros, vosotras	erais	estabais
ellos, ellas, ustedes	eran	estaban

The Present Perfect Tense

In this tense, *ser* and *estar* both translate to "have been." As you might remember, the conjugations are constructed by using a form of the auxiliary verb *haber* ("to have") with the past participle (or *–do*) form of the primary verb: in this case, *sido* and *estado*. For example:

Durante mi vida he sido estudiante, marinero, y vendedor de zapatos.	**During my life I've been a student, sailor, and shoe seller.**
He estado aquí dos horas.	**I have been here for two hours.**
He estado con gripe desde ayer.	**I have had a cold since yesterday.**

The Future Tense

Despite offering the present tense to describe future events, Spanish also has its own strictly future-focused tense.

La semana próxima estaré en Buenos Aires.	**Next week I will be in Buenos Aires.**
Qué será, será.	**What will be, will be.**

The following table contains the conjugations of *ser* and *estar* in the future tense.

THE EVERYTHING LEARNING SPANISH BOOK

Ser and Estar in the Future Tense

Pronoun(s)	Ser	Estar
yo	seré	estaré
tú	serás	estarás
él, ella, usted	será	estará
nosotros, nosotras	seremos	estaremos
vosotros, vosotras	seréis	estaréis
ellos, ellas, ustedes	serán	estarán

A Little Time Travel

Fill in the correct conjugation form based on the context of the sentence. Don't forget to conjugate the verb both according to tense and its subject. To check your answers, see Appendix E.

1. *El señor Ochoa y su esposa* _____ *(hablar) con su vecino a menudo.* (imperfect tense)

2. *En dos días, yo* _____ *(volver) a España.* (future tense)

3. *Si hiciera frío, tú te* _____ *(cubrir) con la manta.* (conditional tense)

4. *Cuando éramos pequeños,* _____ *(vivir) en un apartamento y no en una casa, como ahora.* (imperfect tense)

5. *Marina* _____ *(contestar) que nunca volvería a aquel lugar.* (preterite tense)

6. *Si él abriera la puerta, tú* _____ *(entrar) adentro.* (conditional tense)

7. *Yo* _____ *(pasar) tres años en Nueva York.* (preterite tense)

8. *Nosotros nunca* _____ *(tener) la oportunidad de hablar con él.* (present perfect)

Chapter 9

The Vocabulary of Time

Regardless of how many grammatical tenses a language boasts, when it comes to the concept of time there are really only three general frames of references—past, present, and future—by which to witness daily life. Measuring and telling time is an important part of learning Spanish—and a good way for you to practice your verb tenses!

9

Cardinal Numbers

Spanish employs cardinal and ordinal numerals (as does English). You are probably more familiar with the cardinals—numerals that express quantity and are used for counting: one, two, three, and so on. In fact, Spanish often uses cardinal numerals even when American English would choose ordinals—numerals that show the order of an item in a given series: first, second, third, and so on.

The Basics: 0–15

The single-digit numbers 1 through 9 are the most utilized in Spanish because they are employed alone *and* within larger numbers. All you really need to do is memorize the first nine, plus the word for 0 and 10 through 15; the rest is a matter of combining what you already know. When simply counting, numerals stand alone. Treat them as you would pronouns:

Numbers 0–15

0	cero	8	ocho
1	uno	9	nueve
2	dos	10	diez
3	tres	11	once
4	cuatro	12	doce
5	cinco	13	trece
6	seis	14	catorce
7	siete	15	quince

When enumerating items, however, the numeral is acting as an adjective and precedes the items enumerated. Any number above *uno* requires the use of the plural form of the item (see Chapter 4 for rules on how to add plural endings to nouns). Keep in mind that the actual numeral employed will not be in the plural form for quantities less than 200. For example:

un sacerdote	one priest
una bebida	one drink
cinco dedos	five fingers
cinco quejas	five complaints
ocho vestidos	eight dresses
ocho cortinas	eight curtains

FACT

The cardinal number as a preceding adjective often enumerates the quantity of items. When the cardinal number follows the item(s), it is limiting the discussion to the item in the position described by the number. For example: *cinco volúmenes* (five volumes), as opposed to *volumen cinco* (volume five).

Moving On: 16–99

Double-digit numbers are formed similarly to the way they are formed in English. For example, "21" is "twenty-one." If you know the words for "twenty," "thirty," "forty," and so on, as well as how to count from 1 to 9, you will be able to come up with any number from 1 to 100.

It is pretty much the same in Spanish. First, you need to learn the numbers divisible by 10:

10	*diez*	60	*sesenta*
20	*veinte*	70	*setenta*
30	*treinta*	80	*ochenta*
40	*cuarenta*	90	*noventa*
50	*cincuenta*		

The rules are slightly different for numbers 16 through 29 than for 30 through 99. Take a look at how the numbers 16 through 29 are formed:

16	diez y seis	dieciséis	23	veinte y tres	veintitrés
17	diez y siete	diecisiete	24	veinte y cuatro	veinticuatro
18	diez y ocho	dieciocho	25	veinte y cinco	veinticinco
19	diez y nueve	diecinueve	26	veinte y seis	veintiséis
20	veinte		27	veinte y siete	veintisiete
21	veinte y uno	veintiuno	28	veinte y ocho	veintiocho
22	veinte y dos	veintidós	29	veinte y nueve	veintinueve

For numbers 30 through 99, the rule is exactly the same, and there is no need to combine the number into one word: The two components remain connected by a *y* (and). Here are a few examples:

36	treinta y seis
48	cuarenta y ocho
59	cincuenta y nueve
81	ochenta y uno

Next Up: Hundreds

In Spanish, you rarely if ever say "one hundred"—instead, you simply say *cien* (hundred). Any number between 101 and 199 uses the term *ciento* in combination with the numerals specified in the previous section. Notice that a conjunction is not used between the "hundred" and "ten" words:

116	ciento dieciséis
131	ciento treinta y uno
177	ciento setenta y siete

Multiples of 100 are *cientos*. To create a specific number of "hundred" units, all you really need to do is combine the number of 100s with *cientos:*

200	*doscientos*	600	*seiscientos*
300	*trescientos*	700	*setecientos*
400	*cuatrocientos*	800	*ochocientos*
500	*quinientos*	900	*novecientos*

ALERT!

Notice that the words for 500, 700, and 900 do not follow the regular numeral + *cientos* pattern. To review, they are: *quinientos* (500), *setecientos* (700), and *novecientos* (900).

It follows, then, that for numbers 201 to 999, the process for putting together the numbers goes like this:

206	*doscientos seis*
331	*trescientos treinta y uno*
447	*cuatrocientos cuarenta y siete*
650	*seiscientos cincuenta*
809	*ochocientos nueve*

Keep in mind: You should use *y* only between the "tens" and the "units" values. Otherwise, the *y* is omitted (so, *treinta y ocho,* but *trescientos ochenta*). Also, the numbers containing "hundreds" parts do conform to the gender of the nouns they modify. For example: *trescientas casas* (300 homes), *quinientas veintiuna quejas* (521 complaints).

Moreover: Thousands

Like *cien, mil* (thousand) generally exists without a preceding article. Unlike *ciento,* however, *mil* does not take on any endings when it is part of a number. For any number of thousands above 1,000, simply place the number of thousands before *mil (dos mil, tres mil,* and so on). For example:

1,216	*mil doscientos dieciséis*
2,331	*dos mil trescientos treinta y uno*
3,477	*tres mil cuatrocientos setenta y siete*
5,000	*cinco mil*
45,783	*cuarenta y cinco mil setecientos ochenta y tres*

Spanish provides two equivalent constructions to express the collective noun "thousands"—*miles de* + noun or *millares de* + noun. For example: *Miles de personas votan. Millares de personas votan.* (Thousands of people vote.) Preference for one expression over the other is largely a regional issue.

Note that when you write in Spanish, you use a period instead of a comma to separate the digits in numbers greater than 1,000, and vice versa for the sign used to denote decimal points.

Period and Comma in Spanish Numbers

Spanish	English
3.000	3,000 (three thousand)
4,7	4.7 (four point seven)

Last but Not Least: Millions and Beyond

This is a time to recall the warning on misleading cognates from the first chapter. Though some Spanish and American English numbers do coincide (like million and *millón*), larger numbers do not. Compare:

millón	**million**
mil millones	**one billion**
billon	**one trillion**

Use the following examples to practice what you have just learned.

1,000,001	*un millón uno*
2,000,002	*dos millones dos*
1,000,000,345	*mil millones, trescientos cuarenta y cinco*
14,500,900,005	*catorce mil quinientos millones, novecientos mil, cinco*
1,000,100,700,000	*un billón, cien millones, setecientos mil*

A subtle change in meaning occurs when you begin using numbers in the millions and larger. You already know that "hundreds" and "thousands" no longer describe the quantity of things, but that they themselves become the objects of discussion. This is generally true of one million and beyond. Whereas you can say *cien mujeres* (100 women), you cannot say *un millón mujeres*—the correct phrase would be *un millón de mujeres* (one million women), where *de mujeres* describes the million. If you are talking of an unspecified number of books ranging in the millions, then you would say *millones de libros*.

FACT

With regard to the use of a number as an adjective or a noun, *de* is inserted between a specific number and the accompanying items only for numbers specified to the nearest (whole) million and above. For example: *dos millones de pesos* (two million pesos), but *dos millones tres pesos* (two million and three pesos).

Practice Counting

First, practice recognizing Spanish numbers that you encounter. Below, fill in the correct digits of a number expressed in Spanish.

1. *dieciocho* _____
2. *veintidós* _____
3. *cincuenta y cuatro* _____
4. *noventa y tres* _____
5. *ciento catorce* _____
6. *doscientos setenta y nueve* _____

7. *quinientos sesenta y dos* _____

8. *setecientos treinta y cinco* _____

Next, practice translating from English into Spanish:

1. 18   _____

2. 89   _____

3. 226   _____

4. 345   _____

5. 1,512   _____

6. 10,587   _____

7. 22,713   _____

8. 3,080,000   _____

Ordinal Numbers

When ordinal numbers describe a noun's position in a series, they act as adjectives and generally come before the noun they are modifying. Unlike cardinal numbers, ordinal numbers correspond in gender and number with the noun they describe. For example:

el primer día	**the first day**
la primera semana	**the first week**
los primeros días	**the first days**
las primeras semanas	**the first weeks**

On its own, an ordinal may express a "position" as a place, rather than a description, as in this sentence:

Yo salí de la casa primero.   **I left the house first.**

The following table presents ordinal numbers. Unless otherwise noted, this general form is the same as the masculine singular form.

Cardinal Numbers

primer, primero	first	*octavo*	eighth
segundo	second	*noveno*	ninth
tercer, tercero	third	*décimo*	tenth
cuarto	fourth	*undécimo*	eleventh
quinto	fifth	*duodécimo*	twelfth
sexto	sixth	*decimotercero*	thirteenth
séptimo	seventh	*decimocuarto*	fourteenth

Recall what happens to *uno* when used to describe quantity with respect to a masculine noun. As you might remember, "one car" in Spanish would be translated as *un coche*. That is, *uno* loses the final *–o* before a masculine noun. The same is true with the ordinals *primero* and *tercero* when they precede the noun they modify. For example: *el primer coche* (the first car) and *el decimotercer coche* (the thirteenth car).

Before you go on to the next section, take a look at the following sentences that contain ordinal or cardinal numbers and listen to them on Track 42.

TRACK 42

*De joven, Eliza ganó dos
    trofeos de fútbol.*
**When she was young, Eliza won two
    soccer trophies.**

*Él salió en primer puesto
    en la competencia.*
**He came out in first place in
    the competition.**

María vive en el apartamento ocho.
María lives in apartment eight.

*Los políticos asignan miles de
    millones de dólares cada año.*
**Politicians allocate thousands of
    millions of dollars each year.**

*Nací en el año mil novecientos
    cincuenta y seis.*
I was born in the year 1956.

*Treinta y siete más diez son
    cuarenta y siete.*
Thirty-seven plus ten is forty-seven.

*Patricio es el cuarto hijo de
    Roberto y Alicia.*
**Patrick is Robert and Alicia's fourth
    child.**

Days of the Week

To help you review the ordinal numbers, how about learning the days of the week? The following list answers the question *¿Cuáles son los días de la semana?* (What are the days of the week?) For a list of days of the week, refer to the table that follows.

TRACK 43

El lunes es el primer día de la semana.

Monday is the first day of the week.

El martes es el segundo día de la semana.

Tuesday is the second day of the week.

El miércoles es el tercer día de la semana.

Wednesday is the third day of the week.

El jueves es el cuarto día de la semana.

Thursday is the fourth day of the week.

El viernes es el quinto día de la semana.

Friday is the fifth day of the week.

El sábado es el sexto día de la semana.

Saturday is the sixth day of the week.

El domingo es el séptimo día de la semana.

Sunday is the seventh day of the week.

Days of the Week

lunes	Monday
martes	Tuesday
miércoles	Wednesday
jueves	Thursday
viernes	Friday
sábado	Saturday
domingo	Sunday

Other words that will help you set the sentence in the correct time frame include the following (listed in chronological order):

Time Vocabulary

el año pasado	last year
la semana pasada	last week
anteayer	day before yesterday
ayer	yesterday
este año	this year
esta semana	this week
hoy	today
mañana	tomorrow
pasado mañana	day after tomorrow
la próxima semana	next week
el próximo año	next year

The following set of examples illustrates how these vocabulary words work within the Spanish sentence:

TRACK 44

Esta semana he estado enfermo con un resfriado.	**This week I have been sick with a head cold.**
Toda la semana pasada, estuve de vacaciones.	**I was on vacation all last week.**
Estaré en las Islas Galápagos la semana próxima.	**I will be in the Galápagos Islands next week.**
Este año tendré un empleo nuevo.	**This year I will have a new job.**
El año pasado, estaba en Santo Domingo.	**Last year I was in Santo Domingo.**
El próximo año, estaré en Madrid.	**Next year, I will be in Madrid.**

To use *ser* in expressing time and days of the week, follow the format of the following question and answer: *¿Qué día es hoy?* (What day is it today?) *Hoy es lunes.* (Today is Monday.) Consequently, you would say *mañana es martes, en dos días es miércoles, en tres días es jueves,* and so on.

You know how to say what day it is, but what about the date? In Spanish, the date is known as *la fecha: ¿Cuál es la fecha de hoy?* (Which is the date today?) *Hoy es lunes, el catorce de junio.* (Today is Monday, June 14.) *De hoy en ocho días, es martes, el veintidos de junio.* (Eight days from today, it is Tuesday, June 22.)

Days of the Week

See if you can translate the following sentences into Spanish. Remember to use the appropriate articles. Use your English-to-Spanish and Spanish-to-English dictionary to look up words you don't already know.

1. Yesterday I was sick. (all day, but not today)

   _____

2. Saturday, I was with Elena.

   _____

3. Sunday I will be in Florida.

   _____

4. I am better since last week.

   _____

5. I work Tuesdays.

   _____

6. The birthday party is on the twenty-fifth.

   _____

The Months and Seasons

Moving on from days of the week, let's look at the months of the year and the four seasons. The list of *los meses* (the months) in Spanish appears in the following table.

TRACK 45

Months of the Year

enero	January
febrero	February
marzo	March
abril	April
mayo	May
junio	June
julio	July
agosto	August
septiembre	September
octubre	October
noviembre	November
diciembre	December

There is a slight difference in handling days, seasons, and months. Unless replaced by other modifiers such as "each," a definite article precedes days and seasons: *el lunes* (Monday), *la primavera* (spring). However, months are only specified by the definite article when speaking about a specific time when an event occurred or will occur: *en enero* (in January).

In Spanish, the four seasons of the year correspond to the English winter, spring, summer, and fall. The seasons are listed in the following table.

TRACK 46

Seasons of the Year

el invierno	winter
la primavera	spring
el verano	summer
el otoño	autumn, fall

¿Cuáles son los meses del año?

Translate the following sentences, which answer the question, "What are the months of the year?" Use your English-to-Spanish and Spanish-to-English dictionary to look up words you don't already know.

1. January is the first month of the year.

   _____

2. May is the fifth month of the year.

   _____

3. September is the ninth month of the year.

   _____

4. I was in Europe for two years.

   _____

5. I am thinking about going to Mexico next December.

   _____

6. Each June I am ready to travel.

   _____

Asking and Telling Time

What time is it? It's a common enough question. In Spanish, *tiempo* refers to the general concept of "time." Curiously enough, however, it also means "weather." If you ask someone about *el tiempo*, the person will probably give you a weather report, rather than the time. You will be better served by thinking in terms *la hora* (the hour). The most common ways to ask the time are these phrases:

¿Qué hora es?
¿Qué horas son?

Before going any farther, keep in mind that both phrases are referring to a particular time. Though essentially employing the same words, each phrase is relying on a different number of *la hora. En inglés* (in English), the questions are translated exactly the same, "What time is it?" Depending on the region, native speakers may be inclined to prefer one phrase to the other. Many speakers may even employ both. The possible responses may be:

Es la una.	**It's one o'clock.**
Son las dos.	**It's two o'clock.**
Son las once.	**It's eleven o'clock.**
Son las doce en punto.	**It's twelve o'clock on the dot.**

Did you notice that only one response employed the present tense singular form of *ser (son)*? That's because whenever you speak of any full hour other than *la una*, you are talking about more than one *hora* and, as a consequence, must use the plural form of *ser.* So, *¿Qué hora es?* can be taken to mean that the person asking the question assumes it to be approximately 1:00. On the other hand, *¿Qué horas son?* may refer to the assumption that it is not 1:00. Many people choose *¿Qué horas son?* as their standard time-asking question, since the probability of it not being between 1:00 and 1:59 is one in twelve, or maybe even one in twenty-four!

FACT

In Spain and Latin American countries, time is generally noted with respect to a twenty-four-hour clock (particularly in written form). Depending on the country, you may see 2 P.M. written as 1400, 14h00m, 14:00, or 14'00; and 2:30 A.M. may be written as 02.30, 02h30m, 02:30, or 02'30.

In actual conversation, however, the hour is treated much as in English—it is differentiated by the part of the day:

Spanish	English	When to Use
de la madrugada	of the early morning	until dawn
de la mañana	of the morning	until noon
de la tarde	of the afternoon/ of the evening	before sunset
de la noche	of night	after sunset until midnight

Here are some examples:

Son las dos de la madrugada.	**It's two in the early morning.**
Son las seis de la mañana.	**It's six in the morning.**
Son las dos de la tarde.	**It's two in the afternoon.**
Son las diez de la noche.	**It's ten at night.**

But what are the chances that the time will be exactly six or two or ten? Generally, these rules would apply:

- Minutes 1 through 30 are "added" to *la hora*.
- Minutes 31 through 59 are "subtracted" from *la hora* with *menos* (minus).
- You can also tell time by dividing the hour in half (*media*) and in quarters (*cuartos*).

For example:

TRACK 47

1:23 p.m.	*la una y veintitrés de la tarde*
9:17 p.m.	*las nueve y diecisiete de la noche*
12:37 a.m.	*la una menos veintitrés de la mañana*
5:49 a.m.	*las seis menos once de la mañana*

13:15 p.m.	*la una y cuarto de la tarde*
1:30 a.m.	*la una y media de la madrugada*
13:45 p.m.	*las dos menos cuarto de la tarde*

Additional vocabulary words to help answer the question *¿A qué hora . . . ?* (At what time . . . ?) are listed in the following table.

Additional Vocabulary for Telling Time

el mediodía	noon
por la mañana	in the morning
la madrugada	dawn
por la tarde	in the afternoon/evening
la medianoche	midnight
por la noche	in the night

Though a standard does exist for telling time, nonstandard ways of doing so have taken hold in some areas, particularly in the United States. It's not that these ways are wrong—it's just that they are not widely employed. Here are some you might encounter:

¿Tiene la hora? or *¿Tiene hora?*	**Do you have the time?**
Son las seis y quince.	**It's six fifteen.**
Son las siete y cincuenta y cinco.	**It's seven fifty-five.**
Faltan diez para las tres.	**Ten minutes remain before three.**

What Time Is It?

Try your hand at these times:

1. It's a quarter to three in the afternoon.

2. It's seven-thirty in the morning.

_____

3. It's midnight.

_____

4. 14:36

_____

5. 8:23

_____

6. 4:42

_____

Chapter 10

Important Verbs to Know

The Spanish language has a plethora of verbs—some are regular in all their conjugations, and others have various irregularities. This chapter will examine a few irregular verbs that are frequently found in the Spanish sentence. These verbs are connected with concepts that are important to learn, and will help you master other areas of the Spanish language as you examine each one.

To Have and to Have To: Tener

So far you've looked in detail at two Spanish words used to describe your-self and your existence—*ser* and *estar*. Now it's time to meet *tener*, one of those verbs it's hard to get along without. *Tener* corresponds to descriptions of experience. In its simplest form, it means "to have." To learn how to conjugate *tener* in the present tense, refer to the following table.

Conjugating Tener in Present Tense

yo tengo	I have
tú tienes	you have (informal, singular)
él, ella, usted tiene	he, she, it has; you have (formal, singular)
nosotros, nosotras tenemos	we have
vosotros, vosotras tenéis	you have (informal, plural)
ellos, ellas, ustedes tienen	they have, you have (formal, plural)

Tengo un coche rojo.	**I have a red car.**
Marisela tiene un paraguas azul.	**Marisela has a blue umbrella.**
¿Cuántos años tiene usted?	**How old are you?**

Experience with Tener

Tener may also be used in expressions where it means something like "to be," physically, mentally, or emotionally. This means that, oddly enough, *tener* may appear in many of the same situations as the *estar con* combination. Take a look at the following table.

Tener Used as "To Be"

Spanish	Literally	English
tengo celos	I am (experiencing) jealousy	I am jealous
tengo fiebre	I am (experiencing) fever	I am feverish
tengo frío	I am (experiencing) cold	I am cold
tengo hambre	I am (experiencing) hunger	I am hungry

Spanish	Literally	English
tengo miedo	I am (experiencing) fear	I am afraid
tengo sed	I am (experiencing) thirst	I am thirsty
tengo sueño	I am (experiencing) sleepiness	I am sleepy
tengo vergüenza	I am (experiencing) shame	I am embarrassed

To be more specific, you can then add modifiers to clarify what you are experiencing. Pick one of two modifiers—*mucho* (much, many) or *poco* (few, little). Remember: The modifiers must adopt the gender and number of the condition.

¿Mucho o Poco? (Many or Few?)

Tengo miedo.	*Tengo mucho miedo.*	*Tengo poco miedo.*
Tengo sed.	*Tengo mucha sed.*	*Tengo poca sed.*
Tengo celos.	*Tengo muchos celos.*	*Tengo pocos celos.*

But there's more. Take a look at the following examples, which also rely on the verb *tener*:

TRACK 48

Tengo cuidado.	I am careful.
Tengo la culpa.	I am at fault.
Tengo éxito.	I am successful; I have success.
Tengo quince años.	I am fifteen years old; I have reached fifteen years.
Tengo razón.	I am in the right; I am right.
Tengo suerte.	I am lucky; I have luck.

An Infinitive Construction: Tener Que

Up to this point you've seen the infinitive only as a point of reference to determine meaning and conjugation. You may recall that the infinitive also allows you to speak of an action without really needing to make it active, or attribute it to an actor. For example:

Aprendo a nadar. **I am learning to swim.**

An interesting manifestation of this use of the infinitive can be seen in the expression of obligation that is created when *tener* combines with *que* ("what/that," though not translated in this situation) and the infinitive. In this case, the *tener que* construction may be translated as "have to" or "has to":

Tengo que ir a casa.　　　　　　　　**I have to go home.**

Conjugating Tener Through the Spanish Tenses

In the preterite tense, *tener* describes an experience, or sensation, that is known to have ended and, as a result, is tied only to the past, often as a single event. For example:

Anoche tuve poca hambre.　　　　　**I was not very hungry last night.**

Notice that the conjugations do not follow the regular *–er* verb rules. The base changes to *tuv–*, and the endings are slightly different as well. Refer to the following table for the irregular preterite conjugations of *tener*.

Conjugating Tener in Preterite Tense

yo tuve	I had
tú tuviste	you had (informal, singular)
él, ella, usted tuvo	he, she, it had; you had (formal, singular)
nosotros, nosotras tuvimos	we had
vosotros, vosotras tuvisteis	you had
ellos, ellas, ustedes tuvieron	they had, you had (plural)

Luckily, *tener* follows regular verb rules in the imperfect tense. The imperfect is characterized by its ongoing development in the past, rather than by its termination, which is vague. Here are a few examples with respect to the imperfect form of *tener:*

Hace muchos años, tenía un mascota.	**Several years ago, I had a pet.**

As you may remember, the present perfect tense characterizes an experience as having occurred in the recent past:

He tenido sueño todo el día.	**I have been sleepy all day.**

Finally, in the the future tense, *tener* describes a future state, bounded or unbounded by reference to time. Note that while the endings for conjugating *tener* in the future tense are regular, the base is not *tener–* but *tendr–*.
For example:

Tendré treinta y seis años en julio.	**I will be thirty-six years old in July.**

Working with Tener

Translate the following sentences using the verb *tener*. Use your English-to-Spanish and Spanish-to-English dictionary to look up words you don't already know.

1. I have to drive the car.

   _____

2. You (formal) will have to go at four.

   _____

3. They had to read the book (and did).

   _____

4. I have to dance with Fabian.

   _____

5. You (informal) have to attend the wedding.

   _____

Haber: To Have or to Be?

This verb should be familiar to you—it is the auxiliary verb "to have" that you've been introduced to when learning about the present perfect tense.

He sido plomero.	**I have been a plumber.**

However, *haber* can be found in other types of constructions as well. One of the most common usages for this verb is in the "impersonal third-person" present-tense form *hay.* Because it is used as both singular and plural, it may be translated as either "there is" or "there are," depending on the context. As such, it may be used to:

1. Ask questions characterized by existence:

   ¿Hay alguién aquí?　　　　**Is there someone here?**

2. State the existence of something:

   Hay pan fresco en la cocina.　　**There is fresh bread in the kitchen.**

3. State a broad "impersonal" obligation (lacking a specific subject, sometimes translated into English as "one") in the form of *hay* + *que* + infinitive:

   Hay que luchar por la vida.　　**One must fight for one's life.**

There are two important distinctions to be made regarding *hay* and other verbs with similar uses. First, there is a tendency to confuse *hay* with forms of *estar.* It is best to distinguish them by noting that whereas *estar* expresses the position or location of someone or something, *hay* refers to that someone's or something's very existence. Compare:

Está en casa.	**He is at home.**
Hay alguien en casa.	**There is someone at home.**

Second, there is also a tendency to confuse *hay* with *tener* within a *tener que* + infinitive phrase. Remember that while both expressions express an obligation, *tener que . . .* has a specific subject (and *tener* is conjugated according to that subject), whereas the *hay que . . .* construction expresses an obligation not specifically assigned to a particular individual. Compare:

Hay que comprarlo.	**Someone should buy it.**
Tengo que comprarlo.	**I have to buy it.**

Other Uses and Applications of Haber

As an auxiliary verb, *haber* plays an important role in forming compound tenses. Though these tenses are really beyond the scope of this book, here's a short preview of what to expect.

When it comes to verb tenses, recall that a completed action is described as being "perfect." This being the case, you will often find a form of *haber* helping the past participle of a verb achieve this completion. You've already seen this occur in the present perfect, where *haber* is conjugated in the present tense to bring the completed action of a recent past into closer focus by means of the present. For example:

Yo he terminado el trabajo.	**I have finished the work.**
¿Te has duchado ya?	**Have you already showered?**

In the past perfect (or pluperfect) tense, the past participle remains, but *haber* is conjugated in the imperfect.

Haber Conjugated in the Imperfect Tense

yo había

tú habías

él, ella, usted había

nosotros, nosotras habíamos

vosotros, vosotras habíais

ellos, ellas, ustedes habían

The key to understanding this tense is the use of "had" in its translation. The focus on completed action is now shifted from the present back to the past. For example:

Yo ya había terminado el trabajo.	**I had already finished the work.**
¿Te habías duchado ya?	**Had you already showered?**

Similarly, *haber* also appears in the future perfect tense.

Haber in the Future Perfect Tense

yo habré

tú habrás

él, ella, usted habrá

nosotros, nosotras habremos

vosotros, vosotras habréis

ellos, ellas, ustedes habrán

This compound tense is used in two situations:

1. To describe an action as something that "will have" occurred by a deadline of sorts:

Yo habré terminado el trabajo *para las dos.*	**I will have finished the work** **by two.**

2. To describe an action as something that "must have" occurred, though there is a very slight chance that it hasn't:

Me habré equivocado.	**I must have been mistaken.**

The last compound tense in the indicative mood is the conditional perfect. This tense is the hardest to grasp because the focus of the completed action is not a single point in time but a continuum. See the following table for conditional-tense conjugations of *haber*.

Haber Conjugated in Conditional Perfect Tense

yo habría

tú habrías

él, ella, usted habría

nosotros, nosotras habríamos

vosotros, vosotras habríais

ellos, ellas, ustedes habrían

There are four uses for the conditional perfect. They include:

1. Expressing a future action sandwiched between two events:

   Usued me aseguró que habría pintado la casa antes de entregármela.

   You assured me that you would have painted the house before giving it to me.

2. Expressing an action that failed because of some hindrance:

   Yo habría terminado el trabajo, pero no tenía las herramientas adecuadas.

   I would have finished the work, but I did not have the appropriate tools.

3. Expressing an expansive past probability, allowing for conjecture or approximation. Looking at a situation may assist in getting a better handle on this use. If someone were to ask, "Why is Tom not in his office?" one possible response is, "He must have become ill" (the future perfect). But if the question was posed as a past event, "Why was Tom not in his office?" a possible response to this query is, "He must have been ill" (conditional perfect; *se habría enfermado*). Remember: Both responses express probabilities, but the former forms a conjecture that begins in the future, and the latter forms one rooted in the past.

To Finish: Acabar

You will discover that in addition to *tener* and *haber*, there are multitude expressions that can be gotten from only a few simple words. And, as you have seen with *estar*, prepositions can make quite a significant addition to a verb. Take the word *acabar* (to finish). In its most basic form, it conjugates as a regular *–ar* verb.

Conjugating Acabar in the Present Tense

yo acabo	I finish
tú acabas	you finish (informal, singular)
él, ella, usted acaba	he, she finishes; you finish (formal, singular)
nosotros, nosotras acabamos	we finish
vosotros, vosotras acabais	you finish (informal, plural)
ellos, ellas, ustedes acaban	they finish; you finish (formal, plural)

By itself, *acabar* is used exactly as you would expect:

Hoy acabo la tarea.   **Today I finish the homework.**

It also conjugates as a regular *–ar* verb in other tenses, such as the imperfect and the future (see the following examples):

Raúl acabará sus vacaciones la semana próxima.   **Raul will be finishing his vacation next week.**

When combined with the preposition *con* (with), *acabar* is used in the sense of "to destroy," "finish off," or "to break."

Mañana acabo con todo.   **Tomorrow I will finish off everything.**

In Conversation

In conversation, *acabar* often appears in combination with *de* + infinitive, such as in the following sentences:

Acabamos de nadar.   **We have just finished swimming.**

Notice that this construction requires you to use the present tense to consider a recent action performed to its end. Though you will find the *acabar de* + *infinitivo* in other tenses, the immediacy related to a completed act is only apparent within the present and imperfect tenses, where the conjugated action itself is considered in midstate. Key to understanding the *acabar de* + *infinitivo* construction in the imperfect is that it describes the period soon after an action was completed as a setting for something else to occur. For example:

Acabábamos de nadar.   **We had just finished swimming.**

Working with Acabar

Translate the following sentences into Spanish using *acabar*. Use your English-to-Spanish and Spanish-to-English dictionary to look up words you don't already know. Check your answers in Appendix E.

1. I finish work at three.

_____

2. I have just finished eating.

_____

3. They have just finished conversing.

_____

4. She has just lost her keys.

_____

5. You (formal, plural) finished on time.

_____

To Go: Ir

As you've already seen with *tener*, *haber*, and *acabar*, the right combination of verb and preposition can add significantly to your expressive potential. The next verb introduced in this chapter will further enhance this potential to an astounding degree. Ir is among the most useful, most versatile, and most difficult verbs to master, but your command of this verb will serve you well. Its meaning is simple—"to go"—but as in English, its reach is farther than the two letters would suggest.

Ir is one of the few "innately" irregular verbs—its irregularities are specific to itself and have simply evolved without pronunciation concerns. Take a look at its different tenses and see how the verb changes across time.

Conjugating Ir in the Present, Preterite, Imperfect, and Future

Pronoun	Present	Preterite	Imperfect	Future
yo	*voy*	*fui*	*iba*	*iré*
tú	*vas*	*fuiste*	*ibas*	*irás*
él, ella, usted	*va*	*fue*	*iba*	*irá*
nosotros, nosotras	*vamos*	*fuimos*	*íbamos*	*iremos*
vosotros, vosotras	*vais*	*fuisteis*	*ibais*	*iréis*
ellos, ellas, ustedes	*van*	*fueron*	*iban*	*irán*

FACT

As you might remember, the present perfect tense is formed with the conjugation of the verb *haber* and the past participle form of the main verb. The past participle of *ir* is *ido*. You will see examples of *ir* in the present perfect tense among the sample sentences that follow.

A significant step in understanding how *ir* is used involves coming to the realization that "to go" requires direction. Take a look at the following sentences and listen along on Track 49.

TRACK 49

¿Vas a la carnicería?	**Are you going to the butcher shop?**
Ellas van a la sinagoga.	**They go to the synagogue.**
Mauricio fue a la boda de su mejor amigo.	**Mauricio went to his best friend's wedding.**
¿Adónde fuiste ayer?	**Where did you go yesterday?**
Marta iba a las fiestas de la escuela.	**Marta used to go to the school parties.**
He ido a varios conciertos.	**I have gone to various concerts.**
¿Has ido al Japón?	**Have you gone to Japan?**
¿Irás al cine el sábado?	**Will you go to the movies on Saturday?**
Van a ser las dos de la tarde.	**It is going to be two in the afternoon.**

An important construction to keep in mind is that of the *ir a + infinitivo*. With it you can describe an immediate future (the beginning of an action) or an intention. In English, the equivalent construction is "to be going to." For example:

Voy a comprar una bicicleta.	**I am going to buy a bicycle.**
Voy a comer un bistec.	**I am going to eat a steak.**
Iban a visitar el museo.	**They were going to visit the museum.**

Using Ir

Translate the following sentences into Spanish. Use your English-to-Spanish and Spanish-to-English dictionary to look up words you don't already know. Check your answers in Appendix E.

1. We intend to wait for them in the store.

   _____

2. I am going to listen to the music.

   _____

3. She is going to go to the concert today.

   _____

4. They were going to swim, but it did not happen.

   _____

5. We are going to leave on vacation.

   _____

To Know: Saber and Conocer

By now you've undoubtedly noticed how subtle the difference between words can be. You've experienced "to be" in the forms of *ser, estar, tener,* and *hacer.* You'll be glad to know that as soon as you master those words, there are several others to challenge your curiosity—and the Spanish words meaning "to know" are among them.

The idea of "knowing" in Spanish is divided between two words—*saber* and *conocer.* Take a look at their present tense conjugations in the following table.

Conjugating Saber and Conocer in the Present Tense

Pronoun	Saber	Conocer
yo	*sé*	*conozco*
tú	*sabes*	*conoces*
él, ella, usted	*sabe*	*conoce*
nosotros, nosotras	*sabemos*	*conocemos*
vosotros, vosotras	*sabéis*	*conocéis*
ellos, ellas, ustedes	*saben*	*conocen*

Although both *saber* and *conocer* may be translated as "to know," they deal with different concepts. *Saber* conveys knowledge of a fact or a skill, and *conocer* with familiarity, be it with people, places, or things. These differences are outlined in the following table.

Saber Versus Conocer

Saber	Conocer
to know that . . .	to be acquainted with, or well versed in . . .
to know facts	to know people (remember to include the personal *a*)
to know information	to be familiar with places and things

To review, compare the following pairs:

Yo sé como llegar a tu casa. Yo conozco la ruta a tu casa.

I know how to arrive at your house. I am familiar with the route to your house.

Ella no sabe quien llamó. Ella no le conoce a ella.

She doesn't know who called— she doesn't have that information. She is not acquainted with her— she has never met her.

Constructions with Saber

Here are a few constructions with *saber* that are useful to know:

Saber + Que (To Know That)

Sé que la casa está lejos de aquí.	*I know that the house is far from here.*
Lorena sabe que Juan es buena persona.	*Lorena knows that John is a good person.*

Saber + Infinitivo (To Know How To)

¿Sabes nadar?	**Do you know how to swim?**
No sabemos patinar.	**We don't know how to skate.**

Using Saber and Conocer

Translate the following sentences into Spanish. Use your English-to-Spanish and Spanish-to-English dictionary to look up words you don't already know. Check your answers in Appendix E.

1. I know how old Antonio is.

   _____

2. María knows how to drive well.

   _____

3. I don't know his brother.

   _____

4. We know that respect and communication are essential in a relationship.

   _____

5. He knows Acapulco well because he travels there a lot.

   _____

Chapter 11

Present-Tense Irregular Verbs I

Not all verbs fit the regular-verb molds you've learned so far (*ser*, *estar*, *tener*, and *haber* are among the irregular verbs you already know). When you conjugate irregular verbs, you need to know how their bases change in various conjugations. This chapter will introduce you to verbs that are irregular in the present tense.

What's the Explanation?

For one reason or another, irregular verbs cannot keep their infinitive bases in some or all of their conjugated forms. What are the reasons behind these irregularities? Some irregularities are actually "regular"; that is, the changes that verbs undergo run consistently across verb groups. You will see that group irregularities also depend on similar letter substitutions.

Some irregularities result from spelling accommodations describing changes that occur to keep pronunciation consistent. A few verbs are "naturally" irregular (most often these are words that have been present in Spanish for a long time, and have changed radically over centuries; *ser* is a good example—it is irregular in most of its conjugated forms). Fortunately, only a small fraction of all Spanish verbs are irregular.

Irregular Verbs

andar	to walk
asir	to seize
caber	to fit (into)
caer	to fall
dar	to give
saber	to know
decir	to say
salir	to leave
haber	to have/be
hacer	to do, to make
ir	to go
oír	to hear
poder	to be able (to)
poner	to place, to put
producir	to produce
querer	to want

Irregular Verbs

traer	to bring
valer	to be valued
venir	to come
ver	to see

As you learn each verb, check to see whether it is regular or irregular. If it happens to be irregular, try to see if its irregularity is the same as that of another verb you are already familiar with—then, all you'll need to do is memorize how to conjugate one irregular verb instead of two. For example, did you know that *estar* and *tener* behave similarly in the preterite tense?

A Good Strategy

Keep a notebook with a list of the irregular verbs you think you will more than likely need. At first, limit them to about ten verbs throughout all tenses, but keep adding another verb or two every week. The progress may seem slow, but all you really need to do is become aware of the potential irregularity of a verb. At that point you can do what native speakers do—consult a Spanish verb manual or an online verb-conjugation search engine. Also available for your reference is a condensed verb chart in Appendix D.

Reviewing What You Already Know

As you may remember, the present tense verbs are formed by dropping their infinitive endings *–ar*, *–er*, or *–ir*, and adding appropriate endings based on the person and number of the verb's subject (refer to Chapter 5 for a more thorough review). The following three tables list the present tense verb endings for your review.

Regular –Ar Verbs

Pronoun	Ending	Sample Verb Conjugation
	–ar	*ganar* (to win, earn)
yo	–o	*gano*
tú	–as	*ganas*
él, ella, usted	–a	*gana*
nosotros, nosotras	–amos	*ganamos*
vosotros, vosotras	–áis	*ganáis*
ellos, ellas, ustedes	–an	*ganan*

Regular –Er Verbs

Pronoun	Ending	Sample Verb Conjugation
	–er	*beber* (to drink)
yo	–o	*bebo*
tú	–es	*bebes*
él, ella, usted	–e	*bebe*
nosotros, nosotras	–emos	*bebemos*
vosotros, vosotras	–éis	*bebéis*
ellos, ellas, ustedes	–en	*beben*

Regular –Ir Verbs

Pronoun	Ending	Sample Verb Conjugation
	–ir	*recibir* (to receive)
yo	–o	*recibo*
tú	–es	*recibes*
él, ella, usted	–e	*recibe*
nosotros, nosotras	–imos	*recibimos*
vosotros, vosotras	–ís	*recibís*
ellos, ellas, ustedes	–en	*reciben*

Group Irregularities

Group irregularities (that is, irregularities that occur in patterns, among certain groups of verbs) generally result from vowel-focused modifications. Letter substitutions often occur across person and number, without affecting the employment of the regular verb endings.

Let's take a look at the first type of group irregularity, a diphthong base change from *e* to *ie*. This change occurs with many irregular verbs, across all three conjugation groups (among *ar*, *er*, and *ir* verbs). As an example, take a look at how to conjugate *calentar* (to warm up, heat).

Diphthong Base Change from E to IE

	–ar	*calentar* (to warm up, heat)
yo	–o	*caliento*
tú	–as	*calientas*
él, ella, usted	–a	*calienta*
nosotros, nosotras	–amos	*calentamos*
vosotros, vosotras	–áis	*calentáis*
ellos, ellas, ustedes	–an	*calientan*

FACT

Take a look at the *nosotros* and *vosotros* forms of *calentar*. As you can see, they are the only two forms that do not undergo a base change. As you'll notice with most irregular Spanish verbs, these two forms rarely undergo a base change.

The group of verbs that act similarly to *calentar* is not small. Refer to the following table for the infinitives and a sample conjugation (in the *yo* form, to show which vowel undergoes the change and the *nosotros* form, where the root doesn't change).

List of Verbs with Base Change from E to Ie

Verb	Yo Form	Nosotros Form	English
advertir	advierto	advertimos	to warn
apretar	aprieto	apretamos	to tighten
arrendar	arriendo	arrendamos	to rent, lease
ascender	asciendo	ascendemos	to ascend
cerrar	cierro	cerramos	to close
comenzar	comienzo	comenzamos	to begin
confesar	confieso	confesamos	to confess
convertir	convierto	convertimos	to convert
defender	defiendo	defendemos	to defend
discernir	discierno	discernimos	to discern
empezar	empiezo	empezamos	to begin
encender	enciendo	encendemos	to light
entender	entiendo	entendemos	to understand
enterrar	entierro	enterramos	to bury
extender	extiendo	extendemos	to extend
herir	hiero	herimos	to injure
hervir	hiervo	hervimos	to boil
mentir	miento	mentimos	to lie, deceive
merendar	meriendo	merendamos	to eat a snack (before dinner)
negar	niego	negamos	to deny
pensar	pienso	pensamos	to think
perder	pierdo	perdemos	to lose
preferir	prefiero	preferimos	to prefer
quebrar	quiebro	quebramos	to break
querer	quiero	queremos	to want
recomendar	recomiendo	recomendamos	to recommend
sentir	siento	sentimos	to feel

Verb Practice #1

Translate the following sentences using the appropriate verb forms. Use your English-to-Spanish and Spanish-to-English dictionary to look up words you don't already know.

1. I rent my dwelling.

   _____

2. What (are) you (informal, singular) think(ing)?

   _____

3. Today you (formal) start the new job.

   _____

4. On Fridays we scrub the floors.

   _____

5. They want to go out to eat.

   _____

6. We warn of the danger.

   _____

Keep in mind that group irregularities are often limited to specific tenses and persons. Many of the words above follow the regular conjugations in other tenses. For example: *Hoy meriendo en casa.* (I snack at home today.) but *Ayer, merendé en un restaurante.* (Yesterday I snacked at a restaurant.)

Diphthong Base Change from O to UE

Another common diphthong base change among –*ar* and –*er* verbs (though not in –*ir* verbs) is when the base vowel *o* changes to *ue*. Just as with the previous group of verbs, the *nosotros* and *vosotros* forms retain the base as it appears in the infinitive form. The following table provides a sample conjugation for the verb *mostrar* (to show). Notice that only the base of this verb is irregular—the endings remain the same as for any regular *–ar* verb.

Diphthong Base Change from O to UE

	–ar	*mostrar* (to show)
yo	–o	*muestro*
tú	–as	*muestras*
él, ella, usted	–a	*muestra*
nosotros, nosotras	–amos	*mostramos*
vosotros, vosotras	–áis	*mostráis*
ellos, ellas, ustedes	–an	*muestran*

The following table lists common verbs that belong to the same group as *mostrar* and behave in a similar way.

List of Verbs with Base Change from O to UE

Verb	Yo Form	Nosotros Form	English
absolver	*absuelvo*	*absolvemos*	to absolve
almorzar	*almuerzo*	*almorzamos*	to eat lunch
apostar	*apuesto*	*apostamos*	to bet
avergonzar	*avergüenzo*	*avergonzamos*	to embarrass
colgar	*cuelgo*	*colgamos*	to hang, suspend
comprobar	*compruebo*	*comprobamos*	to verify, check
demostrar	*demuestro*	*demostramos*	to demonstrate
devolver	*devuelvo*	*devolvemos*	to return
encontrar	*encuentro*	*encontramos*	to find, encounter
moler	*muelo*	*molemos*	to grind
morder	*muerdo*	*mordemos*	to bite

Verb	Yo Form	Nosotros Form	English
mover	*muevo*	*movemos*	to move
poder	*puedo*	*podemos*	to be able to
remover	*remuevo*	*removemos*	to remove, dig
rogar	*ruego*	*rogamos*	to beg
soltar	*suelto*	*soltamos*	to release, let go
soñar	*sueño*	*soñamos*	to dream
volar	*vuelo*	*volamos*	to fly
volver	*vuelvo*	*volvemos*	to return

Verb Practice #2

Translate the following sentences using the appropriate verb forms. Use your English-to-Spanish and Spanish-to-English dictionary to look up words you don't already know.

1. I eat lunch at noon.

   _____

2. Tomorrow they fly to San Diego.

   _____

3. I hang the shirts.

   _____

4. You (informal, singular) show houses.

   _____

5. She finds a coin on the floor.

   _____

6. I don't dream much.

   _____

ALERT!

There is a special case to the "*o* to *ue* group" irregularity. Fortunately, it is limited to one verb, *oler* (to smell). In addition to transforming the *o* to *ue*, as in other cases, there is an additional *h* added to the beginning of the word: *yo huelo, tú hueles, él huele, nosotros olemos, vosotros oléis, ellos huelen.*

Base Change from E to I

Another group of verbs, exclusively from the *–ir* category, undergoes a base change where the letter *e* changes to *i*. Once again, the *nosotros* and *vosotros* forms are the only ones not subject to this change. An example of this group is the verb *repetir* (to repeat)—see the following table on how it is conjugated.

Diphthong Base Change from E to I in –Ir Verbs

	–ir	*repetir* (to repeat)
yo	*–o*	*repito*
tú	*–es*	*repites*
él, ella, usted	*–e*	*repite*
nosotros, nosotras	*–imos*	*repetimos*
vosotros, vosotras	*–ís*	*repetís*
ellos, ellas, ustedes	*–en*	*repiten*

The following table presents a list of verbs similar to *repetir* in their behavior in the present tense.

List of Verbs with Base Change from E to I

Verb	Yo Form	Nosotros Form	English
competir	compito	competimos	to compete
despedir	despido	despedimos	to see off, fire
freír	frío	freímos	to fry
impedir	impido	impedimos	to impede
medir	mido	medimos	to measure
reír	río	reímos	to laugh
rendir	rindo	rendimos	I hand over
servir	sirvo	servimos	to serve
sonreír	sonrío	sonreímos	to smile
vestir	visto	vestimos	to dress

The following words also belong to the same group—in each one, the *e* changes to *i*. However, they are also irregular in other respects (described in the following sections of the chapter). For now, simply look at how they have been conjugated.

Base Change from E to I and Additional Irregularities

	–ir	conseguir (to obtain)	corregir (to correct)	elegir (to elect)	seguir (to follow)
yo	–o	consigo	corrijo	elijo	sigo
tú	–es	consigues	corriges	eliges	sigues
él, ella, usted	–e	consigue	corrige	elige	sigue
nosotros, nosotras	–imos	conseguimos	corregimos	elegimos	seguimos
vosotros, vosotras	–ís	conseguís	corregís	elegís	seguís
ellos, ellas, ustedes	–en	consiguen	corrigen	eligen	siguen

Verb Practice #3

Translate the following sentences using the appropriate verb forms. Use your English-to-Spanish and Spanish-to-English dictionary to look up words you don't already know.

1. I (am) boil(ing) eggs.

   _____

2. We elect the president.

   _____

3. You (formal, plural) always follow all the rules.

   _____

4. They follow the soaps.

   _____

5. You (informal, plural) are dressing a baby.

   _____

6. How tall are you (informal, singular)? (Literally: How much do you measure?)

   _____

Chapter 12

Present-Tense Irregular Verbs II

Now that you have taken a break and have come back rested, you can learn the other types of irregular verbs: verbs that undergo spelling accommodations, verbs that gain or lose an accent mark in particular conjugations, and verbs that, for one reason or another, are innately irregular (that is, don't fall into any particular category).

Spelling Accommodations

Think back to that table of verbs with two irregularities in the previous chapter. Take *corregir*, for instance. You might have expected "I correct" to be translated as *corrigo*. Instead, you saw it listed as *corrijo*. The *j* is used in place of the *g* so as to maintain the hard "hh" sound that is in the original word, *corregir* (coh-rreh-HHEER). Without this modification you would have had to pronounce it "coh-rreh-GHEER"—as you may remember, *g* is pronounced "hh" before *e* or *i*, and "gh" when it precedes any other letter.

The rule, then, is that when a verb ends with a *–ger* or *–gir*, the *g* changes to *j* whenever the verb ending does not end in an *e* or *i*—that is, the change only occurs in the *yo* form.

Spelling Accommodation in Verbs That End with –GER and –GIR

	–er	coger (to grab, take)	–ir	fingir (to fake)
yo	–o	cojo	–o	finjo
tú	–es	coges	–es	finges
él, ella, usted	–e	coge	–e	finge
nosotros, nosotras	–emos	cogemos	–imos	fingimos
vosotros, vosotras	–éis	cogéis	–ís	fingís
ellos, ellas, ustedes	–en	cogen	–en	fingen

The following table presents other verbs that undergo a *g* to *j* change. Again, compare the *yo, nosotros,* and *ellos/ellas/ustedes* forms.

–GER and –GIR Verbs with Spelling Change from G to J

Verb	Yo Form	Nosotros Form	Ellos/Ellas/Ustedes Form	English
emerger	*emerjo*	*emergemos*	*emergen*	to emerge
escoger	*escojo*	*escogemos*	*escogen*	to choose
exigir	*exijo*	*exigimos*	*exigen*	to demand
proteger	*protejo*	*protegemos*	*protegen*	to protect
recoger	*recojo*	*recogemos*	*recogen*	to collect, gather
restringir	*restrinjo*	*restringimos*	*restringen*	to restrict
surgir	*surjo*	*surgimos*	*surgen*	to surge, appear

Verbs That End in –GUIR

In verbs that end in *–guir,* the *g* is pronounced as the "g" in "get"—the *u* is silent because it is there to keep the *g* hard (remember, *–gir* would sound like "hheer"). As you conjugate these verbs, you are trying to maintain a consistency of sound, which is why you need a modification in the *yo* form. Take a look at the following table to see if you can figure out what is going on.

–GUIR Verbs That Drop the U in the Yo Form

Verb	Yo Form	Nosotros Form	Ellos/Ellas/Ustedes Form	English
conseguir	*consigo*	*conseguimos*	*consiguen*	to obtain
extinguir	*extingo*	*extinguimos*	*extinguen*	to extinguish
perseguir	*persigo*	*perseguimos*	*persiguen*	to pursue

As you can see, when you are conjugating verbs that end in *–guir,* you need to drop the *u* in the *yo* form. To do otherwise would be to change the hard *g* in *–guir* from "g" as in "get" to "gw" as in "Gwen." For example: *consigo* would be *consiguo,* which would be pronounced "kohn-SEEH-gwoh."

Verb Practice #4

Translate the following sentences using the appropriate verb forms. Use your English-to-Spanish and Spanish-to-English dictionary to look up words you don't already know.

1. I take the small piece.

   _____

2. I choose the yellow apple.

   _____

3. I protect the family.

   _____

4. I gather the clothes from the floor.

   _____

5. I demand attention.

   _____

Other –UIR Verbs

This spelling accommodation focuses on other verbs that end in –uir. The modification is straightforward. The *i* is replaced by a *y* and the personal endings follow. The following table presents the conjugation of *huir* (to flee).

Spelling Accommodation in Other –UIR Verbs

	–ir	huir (to flee)
yo	–o	huyo
tú	–es	huyes
él, ella, usted	–e	huye
nosotros, nosotras	–imos	huimos
vosotros, vosotras	–ís	huís
ellos, ellas, ustedes	–en	huyen

For the other verbs that behave like *huir* in the present tense, refer to the following table.

Other –UIR Verbs That Undergo I to Y Change

Verb	Yo Form	Él/Ella/ Usted Form	Nosotros Form	English
construir	*construyo*	*construye*	*construimos*	to construct
contribuir	*contribuyo*	*contribuye*	*contribuimos*	to contribute
destruir	*destruyo*	*destruye*	*destruimos*	to destroy

You may be wondering why the *i* needs to be replaced at all, and why it is kept in the *nosotros* form. Notice that in the infinitive and in the *nosotros* form, the weak vowels have only themselves to contend with. They share the same strength and are each given equal weight. You've seen before how one weak vowel reacts when it is adjacent to a strong one—the *i* tends to adopt a "y" sound and the *u* a "w" sound. In this case, the *u* must retain its own sound, and the only way to keep it independent is to convert the *i* to *y* and thus make the separation between *u* and a strong vowel clearer with a more explicit "y" sound.

Verbs That End with a Consonant and –CER

Verbs that end in –*cer* undergo spelling-accommodation changes in the *yo* form for the same reason that the –*guir* verbs undergo a change from *g* to *j*—in order to keep the pronunciation consistent. There are two changes that may occur.

FACT

–*Cer* verbs must undergo a change in the *yo* form because if the –*er* is simply replaced by an *o*, the "s" sound produced by the *ce* combination in –*cer* would be transformed to a hard "k" sound.

The first scenario is that the base's final *c* may change to *z*. This occurs with verbs where the *–cer* ending is preceded by a consonant. For example, take the word *convencer* (cohn-vehn-SEHR), meaning "to convince." If you want to ascribe that action to yourself, you would say, "cohn-VEHN-soh," so it should be spelled *convenzo*. If you followed the regular-verb rule, you would have ended up with *convenco* (cohn-VEHN-coh) and, as a result, confuse a whole bunch of people. Refer to the following table for verbs that undergo this particular type of spelling accommodation.

Spelling Accommodation from C to Z

	–er	convencer (to convince)	ejercer (to practice)	vencer (to conquer)
yo	–o	convenzo	ejerzo	venzo
tú	–es	convences	ejerces	vences
él, ella, usted	–e	convence	ejerce	vence
nosotros, nosotras	–emos	convencemos	ejercemos	vencemos
vosotros, vosotras	–éis	convencéis	ejercéis	vencéis
ellos, ellas, ustedes	–en	convencen	ejercen	vencen

Verb Practice #5

Translate the following sentences using the appropriate verb forms. Use your English-to-Spanish and Spanish-to-English dictionary to look up words you don't already know.

1. Intolerance destroys society.

   _____

2. You (plural, formal) construct homes.

   _____

3. We flee from the police.

   _____

4. Michelle contributes to her church.

_____

5. You (informal, singular) flee from responsibility.

_____

ALERT!

As you have already seen, a verb may undergo more than one change. In the first-person present-tense conjugation of *torcer* (to turn), for example, two changes occur: the *o* is replaced by *ue*, and the *–cer* changes to *–zo*: *tuerzo* (I turn), *tuerces* (you turn), *tuerce* (he, she, it turns; you turn), *torcemos* (we turn), *torcéis* (you turn), *tuercen* (they turn, you turn).

Verbs That End with a Vowel and –CER

If the letter that precedes the *–cer* ending in a verb is a vowel, the verb undergoes a slightly different transformation in the *yo* form of the present tense: In this case, the *–cer* ending changes to *–zco*. (This transformation is one of the many remnants left over from Latin.) The reasoning behind this transformation is similar—it is done to keep the *ce* sound that is voiced by the *z* in *–zco*.

Example of Spelling Accommodation from C to ZC

	–er	*ofrecer* (to offer)
yo	*–o*	*ofrezco*
tú	*–es*	*ofreces*
él, ella, usted	*–e*	*ofrece*
nosotros, nosotras	*–emos*	*ofrecemos*
vosotros, vosotras	*–éis*	*ofrecéis*
ellos, ellas, ustedes	*–en*	*ofrecen*

There are quite a few other verbs in Spanish that undergo this transformation in the *yo* form of the present tense.

Verbs with Spelling Accommodation from C to ZC

Verb	Yo Form	Él/Ella/Usted Form	English
agradecer	agradezco	agradece	to thank (for), give thanks
aparecer	aparezco	aparece	to appear
apetecer	apetezco	apetece	to desire, crave
conocer	conozco	conoce	to be acquainted
crecer	crezco	crece	to grow
desaparecer	desaparezco	desaparece	to disappear
desobedecer	desobedezco	desobedece	to disobey
embellecer	embellezco	embellece	to embellish, beautify
empobrecer	empobrezco	empobrece	to impoverish
enriquecer	enriquezco	enriquece	to enrich
envejecer	envejezco	envejece	to grow old
establecer	establezco	establece	to establish
favorecer	favorezco	favorece	to favor
florecer	florezco	florece	to flower, flourish
merecer	merezco	merece	to deserve
nacer	nazco	nace	to be born
obedecer	obedezco	obedece	to obey
padecer	padezco	padece	to suffer
parecer	parezco	parece	to seem, appear

Of course, there are some exceptions to this general rule of thumb. Take a look at the verbs *hacer* (to do), *cocer* (to cook), and *mecer* (to sway, rock), conjugated in the following table. Their *yo*-form conjugations do not follow the rule established for verbs that end in *–cer* preceded by a vowel.

Exceptions to Verbs with Spelling Change from C to ZC

	–er	*hacer* (to do)	*cocer* (to cook)	*mecer* (to sway)
yo	–o	*hago*	*cuezo*	*mezo*
tú	–es	*haces*	*cueces*	*meces*
él, ella, usted	–e	*hace*	*cuece*	*mece*
nosotros	–emos	*hacemos*	*cocemos*	*mecemos*
ellos, ellas, ustedes	–en	*hacen*	*cuecen*	*mecen*

Verbs That End in –UCIR

Treat verbs that end in *–ucir* as verbs that end in *–cer* preceded by a vowel (see previous section). That is, the *c* is transformed to a *zc* in the *yo* form of these verbs following the same rule of spelling accommodation. Use the conjugation of *traducir* as an example.

Example of Spelling Accommodation from C to ZC

	–ir	*traducir* (to translate)
yo	–o	*traduzco*
tú	–es	*traduces*
él, ella, usted	–e	*traduce*
nosotros, nosotras	–imos	*traducimos*
vosotros, vosotras	–ís	*traducís*
ellos, ellas, ustedes	–en	*traducen*

For a list of other *–ucir* verbs that behave similarly to *traducir*, refer to the following table.

Verbs with Spelling Accommodation from C to ZC

Verb	Yo Form	Él/Ella/Usted Form	English
conducir	*conduzco*	*conduce*	to drive (a car)
deducir	*deduzco*	*deduce*	to deduce
introducir	*introduzco*	*introduce*	to introduce
lucir	*luzco*	*luce*	to shine
producir	*produzco*	*produce*	to produce

Verb Practice #6

Translate the following sentences using the appropriate verb forms. Use your English-to-Spanish and Spanish-to-English dictionary to look up words you don't already know.

1. I give thanks for the help.

   _____

2. I do exercises in the morning.

   _____

3. I obey the rules.

   _____

4. The cow produces milk.

   _____

5. The radio program introduces new singers.

   _____

Adding Accent Marks to Weak Vowels

With Spanish verbs ending in *–uar*, some ending in *–iar*, and a few in *–ar*, the present tense conjugations might sometimes require that the ordinarily weak vowels hold their own with the strong ones. In spelling, such vowels must be denoted with an accent mark. Look at what happens to *aislar* (to isolate), *enviar* (to send), and *actuar* (to act).

Verb Conjugations That Require Additional Accent Marks

	–ar	*aislar* (to isolate)	*enviar* (to send)	*actuar* (to act)
yo	*–o*	*aíslo*	*envío*	*actúo*

tú	–as	aíslas	envías	actúas
él, ella, usted	–a	aísla	envía	actúa
nosotros, nosotras	–amos	aislamos	enviamos	actuamos
vosotros, vosotras	–áis	aisláis	enviáis	actuáis
ellos, ellas, ustedes	–an	aíslan	envían	actúan

Other examples of verbs that require accent marks in present tense conjugations (except, of course, in the *nosotros* and *vosotros* forms) are listed in the following table.

Other Verbs That Require Additional Accent Marks

Verb	Yo Form	Él/Ella/Usted Form	Nosotros Form	English
ahijar	ahíjo	ahíja	ahijamos	to adopt
aullar	aúllo	aúlla	aullamos	to howl, shriek
continuar	continúo	continúa	continuamos	to continue

Unfortunately, this rule does not hold up for every –iar verb. The only way to know whether the *i* is accented is to memorize the exceptions. Look at the following table. Note that for each verb, the *i* is either accented in all the forms except *nosotros* and *vosotros*, or is not accented in any of the present tense conjugations (except of course the accented *vosotros* ending –áis).

Accent Irregularities in –IAR Verbs

Verb	Yo Form (with i)	Verb	Yo Form (with i)
abreviar (to abbreviate)	abrevio	averiar (to damage)	averío
acariciar (to caress/pet)	acaricio	confiar (to confide in)	confío
copiar (to copy)	copio	desviar (to deviate)	desvío
estudiar (to study)	estudio	guiar (to guide)	guío
rumiar (to ruminate)	rumio	vaciar (to empty)	vacío

Verb Practice #7

Translate the following sentences using the appropriate verb forms. Use your English-to-Spanish and Spanish-to-English dictionary to look up words you don't already know.

1. I send Christmas cards.

_____

2. Marcela adopts a kitten.

_____

3. The story continues for another thirty pages.

_____

4. Sandra pets the zoo animals.

_____

5. Adam and Berta study medicine.

_____

Innate Irregularities

Recall that innate irregularities are those specific to verbs rather than groups of verbs. That is, the irregularities are not shared by different verbs across the three conjugations and are not simply spelling accommodations made to maintain consistent pronunciation.

Some verbs ending in *–er* or *–ir* may undergo a change in the *yo* form, where the ending becomes *–go*. This group may be divided into two sub-categories: Some remain regular verbs in other forms, while others undergo base changes in second-, third-, or first-person plural forms.

Verbs that remain regular in all but the *yo* form are listed in the following table.

Verbs That End in –GO in the Yo Form

–Er/–Ir Verb	Yo Form	Él/Ella/Usted Form	English
caer	caigo	cae	to fall
hacer	hago	hace	to do
poner	pongo	pone	to put, place
salir	salgo	sale	to leave, go out

Other verbs, however, are irregular in more than one way. That is, in addition to the –go ending in the yo form, they undergo other irregularities in the base, such as an i to ie change (in venir and tener), an i to y change (see oír), or an e to i change (like in the verb decir). The following table provides these verbs' conjugations in the present tense.

Verbs with the –GO Transformation and Other Base Irregularities

	venir (to come)	tener (to have)	oír (to hear)	decir (to say)
yo	vengo	tengo	oigo	digo
tú	vienes	tienes	oyes	dices
él, ella, usted	viene	tiene	oye	dice

Verbs with the –GO Transformation and Other Base Irregularities

nosotros, nosotras	venimos	tenemos	oímos	decimos
vosotros, vosotras	venís	tenéis	oís	decís
ellos, ellas, ustedes	vienen	tienen	oyen	dicen

Verb Practice #8

Translate the following sentences using the appropriate verb forms. Use your English-to-Spanish and Spanish-to-English dictionary to look up words you don't already know.

1. I hear noises at night.

2. Do you (formal, singular) hear her?

_____

3. Ricardo does exercises at night.

_____

4. They come to visit.

_____

5. You (informal, plural) come to visit your parents.

_____

Additional Irregular Verbs

Some irregular verbs do not seem to fit into any category. These verbs include *ir* (to go), *haber* (to have/be), and *caber* (to fit). You've already come across *ir* and *haber; caber* is conjugated in the following table. Please note that despite a radical change in the *yo* form, *caber* is actually regular in the other forms of the present tense.

Conjugating Caber in the Present Tense

	caber (to fit)
yo	*quepo*
tú	*cabes*
él, ella, usted	*cabe*
nosotros, nosotras	*cabemos*
vosotros, vosotras	*cabéis*
ellos, ellas, ustedes	*caben*

Chapter 13

In Addition to the Verb: Direct and Indirect Objects

13

You've learned about the subject of the sentence, and you've already covered quite a lot of ground on verbs. So what's next? Well, most of the time the subject and verb need an object, the target of the action done by the actor, so to speak. This chapter will give you a solid overview of direct and indirect objects and object pronouns.

Transitive and Intransitive Verbs

Now that you've learned both regular and irregular verb forms of the present-tense verbs, you might say that you can put together the most rudimentary sentences:

Luce.	**It shines.**
Salto.	**I jump.**
Devuelvas.	**You return.**
Competimos.	**We compete.**

These sentences describe simple actions. They are complete and self-contained. In some dictionaries, you will see their infinitives marked as *v.i.* (*verbo intransitivo*). Intransitive verbs are those verbs that can stand alone, without the need for further explanation.

But don't you feel like there is something missing? Some verbs may require an object—something that the verb acts upon. These verbs might be marked as *v.t.* (*verbo transitivo*)—transitive verb. For example, you can say, "I agree," which means "agree" is an intransitive verb. But you can't say, "I need," something is missing—you need *something*. That means "to need" is a transitive verb—it has to transition to an object, "a plan," "it," "something to eat," and so on.

Direct Objects

The word that a transitive verb needs to complete the phrase is known as the direct object. For examples of phrases with transitive verbs, as well as their corresponding direct objects, take a look the following table.

Transitive Verbs and Corresponding Direct Objects

Transitive Verb Phrase	Direct Object	Question It Answers
I used to read . . .	newspapers.	(What did I used to read?)
I saw . . .	Roberto.	(Whom did I see?)

Transitive Verb Phrase	Direct Object	Question It Answers
I drove . . .	a car.	(What did I drive?)
I should thank . . .	Marcos.	(Whom should I thank?)
I will search for . . .	the keys.	(What will I search for?)
I will search for . . .	María.	(Whom will I search for?)

The following are some examples of transitive verbs and direct objects in Spanish.

TRACK 50

Leía dos periódicos cada día.	**I used to read two newspapers every day.**
Dejé mi coche en el garaje.	**I left my car at the garage.**
Agradezco a Marco sus atenciones.	**I thank Marco for his attention.**
Buscaré las llaves del coche.	**I will search for the car keys.**
Buscaré a María en su trabajo.	**I will look for Maria at her job.**

In these sentences, the newspapers, the car, the attention, the keys, and Maria all "act" as direct objects—objects that receive directly the actions of the sentence's verb.

Direct-Object Pronouns

You have already learned about subject pronouns—pronouns that replace nouns to make the sentence shorter. For example, instead of saying "the girl from sixth grade, the one with short hair," you can simply say "she." Similarly, you can replace objects with object pronouns.

Let's say that you are talking about Maria. Maybe you searched for Maria at a party, or embraced Maria. In this example, "Maria" acts as a direct object. However, once you're talking about Maria, you can then switch to the direct-object pronoun, "her." The following table lists the direct-object pronouns available to you in Spanish.

Direct-Object Pronouns

singular	plural
me (me)	*nos* (us)
te (you, informal)	*os* (you, informal)
lo, la (you, formal)	*los, las* (you)
lo, la (him, her, it)	*los, las* (them)

This might seem a bit confusing to you. To make sense of all these pronouns, take a look at the following set of examples that illustrates the use of each direct-object pronoun.

TRACK 51

Tú me ves.	**You see me.**
Hermanito, te veo ya.	**Little brother, I already see you.**
No lo encontré en el parque.	**I didn't find him at the park.**
La encontrarás mañana.	**You will meet up with her tomorrow.**
Señor, lo llevo a la calle Ochoa.	**Sir, I'll take you to Ochoa Street.**
Señora, la ayudo enseguida.	**Madam, I'll help you in a second.**
El profesor no nos alabó por el buen trabajo.	**The professor did not praise us for the good work.**
La agente os ayudará.	**The agent will help you.**
Carlos no los miró en el teatro.	**Carlos did not see them at the theater.**
Cuando vemos a las muchachas, no las abrazamos.	**When we see the girls, we don't hug them.**
Las saludaré en la reunión.	**I will greet you at the reunion.**
María y Teresita, las buscaré por la tarde.	**Maria and Teresita, I will look for you in the afternoon.**

Are you beginning to see a pattern here? You probably noticed that in Spanish, the direct object is usually placed *before* and not *after* the verb. The following rules apply to using a direct object in Spanish:

- The direct-object pronoun is placed before the verb that is acting upon it as long as it is standing alone (you'll learn about the few exceptions later).

- The negation of a transitive verb requires that *no* be placed immediately before the direct object.
- Only transitive verbs require the use of a direct-object pronoun.

To Clarify the Direct-Object Pronoun

In addition to the direct object, a Spanish speaker may add an additional phrase to help clarify the meaning of the direct object. For instance, in the phrase *las buscaré*, you might not always know based on the context whether *las* refers to "you" (feminine, formal) or "them" (feminine). To clarify, you might say *las buscaré a ellas* (I'll look for them) or *las buscaré a ustedes* (I'll look for you). *Las* and *a ellas* refer to the same thing—the object "them." The following table provides the relevant clarifying phrase for each object pronoun.

Object Pronouns and Pronoun Phrases

Direct-Object Pronoun	English	Matching Pronoun Phrase
me	me	*a mí*
te	you (informal, singular)	*a ti*
lo	him, it, you (formal, singular)	*a él, a usted*
la	her, it, you (formal, singular, feminine)	*a ella, a usted*
nos	us	*a nosotros, a nosotras*
os	you (informal, plural)	*a vosotros, a vosotras*
los	them, you (formal, plural)	*a ellos, a ustedes*
las	them (feminine), you (formal, plural, feminine)	*a ellas, a ustedes*

For examples of how to use these direct-object phrases to emphasize or clarify who is being acted upon, take a look at the following group of phrases:

Me ven (a mí) bronceado.	**They see me tanned./They see that I'm tanned.**
Te llamaré (a ti) la semana próxima.	**I will call you next week.**
No lo encontré (a él) en el parque.	**I didn't find him at the park.**
No la encontré (a ella) en la casa.	**I didn't find her at home.**
La entiendo completamente (a usted).	**I understand you completely.**
Nos alabé (a nosotros) por el buen trabajo.	**I praised us for the good work.**
Os saludaré (a vosotros) cuando os encontraré.	**I will greet you when I find you.**
Las conocimos (a ellas) en la fiesta.	**We got to know them at the party.**

Object Pronouns

Translate the following sentences and then substitute each direct object with the appropriate direct-object pronoun. Use your English-to-Spanish and Spanish-to-English dictionary to look up words you don't already know. For example:

Conozco a Miguel. Yo lo conozco.	**I know (am acquainted with) Miguel. I know him.**

1. You (formal, singular) have two cars.

_____

2. I am looking for the street.

_____

3. He makes the beds.

_____

4. I put the book on the shelf.

_____

5. Mr. Muñoz, I will see you tomorrow.

_____

Reviewing the Personal A

As you already know, *a* may be translated as "to" and is sometimes used as a preposition of direction. For example:

¿Adónde van?	**Where are you all going?**
Vamos a la playa.	**We are going to the beach.**

However, when discussing it with respect to persons as direct objects, *a* doesn't really have a translation. It is used for nothing more than to indicate which person is the direct object. Take a look at how this plays out with the verb *mirar* (to look, look at):

Miro a mi esposa, a mi hija, *y a mi hijo.*	**I look at my wife, daughter, and son.**
Miro la cartelera encima del *edificio.*	**I look at the billboard on top of the** **building.**

See? No personal *a* is needed for an inanimate object, *la cartelera*. Here are a few more examples:

TRACK 52

Esperaba el bus.	**I was waiting for the bus.**
Esperaba a Beti.	**I was waiting for Betty.**
Visité el museo.	**I visited the museum.**
Visité a mi mamá.	**I visited my mom.**
Escucho la música.	**I listen to the music.**
Escucho al sacerdote.	**I listen to the priest.**

There are some exceptions to keep in mind for the use of the personal *a*. Keep the following points in mind:

- Animals may take a personal *a* if they have some emotional tie or relationship to the speaker. For example: *Amo a mi perrito.* (I love my dear/little dog.) but, *Ví un perro.* (I saw a dog.)
- Direct objects used with *ser, tener,* and *hay* (there is/are) are not preceded by *a*. For example: *Soy Rodolfo* (I am Rodolfo). *Tengo tres primas.* (I have three cousins.)
- Only "concrete" personal direct objects are preceded by a; object abstracts of persons are not. For example: *Busco un hombre inteligente, fiel, y muy divertido.* (I am looking for an intelligent, faithful, and very funny man.)

Using the Personal A

Translate the following sentences, and remember to add a personal *a* where it is appropriate. Use your English-to-Spanish and Spanish-to-English dictionary to look up words you don't already know. To check your answers, see Appendix E.

1. I see Ignacio, Amanda, and Pedro.

   _____

2. Who(m) do you (informal, singular) love?

   _____

3. They have a daughter.

   _____

4. I am a citizen of the United States.

   _____

5. I love my cat.

_____

Indirect Objects

Just as there are nouns or pronouns that directly interact with and complete the action of the verb, there are those that are related to the verb indirectly—they receive the completed action. These receivers are called indirect objects.

Indirect objects represent the nouns and pronouns that answer the questions "to whom" and "for whom" the verb's actions are intended. Take a look at the following sentences and try to figure out which are the direct objects and which are the indirect objects:

- I bought Laura a beverage.
- I will send you a letter.
- I brought my friends lunch.
- I recommend them Jonathan.

The direct objects in the previous examples are "beverage," "letter," "lunch," and "Jonathan." The indirect objects are "Laura," "you," "my friends," and "them." If you had trouble with these sentences, try reworking them so that the indirect objects are set apart:

- I bought a beverage for Laura.
- I will send a letter to you.
- I brought lunch for my friends.
- I recommend Jonathan to them.

Indirect-Object Pronouns

The indirect-object pronouns in Spanish are very similar to the direct objects. In fact, the only point of confusion may be the third-person object pronouns. Take a look at the following tables, which contain pronouns for direct and indirect objects, and compare them.

Direct-Object Pronouns

Singular	Plural
me (me)	*nos* (us)
te (you, informal)	*os* (you, informal)
lo, la (you, formal)	*los, las* (you)
lo, la (him, her, it)	*los, las* (them)

Indirect-Object Pronouns

Singular	Plural
me (to me)	*nos* (to us)
te (to you, informal)	*os* (to you, informal)
le (you, formal)	*les* (you, formal)
le (to him, her, it)	*les* (to them)

ALERT!

Use *le* and *les* for all indirect objects in the third person. *Le* should be used as any indirect-object pronoun in the singular: to him, her, it, or the formal you (*usted*); *les* should be used as any indirect-object pronoun in the plural: to them (whether masculine or feminine), or to you, formal/plural (whether masculine or feminine as well).

The following examples will help you see how the indirect-object pronouns should be used in a Spanish sentence.

TRACK 53

Él me compró una bicicleta.	**He bought me a bicycle.**
Te compré una bicicleta.	**I bought you (informal/singular) a bicycle.**
Le compré una bicicleta.	**I bought you (formal/singular)/him/ her a bicycle.**
Ella nos compró una bicicleta.	**She bought us a bicycle.**

Ella os compró una bicicleta.	**She bought you (informal/plural) a bicycle.**
Les compré una bicicleta.	**I bought you (formal/plural)/them a bicycle.**

To review, here are some points to keep in mind about indirect-object pronouns:

- Indirect-object pronouns refer only to people.
- Indirect-object pronouns are almost always placed before the conjugated verb (exceptions will be covered later in this book).
- When *no* is necessary, place it before the indirect object. For example: *No me compró una bicicleta.* (He did not buy me a bicycle.)
- When *me*, *te*, or *nos* are used within a sentence that also employs a direct-object pronoun, they are placed immediately before the direct-object pronoun. For example: *Me la compró.* (He bought it for me.)
- Much like with the direct-object pronouns, you can use a redundant construction to emphasize who is receiving the completed action. For example: *Me compró a mí una bicicleta.* (He bought me a bicycle.)
- When *le* or *les* is used within a sentence that also employs a direct-object pronoun, it is replaced by *se*, which is then placed immediately before the direct-object pronoun. For example: *Le compré la bicicleta. Se la compré.* (I bought her a bicycle. I bought it for her.)
- In situations where an infinitive follows an active verb, the indirect-object pronoun may be placed either before the active verb or attached to the end of the infinitive, as follows: *Necesitas mandarle el regalo. Le necesitas mandar el regalo.* (You need to send him/her a present.)

The following are some examples of dealing with direct and indirect objects and object pronouns.

TRACK 54

Quiero escribir una carta a Susana.	**I want to write a letter to Susana.**
Le quiero escribir una carta.	**I want to write her a letter.**
Quiero escribirle una carta.	**I want to write her a letter.**

Le quiero escribir a ella una carta.	**I want to write her a letter.**
Quiero escribirle a ella una carta.	**I want to write her a letter.**
Se la quiero escribir.	**I want to write it to her.**
Se la quiero escribir a ella.	**I want to write it to her.**

Indirect-Object Pronouns

Translate these phrases, using the appropriate indirect-object pronouns. Then, convert all the direct and indirect objects to pronouns. Use your English-to-Spanish and Spanish-to-English dictionary to look up words you don't already know.

1. I purchased him a beverage.

   _____

2. I will send you kisses.

   _____

3. I brought you (formal, plural) the book.

   _____

4. I show Berta the painting.

   _____

5. I told her all the news.

   _____

Chapter 14

Family and Friends

In this chapter, you will learn grammatical concepts that will broaden your scope to help you discuss topics related to your family and friends—possessive adjectives and pronouns, the impersonal *ser* construction to help you express possession, and the Spanish diminutives.

Reviewing Possessive Constructions

If you think about it, a part of your identity is dependent on the relationships that you have, the relationships to which you belong. And as you belong to a relationship, the relationship "belongs" to you.

Spanish, as you may remember, does not facilitate the use of contractions to show possession. When you speak of "belonging" *en español,* you often mean that something is part "of" or "from" something else. For example:

Soy hijo de César y Patricia. **I am the son of Cesar and Patricia.**

The preposition *de* links *son* to parents, where the *son* is "of" the parents. Another way of expressing this relationship is:

César y Patricia son los padres **Cesar and Patricia are the parents**
de Álex. **of Alex.**

Possessive Adjectives

You will have to rely on the *de* construction quite often, particularly when speaking of parts of a whole, in general. However, when it becomes redundant, you can always rely on possessive adjectives to do the job—it's quicker and easier. Refer to the a list of possessive adjectives in the following table.

Possessive Adjectives

Possession of One Object	Possession of Multiple Objects	English
mi	*mis*	my
tu	*tus*	your (informal, singular)
su	*sus*	his, her, its, your (formal, singular)
nuestro	*nuestros*	our (masculine/mixed)
nuestra	*nuestras*	our (feminine)
vuestro	*vuestros*	your (informal, plural, masculine/mixed)

Possession of One Object	Possession of Multiple Objects	English
vuestra	vuestras	your (informal, plural, feminine)
su	sus	their, your (formal, plural)

ALERT!

In English, the adjectives used to show possession depend more on the person who has the items than on the items owned (possessed). Thus, you can use "my" to express ownership of a single item as well as many: my book, my books. In Spanish, however, a possessive pronoun will change depending on the number of the noun that it modifies: *mi libro, mis libros.*

To see how possessive adjectives work in Spanish, take a look at the following sentences, and then listen to them on Track 55.

TRACK 55

Tengo mi propia computadora.	**I have my own computer.**
Compré mis libros en la librería.	**I purchased my books at the bookstore.**
Soy tu mejor amigo.	**I am your best friend.**
¿Visitaste a tus padres?	**Did you visit your parents?**
Conducirá su coche.	**He will drive his car.**
No conozco a sus hermanos.	**I don't know her brothers.**
¿Dónde está su libro, Sra. Lopez?	**Where is your book, Mrs. Lopez?**
Necesito sus consejos, Sr. García.	**I need your advice, Mr. Garcia.**
Estoy entusiasmado con nuestro viaje.	**I am excited about our trip.**
Escribiré nuestros nombres, Alicia y Carolina, en el registro.	**I will write our names, Alicia and Carolina, on the register.**
Es cuestión de vuestro agradecimiento.	**It's a question of your gratitude.**
Aquí están vuestras tazas de café.	**Here are your cups of coffee.**
Contaré su historia, la historia de Manuel y Jacinta.	**I'll tell their story, the story of Manuel and Jacinta.**
¿Ustedes buscan sus coches?	**Are you looking for your cars?**

Remember to use a possessive adjective in front of every possessed noun listed. For example: *Hablé con tu hermana y tu primo*. (I spoke with your sister and cousin.)

Don't worry about the potential for confusion when employing possessive adjectives *su* and *sus*—they are generally clear in context. After all, you switch to a possessive adjective only after you've established the subjects or "possessors" in question. After all, you'd never say "her shoes" before you've made it clear to the speaker that you are referring to "Jane's shoes."

Possessive Pronouns

In addition to adjectives, *español* employs pronouns to show possession—the difference is that the possessive pronouns replace rather than describe nouns. Quick example: my books are mine. "My" is a possessive adjective describing "books." "Mine" is a possessive pronoun that replaces "books."

Like possessive adjectives, possessive pronouns reflect the number of items possessed. However, they must also agree in gender. Note that it is the gender and number of the items possessed (*not* the gender and number of the subject or "owner") that determines the gender of the possessive pronoun. Refer to the following table for a comprehensive list of possessive pronouns.

Possessive Pronouns

Possession of One Object	Possession of Multiple Objects	English
mío	*míos*	mine, masculine
mía	*mías*	mine, feminine
tuyo	*tuyos*	yours (of *tú*), masculine
tuya	*tuyas*	yours (of *tú*), feminine
suyo	*suyos*	his, masculine
suya	*suyas*	his, feminine
suyo	*suyos*	yours (of *usted*), masculine

Possession of One Object	Possession of Multiple Objects	English
suya	suyas	yours (of *usted*), feminine
nuestro	nuestros	ours, masculine
nuestra	nuestras	ours, feminine
vuestro	vuestros	yours (of *vosotros*), masculine
vuestra	vuestras	yours (of *vosotros*), feminine
suyo	suyos	theirs, masculine
suya	suyas	theirs, feminine
suyo	suyos	yours (of *ustedes*), masculine
suya	suyas	yours (of *ustedes*), feminine

Check out the following examples.

TRACK 56

Es mi casa. Es mía.	**It's my house. It's mine.**
Son sus regalos. Son suyos.	**They're your presents. They're yours (of usted).**
Son los problemas del profesor. Son suyos.	**They're the professor's problems. They're his.**
Es mi colchón. Es mío.	**It's my mattress. It's mine.**
Es tu corbata. Es tuya.	**It's your tie. It's yours.**
Son mis ideas. Son mías.	**They're my ideas. They're mine.**
Es su cuento. Es suyo.	**It's your story. It's yours (of ustedes).**
Son vuestros libros. Son vuestros.	**They're your books. They're yours.**
Es nuestra bicicleta. Es nuestra.	**It's our bicycle. It's ours.**
Son tus zapatos. Son tuyos.	**They're your shoes. They're yours.**
Es vuestra imágen. Es vuestra.	**It's your image. It's yours.**
Son nuestros coches. Son nuestros.	**They're our cars. They're ours.**

The Verb Ser and Possession

You've already learned that *ser*, a rather versatile Spanish verb, may express "to be" in six particular ways—personal identity, relationships, profession, origin, personality, and character appearance. To these six, you can also add possession. To review the conjugations of the verb *ser*, refer to the following table.

Conjugating Ser

Subject	Present	Preterite	Imperfect	Present Perfect	Future
(yo)	soy	fui	era	he sido	seré
(tú)	eres	fuiste	eras	has sido	serás
(él, ella, usted)	es	fue	era	ha sido	será
(nosotros, nosotras)	somos	fuimos	éramos	hemos sido	seremos
(vosotros, vosotras)	sois	fuisteis	erais	habéis sido	seréis
(ellos, ellas, ustedes)	son	fueron	eran	han sido	serán

The third person of the verb *ser* allows for a possessive construction, like the following two examples:

El coche es mío. Es mi coche.	**The car is mine. It is my car.**
La casa es mía. Es mi casa.	**The house is mine. It is my house.**

This construction works in all of the verb tenses:

Fue mi coche.	**It was/used to be my car (but no longer).**
Era mi coche.	**It was my car (and may or may not be now).**
Ha sido mi coche desde hace cuatro años.	**It has been my car since four years ago.**
Será mi coche.	**It will be my car.**

What if you were talking about more than one car? How can this construction be expressed for plural items? Well, you simply use the third-person plural form of *ser: son* (in the present tense), and so on. Take a look at the following examples:

Son mis metas ahora.	**They are my goals now.**
Son mis metas cada vez que intento.	**They are my goals each time I try.**
Fueron mis metas.	**They were/used to be my goals (but no longer).**
Eran mis metas.	**They were my goals.**
Han sido mis metas desde la universidad.	**They have been my goals since college.**
Serán mis metas de hoy en adelante.	**They will be my goals from now on.**

Ser in Possessive Constructions

Translate the following sentences, using the appropriate forms of *ser* and possessive adjectives and pronouns. Use your English-to-Spanish and Spanish-to-English dictionary to look up words you don't already know.

1. It is my sweater.

2. The telephone is his.

3. They're my trousers.

4. They're (feminine) yours (informal).

5. Good grades will be mine.

6. The eyeglasses are his.

The Family Gathering

In this section you will practice expressing familial relationships. Take a look at the following table, which contains some relevant vocabulary.

Vocabulary: Familial Relationships

el abuelo, la abuela	grandparent; grandfather, grandmother
el ahijado, la ahijada	godchild; godson, goddaughter
el cuñado, la cuñada	brother-in-law, sister-in-law
el esposo, la esposa	spouse; husband, wife (Spain and Latin America)
el hermanastro, la hermanastra	stepbrother, stepsister
el hermano, la hermana	sibling; brother, sister
el hijastro, la hijastra	stepchild; stepson, stepdaughter
el hijo, la hija	child; son, daughter
la madrastra	stepmother
la madre, la mamá (mami)	mother, mom
el marido	husband (Spain)
la mujer	wife (Spain), woman, female
el nieto, la nieta	grandchild; grandson, granddaughter
el niño, la niña	child; boy, girl
la nuera	daughter-in-law
el padrastro	stepfather
el padre, el papá (papi)	father, dad
el primo, la prima	cousin
el sobrino, la sobrina	nephew, niece
el suegro, la suegra	father-in-law, mother-in-law
el varón	male, man
el yerno	son-in-law

Tips and Tricks

In general, there are a few things to remember when speaking of family relationships:

- When talking in general terms, or grouping family members by relationship rather than gender, you will often use the plural of the masculine form of the word. For example: *¿Cuántos hijos tienen Luis y Fanny?* (How many children do Luis and Fanny have?) *¿Quiénes son los padres de Hugo?* (Who are the parents of Hugo?)
- When grouping family members by relationship and gender, you will need to use the plural form of the word in the chosen gender. For example: *¿Cuántas sobrinas tiene César?* (How many nieces does Cesar have?)
- Since the masculine form is often used as the default gender of most categories, sometimes it may be necessary to further specify the male gender. For example: *¿Quiénes son los hijos (varones) de Luis y Fanny?* (Who are the sons of Luis and Fanny?)

Members of the Family

Translate the following sentences, using the vocabulary you have just learned, and the appropriate forms of *ser*. Use your English-to-Spanish and Spanish-to-English dictionary to look up words you don't already know.

1. The Garcías were my neighbors last year.

   _____

2. I (fem.) am your friend.

   _____

3. He is my husband.

   _____

4. They are my children.

_____

5. I (masc.) am yours.

_____

Diminutives

When you hear a family member addressed in Spanish, you may not hear the standard relation terms you just saw above. In fact, you are more likely to hear variations on those terms. This is true because Spanish allows diminutive suffixes to be added to the ends of nouns. These suffixes are there to signal how the speaker feels about the person (or object) being described.

You will often encounter the _–ito_ and _–ita_ suffixes attached to masculine and feminine nouns and some adjectives. In general, they add a quality of "smallness" or "dearness" to the description of a noun.

Although you are probably not aware of it, diminutives also occur in English. For example, compare the following phrases: kitten/kitty, duck/ducky, dog/doggy. The difference is in terms of ease and frequency of usage: In Spanish, any noun can be easily changed to a diminutive by adding the appropriate suffix, and diminutives are used a lot more frequently.

Rules to Follow

When you wish to add a diminutive suffix, you need to keep a few things in mind. In general, nouns that end in vowels have the vowel replaced by the suffix appropriate in gender and number:

Diminutives

la casa (the house)	*la casita* (the little house)
las cucharas (the spoon)	*las cucharitas* (the teaspoons)
el gato (the cat)	*el gatito* (the kitten)
la hermana (the sister)	*la hermanita* (the little/younger sister)
la lámpara (the lamp)	*la lamparita* (the little lamp)
los perros (the dogs)	*los perritos* (the puppies)

As with irregular verbs that require spelling accommodations, some diminutives also require certain modifications to maintain the pronunciation of the transformed nouns. Fortunately, the changes are similar to those you have already encountered.

Recall that if you wish a word to maintain a hard "c" sound, it must be replaced with a *qu* combination when adding a suffix that begins with *e* or *i*: *taco* (taco); *taquito* (little taco). Similarly, *g* is replaced by *gu*: *jugo* (juice), *juguito* (a little juice). *Z* sometimes needs to be replaced by *c*: *pedazo* (piece), *pedacito* (little piece).

If the noun ends in an *n* or *r*, add a *c* before the suffix: *joven* (youth), *jovencito* (young boy); *mujer* (woman), *mujercita* (young girl, woman).

If a noun with more than one syllable ends in *e*, you would also need to add a *c* before the suffix: *mueble* (furniture), *mueblecito* (small piece of furniture). If the first syllable of a two-syllable noun has an *ie* or a *ue*, and the last syllable ends in an *o* or an *a*, add the combination *ec* before the suffix: *cuento* (story), *cuentecito* (short story); *pierna* (leg), *piernecita* (small leg).

Appropriate Use

With respect to proper nouns and relationships, diminutives denote a particular closeness or affection for an individual. Most often, diminutives are used as forms of address. Given the affection that the diminutive implies, not using it may characterize a distance or formality within a relationship.

Keep in mind that diminutives are largely regional and the uses of *–ito* and *–ita* may differ from one country to the next. Other diminutives employed in addition to or instead of these suffixes include:

- *–ico/–ica*: *mata* (bush), *matica* (little bush)
- *–illo/–illa*: *pan* (bread), *panecillo* (bread roll)

Diminutives may also be employed with a limited number of adjectives. However, whereas diminutive nouns show a small size or affection, adding a diminutive suffix to an adjective will generally make its meaning more emphatic. For example: *suave* (soft), *suavecito* (very soft); *viejo* (old), *viejito* (a warm way of calling someone "old").

Working with Diminutives

Write the appropriate *–ito/–ita* diminutives for the following words:

1. *el padre* (the father) _____

2. *la piedra* (the rock) _____

3. *el nieto* (the grandson)_____

4. *el caballo* (the horse) _____

5. *pobre* (poor) _____

Chapter 15

Irregular Verbs: Moving Through Time

As you have seen in Chapters 11 and 12, irregular verbs in the present tense undergo various kinds of changes based on spelling modifications, group irregularities, and "innate" irregularities specific to a particular verb. This chapter will introduce you to how irregular verbs behave in the preterite, imperfect, present perfect, and future.

15

The Preterite Tense

To review, the preterite tense deals with actions that occur in the past and have been completed. For regular-verb conjugations in the preterite, refer to the following table, which conjugates the regular verbs *cantar* (to sing), *aprender* (to learn), and *vivir* (to live).

Verb Conjugations in the Preterite Tense

	–Ar Verbs	–Er and –Ir Verbs
yo	–é (canté)	–í (aprendí, viví)
tú	–aste (cantaste)	–iste (aprendiste, viviste)
él, ella, usted	–ó (cantó)	–ió (aprendió, vivió)
nosotros, nosotras	–amos (cantamos)	–imos (aprendimos, vivimos)
vosotros, vosotras	–asteis (cantasteis)	–isteis (aprendisteis, vivisteis)
ellos, ellas, ustedes	–aron (cantaron)	–ieron (aprendieron, vivieron)

Spelling Accommodations

Whenever a particular conjugation ending threatens to change its pronunciation, the spelling of the verb must be altered to accommodate the correct pronunciation.

AR Verb Irregularities

The first type of spelling accommodation that you might consider is in the verbs that end in *–car*. Because the *yo* ending is *é*, you need to find some way to accommodate the conjugation so that it keeps the "k" sound in *–car*. (You have already come across similar spelling-accommodation changes when learning about the irregular verbs in the present.) For example, take a look at the preterite conjugations of the verb *buscar*.

Conjugating Buscar in the Preterite

	–ar	buscar (to search, look for)
yo	–é	busqué
tú	–aste	buscaste
él, ella, usted	–ó	buscó
nosotros, nosotras	–amos	buscamos
vosotros, vosotras	–asteis	buscasteis
ellos, ellas, ustedes	–aron	buscaron

As you can see, in order to get a conjugation that is pronounced "boos-KEH," the c is changed to *qu*, which spells out *busqué*. For other verbs in this category, refer to the following table.

Other –CAR Verbs

Verb	Yo Form	Él/Ella/Usted Form	English
abarcar	abarqué	abarcó	to take on
clarificar	clarifiqué	clarificó	to clarify
explicar	expliqué	explicó	to explain
practicar	practiqué	practicó	to practice
sacar	saqué	sacó	to get, take out
tocar	toqué	tocó	to touch, play (an instrument)

Another spelling accommodation that occurs in the *yo* form of the preterite conjugation applies to verbs that end in *–gar*. In order to avoid the ending *–gé* (which makes the g soft), the spelling is modified to *–gué*.

Because only the *yo*-form ending of these verbs begins with an *e* (the only other vowel that would similarly influence g is *i*), only one out of the five conjugations is irregular. The following table lists most of the *–gar* verbs, as well as their conjugations in the *yo* form and the *él/ella/usted* form (used as example of the "default" conjugation).

–GAR Verb Conjugations

Verb	Yo Form	Él/Ella/ Usted Form	English
apagar	apagué	apagó	to turn off, put out
entregar	entregué	entregó	to bring, hand over
jugar	jugué	jugó	to play
llegar	llegué	llegó	to arrive
madrugar	madrugué	madrugó	to get up early
pagar	pagué	pagó	to pay
tragar	tragué	tragó	to swallow

The last exception for the first-person singular conjugations in the preterite that apply to –ar verbs are the verbs that end in –zar. When –é is added to the base, z must be replaced by c. This change may seem a bit confusing, since in most of the Spanish dialects, both letters represent the same sound. Unfortunately, this is but another remnant of Spanish's heritage, when z and c had different pronunciations. Again, this spelling accommodation occurs only in the yo form of the preterite. For a list of –zar verbs, refer to the following table.

–ZAR Verb Conjugations

Verb	Yo Form	Él/Ella/ Usted Form	English
abrazar	abracé	abrazó	to embrace, hug
almorzar	almorcé	almorzó	to have lunch
empezar	empecé	empezó	to begin
rezar	recé	rezó	to pray

Base Ending in a Vowel

Look for –er and –ir verbs that have a base ending in a vowel (for example, construir, "to construct/build"—its base ends in a vowel u). In this category, the i in third-person endings –ió and –ieron changes to a y. This switch does not indicate a fundamental change so much as it provides a clarification of emphasis. Remember that the *i* is a weak vowel that is often overpowered by stronger vowels (*a, e,* and *o*) to produce a "y" sound. Recall also that the accented *í* maintains its "ee" sound. An accented *í* would actually change the pronunciation of the word, and yet the "vowel + *i* + strong vowel" combination does not seem to produce a strong enough "y" to tame that mess of open sound. The answer therefore is to adopt the *y* formally. Refer to the conjugations of *construir* (to construct) and *sustituir* (to substitute) in the following table.

Conjugating Construir and Sustituir in the Preterite

	–uir	*construir* (to construct)	*sustituir* (to substitute)
yo	–í	*construí*	*sustituí*
tú	–iste	*construiste*	*sustituiste*
él, ella, usted	–ió	*construyó*	*sustituyó*
nosotros, nosotras	–imos	*construimos*	*sustituimos*
vosotros, vosotras	–isteis	*construisteis*	*sustituisteis*
ellos, ellas, ustedes	–ieron	*construyeron*	*sustituyeron*

In some of the verbs that belong to the same category (verb base ending in a vowel), there's an additional change: *tú, nosotros,* and *vosotros* forms also have an accent mark over the *i*—the accent mark turns the weak *i* ("y") into a strong *í* ("ee"). For a sample conjugation, take a look at *proveer.*

Conjugating Proveer in the Preterite

	–er	*proveer* (to provide)
yo	–í	*proveí*
tú	–iste	*proveíste*
él, ella, usted	–ió	*proveyó*
nosotros, nosotras	–imos	*proveímos*

Conjugating Proveer in the Preterite

vosotros, vosotras	–isteis	proveísteis
ellos, ellas, ustedes	–ieron	proveyeron

Other Verbs in the I to Y Category

Verb	Tú Form	Él/Ella/ Usted Form	Nosotros Form	Ellos/Ellas/ Ustedes Form	English
caer	caíste	cayó	caímos	cayeron	to fall
creer	creíste	creyó	creímos	creyeron	to believe
leer	leíste	leyó	leímos	leyeron	to read

Now it's time to take a break and review what you've learned so far. Then, check out the following exercise to help you practice these irregular-verb conjugations.

Verb Practice #9

Translate the following sentences using the appropriate verb forms. Use your English-to-Spanish and Spanish-to-English dictionary to look up words you don't already know.

1. I searched for my book.

   _____

2. He read the newspaper.

   _____

3. They believed the worst.

   _____

4. I practiced all day.

_____

5. You (formal) possessed courage.

_____

Verbs That End in –DUCIR

In the case of verbs that end with –*ducir,* the irregular changes occur in *all* of the conjugations of the preterite tense. For example, take a look at how to conjugate *conducir* (to drive).

Conjugating Conducir in the Preterite Tense

	conducir (to drive)
yo	*conduje*
tú	*condujiste*
él, ella, usted	*condujo*
nosotros, nosotras	*condujimos*
vosotros, vosotras	*condujisteis*
ellos, ellas, ustedes	*condujeron*

As you can see, three major changes have taken place: The *c* at the end of each base has been changed to *j,* the accent marks that generally appear in some of the preterite forms have all been dropped, and the ending in the third-person plural is –*eron* (and not –*ieron,* as in regular –*er* and –*ir* verbs).

Other verbs that belong to this category appear in the following table.

Sample –DUCIR Verb Conjugations in the Preterite

Verb	Yo Form	Él/Ella/ Usted Form	Ellos/Ellas/ Ustedes Form	English
deducir	*deduje*	*dedujo*	*dedujeron*	to deduce
introducir	*introduje*	*introdujo*	*introdujeron*	to introduce

Verb	Yo Form	Él/Ella/ Usted Form	Ellos/Ellas/ Ustedes Form	English
producir	*produje*	*produjo*	*produjeron*	to produce
traducir	*traduje*	*tradujo*	*tradujeron*	to translate

Another verb that is similar to this group (though, technically, it doesn't belong here) is *decir* (to say). In the preterite, its base changes to *dij–*, and its endings are the same as that of the verbs in this category: *–e, –iste, –o, –imos, –isteis,* and *–eron* (notice that there are no accent marks over these endings).

Group Irregularities

In the preterite, verbs that follow group irregularities may have vowel or consonant base changes. Each group is described in the following sections.

–IR Verbs with Base Change from E to I

A few group-based irregularities have to do with vowel modifications. Some of these may be familiar to you from the present-tense irregular verb conjugations. For example, the following group of *–ir* verbs undergoes a base-vowel change from *e* to *i* in the third-person singular and third-person plural forms of the preterite verb. (Compare the base of the *yo* and *nosotros* forms to the *él/ella/usted* and *ellos/ellas/ustedes* forms in the following table.)

List of Verbs with Base Change from E to I

Verb	Yo Form	Él/Ella/ Usted Form	Nosotros Form	Ellos/Ellas/ Ustedes Form	English
advertir	*advertí*	*advirtió*	*advertimos*	*advirtieron*	to warn
medir	*medí*	*midió*	*medimos*	*midieron*	to measure
mentir	*mentí*	*mintió*	*mentimos*	*mintieron*	to lie
pedir	*pedí*	*pidió*	*pedimos*	*pidieron*	to ask
preferir	*preferí*	*prefirió*	*preferimos*	*prefirieron*	to prefer

Verb	Yo Form	Él/Ella/ Usted Form	Nosotros Form	Ellos/Ellas/ Ustedes Form	English
repetir	*repetí*	*repitió*	*repetimos*	*repitieron*	to repeat
seguir	*seguí*	*siguió*	*seguimos*	*siguieron*	to follow
sentir	*sentí*	*sintió*	*sentimos*	*sintieron*	to feel
servir	*serví*	*sirvió*	*servimos*	*sirvieron*	to serve

–IR Verbs with Base Change from O to U

Although the group of verbs that falls into this category in the present tense is quite large, there are only two verbs (*dormir* and *morir*) that undergo this change in the preterite. Much like with the *e* to *i* change, only the bases of the third-person singular and plural conjugations undergo the change. For the conjugations, see the following table.

Conjugating Dormir and Morir in the Preterite

	–ir	*dormir* (to sleep)	*morir* (to die)
yo	–í	*dormí*	*morí*
tú	–iste	*dormiste*	*moriste*
él, ella, usted	–ió	*durmió*	*murió*
nosotros, nosotras	–imos	*dormimos*	*morimos*
vosotros, vosotras	–isteis	*dormisteis*	*moristeis*
ellos, ellas, ustedes	–ieron	*durmieron*	*murieron*

Verb Practice #10

Translate the following sentences using the appropriate verb forms. Use your English-to-Spanish and Spanish-to-English dictionary to look up words you don't already know.

1. We drove to the party.

_____

2. The salesman repeated the offer.

_____

3. Did you (informal, singular) translate the speech?

_____

4. She introduced her friends.

_____

5. They slept all day.

_____

–ER Verbs with Base Change from A or O to U

The following verbs undergo a base change with the substitution of a _u_ (note that, in some cases, the consonant following the base vowel will change as well, and the endings are also irregular). The _u_ base change applies to all preterite conjugations of each of these verbs.

Verbs with Base Vowel Change to U

	caber (to fit)	poder (to be able to)	poner (to put)	saber (to know, learn)
_yo_	_cupe_	_pude_	_puse_	_supe_
_tú_	_cupiste_	_pudiste_	_pusiste_	_supiste_
él, ella, usted	_cupo_	_pudo_	_puso_	_supo_
nosotros, nosotras	_cupimos_	_pudimos_	_pusimos_	_supimos_
vosotros, vosotras	_cupisteis_	_pudisteis_	_pusisteis_	_supisteis_
ellos, ellas, ustedes	_cupieron_	_pudieron_	_pusieron_	_supieron_

Verbs with Base Change from A or E to I

Another irregularity is the substitution of a base vocalized by an *i*. Again, the best approach for these verbs is to memorize the irregular base and how the endings vary from the regular rule. For the conjugations of *i*-based verbs, refer to the following table.

Verbs with Base Vowel Change to I

	dar (to give)	hacer (to do, to make)	querer (to want)	venir (to come)
yo	di	hice	quise	vine
tú	diste	hiciste	quisiste	viniste
él, ella, usted	dio	hizo	quiso	vino
nosotros, nosotras	dimos	hicimos	quisimos	vinimos
vosotros, vosotras	disteis	hicisteis	quisisteis	vinisteis
ellos, ellas, ustedes	dieron	hicieron	quisieron	vinieron

QUESTION?

What's the correct translation of the verb *querer*?
Though *querer* is generally translated as "to want," it can also mean "to love" and "to like" (as in wanting) For instance: *¿Quiere un té?* means "Would you (formal, singular) like some tea?" The expression *te quiero* translates to "I love you."

You may have noticed that the *hic–* base of the preterite form of *hacer* did undergo an additional change in the third-person singular (*él/ella/usted*) form, where the *c* changed to a *z* (to form *hizo*). This is actually a spelling-accommodation change—think about what would happen if you didn't substitute the *z* for the *c*. You are trying to say "EE-soh"; spelling this conjugation *hico* would force you to change the pronunciation to "EE-koh."

Verb Practice #11

Translate the following sentences using the appropriate verb forms. Use your English-to-Spanish and Spanish-to-English dictionary to look up words you don't already know.

1. We gave Susy the gift.

_____

2. I placed the key on the table.

_____

3. You (informal, plural) wanted a steak.

_____

4. Julio came to Vita's birthday party.

_____

5. You (formal, singular) knew it.

_____

–AER Verbs with Base Consonant Change to J

Consonant-based irregularities are similar to vowel-based ones. They require changes or additions to a letter (in this case a consonant) within the base of the verb. Also note that these conjugations may undergo additional irregularities. For example, the accent marks may be dropped from the first-person singular and third-person singular conjugations. The verbs in the following group gain a *j*.

–AER Verbs with Base Consonant Change to J

	abstraer (to make abstract)	atraer (to attract)	contraer (to contract)	Distraer (to distract)
yo	abstraje	atraje	contraje	distraje
tú	abstrajiste	atrajiste	contrajiste	distrajiste
él, ella, usted	abstrajo	atrajo	contrajo	distrajo
nosotros, nosotras	abstrajimos	atrajimos	contrajimos	distrajimos
vosotros, vosotras	abstrajisteis	atrajisteis	contrajisteis	distrajisteis
ellos, ellas, ustedes	abstrajeron	atrajeron	contrajeron	distrajeron

Mixed Irregularities

Mixed irregularities combine vowel-based and consonant-based irregularities in their verbs. You have already encountered some of these verbs—just think back to the *ser* and *estar* chapter. Do you remember how to conjugate *estar* in the preterite? The base of this verb changes to *estuv–*. Another verb that behaves the same way is *tener (tuv–)*. And there is another verb that belongs to this category: *andar* (to walk). To compare the preterite conjugations of *andar, estar,* and *tener,* refer to the following table.

Conjugating Andar, Estar, and Tener in the Preterite Tense

	andar (to walk)	estar (to be)	tener (to have)
yo	anduve	estuve	tuve
tú	anduviste	estuviste	tuviste
él, ella, usted	anduvo	estuvo	tuvo
nosotros, nosotras	anduvimos	estuvimos	tuvimos
vosotros, vosotras	anduvisteis	estuvisteis	tuvisteis
ellos, ellas, ustedes	anduvieron	estuvieron	tuvieron

Oír (to hear) is another irregular verb that is hard to categorize (as you might remember from looking at its conjugations in the present tense). The following table lists the conjugations of *oír* in the preterite.

Conjugating Oír in the Preterite Tense

	oír (to hear)
yo	*oí*
tú	*oíste*
él, ella, usted	*oyó*
nosotros, nosotras	*oímos*
vosotros, vosotras	*oísteis*
ellos, ellas, ustedes	*oyeron*

Verb Practice #12

Translate the following sentences using the appropriate verb forms. Use your English-to-Spanish and Spanish-to-English dictionary to look up words you don't already know.

1. I abstracted the ideas from the book.

   _____

2. We contracted the measles.

   _____

3. You (informal, plural) walked along the path that day.

   _____

4. You (informal, singular) distracted the driver.

   _____

5. They heard the noise from far (away).

   _____

Irregularities in Other Verb Tenses

The bad news is, we still have a number of tenses to cover. But the good news is, the rest of them aren't nearly as filled with irregularities as the preterite. Take a break, and then move on to review irregulars in the imperfect, present perfect, and the future tense.

Imperfect Tense

In the imperfect tense, the endings always remain the same, just as in the regular-verb conjugations (refer to the following table for a review of regular conjugations in the imperfect tense).

Conjugating –AR Verbs in the Imperfect Tense

Pronoun	Ending	Cantar (To Sing)
yo	–aba	cantaba
tú	–abas	cantabas
él, ella, usted	–aba	cantaba
nosotros, nosotras	–ábamos	cantábamos
vosotros, vosotras	–abais	cantabais
ellos, ellas, ustedes	–aban	cantaban

Conjugating –ER and –IR Verbs in the Imperfect Tense

Pronoun	Ending	Aprender (To Learn)	Vivir (To Live)
yo	–ía	aprendía	vivía
tú	–ías	aprendías	vivías
él, ella, usted	–ía	aprendía	vivía
nosotros	–íamos	aprendíamos	vivíamos
vosotros, vosotras	–íais	aprendíais	vivíais
ellos, ellas, ustedes	–ían	aprendían	vivían

The few irregularities that exist in the imperfect are limited to innate base changes. One such example is the verb *ver* (to see). In the imperfect, the base changes from *v–* to *ve–*, so that you have *veía* (I saw) instead of *vía* (which is wrong and, incidentally, means "way" or "path" in Spanish). Refer to the following table to see how *ver* is conjugated in the imperfect.

Conjugating Ver in the Imperfect Tense

yo	veía
tú	veías
él, ella, usted	veía
nosotros, nosotras	veíamos
vosotros, vosotras	veíais
ellos, ellas, ustedes	veían

Present Perfect Tense

As you may remember, the present perfect is a composite tense—that is, it's made up of two verb parts: *haber* conjugated in the present tense plus a past participle. To review the present-tense conjugations of *haber*, review the following table of regular present-tense conjugations.

Conjugating Verbs in Present Perfect

	–AR Verb	–ER Verb	–IR Verb
yo	he cantado	he aprendido	he vivido
tú	has cantado	has aprendido	has vivido
él, ella, usted	ha cantado	ha aprendido	ha vivido
nosotros, nosotras	hemos cantado	hemos aprendido	hemos vivido
vosotros, vosotras	habéis cantado	habéis aprendido	habéis vivido
ellos, ellas, ustedes	han cantado	han aprendido	han vivido

It follows, then, that the irregularities in the present perfect are really the irregularities in the past participles. The following table contains a list of verbs that have irregular past participles.

Irregular Past Participles

Infinitive	Past Participle	English
abrir	abierto	to open
cubrir	cubierto	to cover
decir	dicho	to say
escribir	escrito	to write
hacer	hecho	to do or make
poner	puesto	to put
resolver	resuelto	to resolve
romper	roto	to break
satisfacer	satisfecho	to satisfy
ver	visto	to see
volver	vuelto	to return

Verb Practice #13

Translate the following sentences using the appropriate verb forms. Use your English-to-Spanish and Spanish-to-English dictionary to look up words you don't already know.

1. I have opened an account.

_____

2. She has put one hundred dollars in the account.

_____

3. They have done the work.

_____

4. You (formal, singular) have satisfied the requirements.

_____

5. We have returned to university.

_____

Future Tense

In the future tense, irregularities are limited to innately irregular verbs. As a result, the endings employed are the same as those used with regular verbs. But first off, let's review regular verb endings in the future tense—refer to the following table for the conjugations.

Conjugating Verbs in Future Tense

	Verb Ending	Cantar (To Sing)	Aprender (To Learn)	Vivir (To Live)
yo	–é	*cantaré*	*aprenderé*	*viviré*
tú	–ás	*cantarás*	*aprenderás*	*vivirás*
él, ella, usted	–á	*cantará*	*aprenderá*	*vivirá*
nosotros, nosotras	–emos	*cantaremos*	*aprenderemos*	*viviremos*
vosotros, vosotras	–éis	*cantaréis*	*aprenderéis*	*viviréis*
ellos, ellas, ustedes	–án	*cantarán*	*aprenderán*	*vivirán*

There is a group of verbs that gain a *d* in the base that is used to put together the future-tense conjugations. These verbs are *poner* (to put), *salir* (to leave), *tener* (to have), and *venir* (to come). Since they have regular endings, the following table includes only some of the future-tense conjugations of these verbs.

Verbs That Gain a D in the Base of Future-Tense Conjugations

Verb	Yo Form	Él/Ella/ Usted Form	Nosotros/ Nosotras Form
poner (to put)	*pondré*	*pondrá*	*pondremos*
salir (to leave)	*saldré*	*saldrá*	*saldremos*
tener (to have)	*tendré*	*tendrá*	*tendremos*
venir (to come)	*vendré*	*vendrá*	*vendremos*

Another group of verbs modifies its base by dropping an *e*. (A likely explanation might be that dropping this vowel shortened the pronunciation of these verbs by a syllable.) For a list of these verbs, refer to the following table.

Verbs That Lose an E in the Base of Future-Tense Conjugations

Verb	Yo Form	Él/Ella/ Usted Form	Nosotros/ Nosotras Form
caber (to fit)	*cabré*	*cabrá*	*cabremos*
poder (to be able to)	*podré*	*podrá*	*podremos*
saber (to know)	*sabré*	*sabrá*	*sabremos*

Finally, there are some verbs that are just hard to classify. You've seen them come up again and again in the chapters on irregular verbs: *decir* (to say), *hacer* (to do), and *querer* (to want). Their conjugations are listed in the following table.

Other Verbs with Irregular Future-Tense Conjugations

Verb	Yo Form	Él/Ella/ Usted Form	Nosotros Form
decir (to say)	*diré*	*dirá*	*diremos*
hacer (to do)	*haré*	*hará*	*haremos*
querer (to want)	*querré*	*querrá*	*querremos*

Verb Practice #14

Translate the following sentences using the appropriate verb forms. Use your English-to-Spanish and Spanish-to-English dictionary to look up words you don't already know.

1. Will you (informal, singular) make the bed?

_____

2. My parents will come on Tuesday.

_____

3. We will not be able to walk more.

_____

4. You (informal, singular) will leave soon.

_____

5. They will want to wash their clothes.

_____

Chapter 16

Impersonal Assertions and the Subjunctive

You probably remember your old English teacher warning everybody about overusing passive-voice sentences like "it was given to me by Eileen" (instead of "Eileen gave it to me"). But sometimes you do need to use impersonal constructions, and you may also want to know how to do so in Spanish. And whereas we rarely use subjunctive mood in English, it's a far more useful concept in Spanish, and worth learning about.

Impersonal Assertions

Most passive-voice constructions in English come with the verb form of "to be." In Spanish, you will often use *ser* as the equivalent. One type of passive-voice construction that uses *ser* is the impersonal assertion. Impersonal assertions are those statements that are said as general truths. They are not bound to time—they may have been true before, may be true now, and might be true in the future. The general rule is that they are expressed in the third person of the present tense with the verb ser.

Recall that the interaction of the verb *ser* (to be) and the object of possession permitted you to say *es mi abrigo* (it's my coat). Following are some examples of impersonal-assertion sentences:

Es malo fumar.	**It's bad to smoke.**
Es bueno hacer ejercicios.	**It's good to exercise.**
Es inteligente tomar notas.	**It's smart to take notes.**

The easiest way to distinguish impersonal constructions is to remember that they do not have a specific subject. Technically, of course, the subject is the pronoun of *ser* (*él* or *ella* for *es*, and *ellos* or *ellas* for *son*, translated into English as "it"), but it does not refer to anything and is never actually present in the meaning of the sentence.

Discussing the Weather

The impersonal construction may be used to discuss *el tiempo* (the weather). However, since the weather is never in a permanent state, the verb *estar* is used instead of ser. (If you need to review the differences between *ser* and *estar*, reread Chapters 6 and 7.)

Estar allows you to describe physical conditions; when employed to describe the environment, *estar* may be translated as "it is." Take a look at the following questions:

¿Cómo está el clima?	**How is the climate?**
¿Cómo está el tiempo?	**How is the weather?**
¿Cómo está afuera?	**How is it outside?**

In reply, all you need to do is say *Está . . .* and a word that would describe the weather. For a list of weather-related vocabulary, check out the following table.

The Vocabulary of Weather

agradable	pleasant
el buen tiempo	nice weather
caluroso	hot
claro	clear
cubierto	covered (with clouds)
despejado	without clouds
frío	cold
helado	freezing
húmedo	humid
lluvioso	rainy
nevado	snowy
nublado	cloudy
con mucho viento	windy

What's the Weather Doing?

You can also use *hacer* to describe what the weather "does" (as opposed to how it "is"). For instance, *hace sol* may be translated as "it's sunny," but this phrase literally stands for "(the weather) makes the sun."

So another way of asking about the weather is *¿Qué tiempo hace?* ("How is the weather?" or "Which weather is going on?") In reply, you would say, *Hace . . .*

Hace buen tiempo.	**The weather is nice.**
Hace calor.	**It's hot.**
Hace frío.	**It's cold.**
Hace viento.	**It's windy.**

Other Weather-Related Verbs

In addition to *estar* and *hacer,* you can use other verbs that describe the weather. Take a look at the following table for some examples. Notice that most of these verbs look like the adverbs you've learned already to describe the weather.

Verbs to Use in Describing the Weather

amanecer	to grow light (at dawn)
anochecer	to grow dark (at night)
granizar	to hail
helar	to freeze
llover	to rain
lloviznar	to drizzle
relampaguear	to flash with lightning
tronar	to thunder

Listen to Track 57 as you review the following examples.

TRACK 57

Amaneció nublado.	**It was cloudy at dawn.**
Anocheció despejado.	**It was clear at nightfall.**
Ya no graniza.	**It's not hailing anymore.**
Hoy ha helado.	**It has been freezing today.**
Llueve a cántaros.	**It rains like cats and dogs.**

Imperative Constructions

Another type of construction that lacks a voiced subject is the imperative construction. The imperative is often called the command mood, though it's not used solely for commands, but also in making requests. When you request, ask, or demand something addressing yourself directly to someone, you are using the imperative.

The imperative mood's concern with the present should make it a fairly easy mood to master. Simply plug in the appropriate endings and place the command within exclamation marks (¡ . . . !) for emphasis. Note that there are only *tú, usted, nosotros, vosotros, and ustedes* forms in the command mood, because you must address a "you" (*nosotros* form, to be explained in greater detail, is a "let's . . ." construction). However, the tricky thing is that endings vary depending on whether the command is positive (do!) or negative (don't!).

Tú in the Imperative

The best way to approach the imperative is by learning the *tú* form. That's because it's the most obvious type of command—you are much more likely to use the imperative with somebody you know well, or somebody who is younger than you.

Positive Commands Addressed to Tú

−AR Verb	−ER Verb	−IR Verb
¡Camina! (Walk!)	¡Bebe! (Drink!)	¡Recibe! (Get!)

Negative Commands Addressed to Tú

−AR Verb	−ER Verb	−IR Verb
¡No camines! (Don't walk!)	¡No bebas! (Don't drink!)	¡No recibas! (Don't get!)

It is understandable if you find these a little confusing. The positive command endings are the same for the imperative *tú* form as they are for the indicative present-tense *él/ella/usted* form: *camina, bebe, recibe*.

Whereas the positive imperatives for *tú* take the same form as the indicative present-tense conjugations of the more formal *usted*, negative imperatives of *tú* seem to invert the present-tense *tú* conjugation endings. *Caminar* takes on the *–es* ending, and *beber* and *recibir* take on the *–as* ending: *no camines, no bebas, no recibas*.

There are only a few verbs that have irregular positive-*tú* command conjugations—that is, verbs that don't simply follow the rules outlined here. These verbs are listed in the following table.

Irregular Verbs

Verb	English	Positive Tú Command	Negative Tú Command
decir	to say	*¡Di!*	*¡No digas!*
hacer	to do	*¡Haz!*	*¡No hagas!*
ir	to go	*¡Ve!*	*¡No vayas!*
poner	to put	*¡Pon!*	*¡No pongas!*
salir	to leave	*¡Sal!*	*¡No salgas!*
ser	to be	*¡Sé!*	*¡No seas!*
tener	to have	*¡Ten!*	*¡No tengas!*
venir	to come	*¡Ven!*	*¡No vengas!*

Vosotros/Vosotras in the Imperative

There is also a *vosotros/vosotras* form for the imperative mood. To make a positive *vosotros* command, drop the final *r* of the verb's infinitive and replace it with a *d: caminad, bebed, recibid*.

The only exception to this rule is the verb *ir* (to go): the positive form in the command mood is *id:*

¡Id a casa ahora mismo!   **Go home immediately!**

To make negative *vosotros* commands, use the present-tense verb endings, but switch the endings of *–ar* and *–er/–ir* verbs, as you've done with the negative *tú* commands: *no caminéis, no bebáis, no recibáis*.

To review the *vosotros/vosotras* command conjugations, see the following table:

Positive Commands Addressed to Vosotros/Vosotras

–AR Verb	–ER Verb	–IR Verb
¡Caminad! (Walk!)	¡Bebed! (Drink!)	¡Recibid! (Get!)

Negative Commands Addressed to Vosotros/Vosotras

–AR Verb	–ER Verb	–IR Verb
¡No caminéis! (Don't walk!)	¡No bebáis! (Don't drink!)	¡No recibáis! (Don't get!)

Usted/Ustedes and Nosotros/Nosotras in the Imperative

The commands or requests addressed to *usted, ustedes, nosotros,* and *nosotras* approach the imperative in the same way as the negative *tú/vosotros/vosotras* commands. That is, you add *–e,–en,* and *–emos* endings to the *–ar* verbs, and *–a, –an,* and *–amos* endings to the *–er* and *–ir* verbs. This rule applies to both positive and negative commands.

Positive Commands to Usted, Ustedes, and Nosotros/Nosotras

	–AR Verb	–ER Verb	–IR Verb
usted	¡Camine!	¡Beba!	¡Reciba!
ustedes	¡Caminen!	¡Beban!	¡Reciban!
nosotros, nosotras	¡Caminemos!	¡Bebamos!	¡Recibamos!

Negative Commands to Usted, Ustedes, and Nosotros/Nosotras

	–AR Verb	–ER Verb	–IR Verb
usted	¡No camine!	¡No beba!	¡No reciba!
ustedes	¡No caminen!	¡No beban!	¡No reciban!
nosotros, nosotras	¡No caminemos!	¡No bebamos!	¡No recibamos!

In the *nosotros/nosotras* form, the commands may be translated in the form of "let's . . ." This means *¡Caminemos!* translates to "Let's walk!"; *¡Bebamos!* is "Let's drink!"; and *¡Recibamos!* may be translated as "Let's receive (something)!"

Irregular Nosotros/Nosotras Conjugations

Some verbs undergo a spelling accommodation in the *nosotros/nosotras* form of the imperative. Verbs that end in *–car*, *–gar*, and *–zar* follow a base consonant change from *c* to *qu*, *g* to *gu*, and *z* to *ce*, respectively (see the following tables for details).

Consonant Change in –CAR Verbs

Verb	English	Imperative Nosotros/Nosotras Form
abarcar	to take on	abarquemos
buscar	to look for	busquemos
practicar	to practice	practiquemos
sacar	to take out	saquemos

Consonant Change in –GAR Verbs

Verb	English	Imperative Nosotros/Nosotras Form
apagar	to turn off	apaguemos
entregar	to hand over	entreguemos
jugar	to play	juguemos
llegar	to arrive	lleguemos

Consonant Change in –ZAR Verbs

Verb	English	Imperative Nosotros/Nosotras Form
abrazar	to embrace	*abracemos*
almorzar	to eat lunch	*almorcemos*
empezar	to begin	*empecemos*
rezar	to pray	*recemos*

Another group of irregular verbs belong to the *–ir* category, and the spelling-accommodation changes involved concern the verb's base vowel. The changes usually occur as follows: from *e* to *i*, and from *o* to *u* (see the following two tables).

Vowel Change from E to I

Verb	English	Imperative Nosotros/Nosotras Form
advertir	to warn	*advirtamos*
medir	to measure	*midamos*
mentir	to lie, deceive	*mintamos*
pedir	to ask, request	*pidamos*

Vowel Change from O to U

Verb	English	Imperative Nosotros/Nosotras Form
dormir	to sleep	*durmamos*
morir	to die	*muramos*

Object Pronouns in Commands

As you learned in Chapter 13, object pronouns generally precede the verb:

Lo vi en la calle.	**I saw him on the street.**
Lo hice a las nueve de la mañana.	**I did it at nine in the morning.**

In positive commands, the object pronoun is attached to the verb of command:

TRACK 58

¡Estúdialo ahora mismo!	**Study it right now!**
¡Bébanlo después de comer!	**Drink it after eating!**
¡Abrámoslo mañana!	**Let's open it tomorrow!**
¡Escúchame!	**Listen to me!**
¡Dame la blusa!	**Give me the blouse!**
¡Dámela!	**Give it to me!**

In some cases, when you add additional syllables to a word, you also need to add an accent mark—unless you intend to pronounce it differently. For example, take a look at *¡Dame!* and *¡Dámela!* According to accent rules, a word that ends in a vowel should be accented on the next-to-last syllable. When you add *la*, you also need to add an accent mark over the *a* in order to keep the pronunciation "DAH-meh-lah" (and not "dah-MEH-lah"). Note that in the last example the indirect object *me* (to me) precedes the direct object *la* (it).

In the negative, however, the object pronouns precede the imperative verb (though, once again, the indirect object comes first, followed by the direct object). Take a look at the following examples:

¡No me escuches!	**Don't listen to me!**
¡No me des la blusa!	**Don't give me the blouse!**
¡No me la des!	**Don't give it to me.**

Reviewing the Imperative

Translate the following sentences, using the information you have just learned. Use your English-to-Spanish and Spanish-to-English dictionary to look up words you don't already know.

1. Listen (you, informal/singular) to the news!

2. Let's decide on a movie!

_____

3. Wait (you, formal/singular) for me at the door!

_____

4. Come (you, informal/singular) here!

_____

5. Don't cry (you, informal/plural)!

_____

6. Look for (you, formal/singular) the key!

_____

7. Don't put (you, informal/plural) it (masculine) here!

_____

8. Let's travel to Mexico together!

_____

9. Don't buy (you, formal/singular) it for her!

_____

10. Bring (you, formal/plural) it to me!

_____

Introducing the Subjunctive

As you saw earlier, an impersonal assertion tries to lend a certain amount of authority or objectivity to a statement. An easy way to create this impression is to use the phrases that lend themselves to its construction. Some of these phrases include:

Es evidente que . . .	**It is evident that . . .**
Es cierto que . . .	**It is certain that . . .**
Es verdad que . . .	**It is true that . . .**
Es seguro que . . .	**It is sure that . . .**
Es indudable que . . .	**It is indubitable that . . .**
Es que . . .	**It is that . . .**

To see how these constructions behave in complete sentences, look at the following examples:

Será feliz quien tiene a quien amar.	**One who has someone to love will be happy.**
Es indudable que los hijos necesitan a su madre.	**There is no doubt that children need their mother.**
Es seguro que el policía lo coje.	**It's sure that the policeman catches him.**

All of these constructions express opinions of certainty in the indicative mood. As you've seen before, this mood can also express some uncertainty, particularly in the compound tenses using a form of *haber*. Recall, however, that usually the uncertainty that can be created is somewhat limited—a probability by definition implies that there is a chance that the contrary may occur, but the deck is stacked in favor of the outcome. The indicative offers the following sentence qualifiers:

A lo mejor voy de vacaciones a Perú.	**I may go on vacation to Peru.**
Quizás llega a tiempo el regalo de Navidad.	**Hopefully the Christmas present arrives on time.**

Tal vez no le gustan los camarones.	**Perhaps she doesn't like shrimp.**
Posiblemente el remedio es demasiado fuerte.	**Possibly the remedy is too strong.**

Though the ability to express uncertainty can be found in the indicative mood, the degree of doubt or opinion is very constrained. To more forcefully express the gray areas of life, you need to consider the subjunctive mood, which may be novel, given its scarce employment in everyday English.

Recall that the mood associated with verbs is the manner by which you decide to communicate or report the world around you. In the indicative, you were concerned with telling how things appeared—a somewhat "objective" accounting. In contrast, the subjunctive takes on a somewhat "subjective" approach. It allows you to express opinions, personal as well as impersonal.

In the present subjunctive, the conjugations are similar to present indicative, except that they're inverted (you've already seen this in the imperative conjugations). Take a look at the following tables for details.

Conjugating –AR Verb Cantar (To Sing) in Present Subjunctive

yo	–e	cante
tú	–es	cantes
él, ella, usted	–e	cante
nosotros, nosotras	–emos	cantemos
vosotros, vosotras	–éis	cantéis
ellos, ellas, ustedes	–en	canten

Conjugating –ER Verb Aprender (To Learn) in Present Subjunctive

yo	–a	aprenda
tú	–as	aprendas
él, ella, usted	–a	aprenda
nosotros, nosotras	–amos	aprendamos
vosotros, vosotras	–áis	aprendáis
ellos, ellas, ustedes	–an	aprendan

Conjugating –IR Verb Vivir (To Live) in Present Subjunctive

yo	*–a*	*viva*
tú	*–as*	*vivas*
él, ella, usted	*–a*	*viva*
nosotros, nosotras	*–amos*	*vivamos*
vosotros, vosotras	*–áis*	*viváis*
ellos, ellas, ustedes	*–an*	*vivan*

As you can see, the *–ar* present subjunctive endings are similar to the *–er* endings of the present indicative. Likewise, the present subjunctive *–er* and *–ir* endings are almost the same as those of the *–ar* present indicative. The one difference is that *yo* and *él/ella/usted* forms are identical in the subjunctive.

So, now that you've got the conjugations down, the next step is to figure out when you need to switch to the subjunctive mood. The following sections will help you figure that out.

A subjunctive phrase rarely stands alone. At the heart of most sentences that use the present subjunctive, there is an indicative phrase that sets the subjunctive in motion by introducing a need or desire to be met, a doubt to be expressed, or an opinion to be made. The short sentence is largely absent in the subjunctive.

Expressing Uncertainty

As you saw earlier, certain "keywords" may be employed to express doubt. Such keywords in the subjunctive include words like "maybe" and "possibly":

Quizás llegue a tiempo el regalo de Navidad.	**Hopefully the Christmas present arrives on time—but there is a good chance that it won't.**
Tal vez no le gusten camarones.	**Perhaps she doesn't like shrimp— but she may.**

Posiblemente el remedio sea demasiado fuerte.	**Possibly the remedy is too strong— but it may be otherwise.**

Although the sentences are very similar to the ones you've seen previously, the fact that you are using the subjunctive lends them a sense of uncertainty—hence the additional phrases included in the translations. Other tags of uncertainty specifically useful in the subjuntive include "it's doubtful that" and "it might be that":

Es dudoso que Mario saque buena nota en la prueba.	**It is doubtful that Mario gets a good grade on the test.**
Es posible que lo llame por teléfono mañana.	**It's possible that I might call him tomorrow.**
Puede ser que compre un coche usado.	**It might be that I'll purchase a used car.**
Puede que el dueño cambie de idea.	**It could be that the owner changes his mind.**

Notice in the sample sentences above how *que* introduces the subjunctive phrase, a common way of signaling the subjunctive. Often, the subjunctive is found as a dependent clause that relies on a main independent and indicative clause to exist.

The following are groups of verbs that take on a subjunctive *que* clause:

The Subjunctive Que Clause

Doubt or Uncertainty	
dudar	to doubt
no estar seguro	not to be sure
imaginarse	to expect
Hope or Necessity	
esperar	to hope, to expect
necesitar	to need
querer	to want
preferir	to prefer

Emotional State	
alegrar	to make happy
enojar	to make angry
gustar	to like
sentir	to feel
sorprender	to surprise

Telling or Asking	
aconsejar	to advise
decir	to say
exigir	to demand
insistir	to insist
pedir	to ask
prohibir	to forbid
rogar	to beg

Here are some examples:

Dudamos que usted tenga suficiente valor.	**We doubt that you have enough courage.**
Ellos prefieren que nieve.	**They prefer that it snowed.**
Me enoja que vosotros todavía no vayáis a la escuela.	**It makes me angry that you still don't go to school.**
Ojalá que el próximo año sea mejor.	**Let's hope that next year is better.**

A Subjunctive Matter

Fill in the correct form for the given verb for each sentence. Note that some should be in the present indicative while others in the present subjunctive.

1. *Dudo que este empleo _____ mucho. (pagar)*

2. *Es malo que nosotros no _____ listos. (estar)*

3. *Es posible que el presidente no* _____ *en la Casa Blanca, pero no lo creo. (estar)*

4. *Me gusta que ella* _____ *en este vecindario. (vivir)*

5. *Los estudiantes piden que el director de la escuela* _____ *al nuevo profesor por otro. (sustituir)*

6. *Yo dudo que* _____ *posible entrar por esta puerta sin ningún ruido. (ser)*

7. *No hay duda de que la película* _____ *en un momento. (empezar)*

8. *Es interesante que vosotros* _____ *tanto dinero por estos boletos. (pagar)*

Perfect Tenses in the Subjunctive

The subjunctive mood also has two perfect tenses: the present perfect and past perfect. These tenses are not used frequently and will only be given a brief introduction here.

The rules for using subjunctive in the perfect tenses are the same as in the present subjunctive for the most part. Like all perfect tenses, perfect subjunctives (past and present) pair *haber* with the past participle.

The present-perfect subjunctive is used when the main verbal clause is in the present tense. The following table lists the present-perfect conjugations of *haber*.

Present-Perfect Conjugations of Haber

yo	*haya*
tú	*hayas*
él, ella, usted	*haya*
nosotros, nosotras	*hayamos*
vosotros, vosotras	*hayáis*
ellos, ellas, ustedes	*hayan*

Here are some examples of how the present-perfect subjunctive may be used:

Quiero que hayan terminado el examen.	**I want them to have finished the test.**
Ella busca a una persona que haya visitado este museo.	**She is looking for a person who has visited this museum.**

The past-perfect subjunctive is the subjunctive equivalent of a perfect past tense, and it is often used when the main verbal clause of the sentence is in preterite, imperfect, or conditional tense. First, the past perfect subjunctive conjugations of *haber.* (Note these are the imperfect subjunctive endings.)

Past-Perfect Conjugations of Haber

yo	*hubiera*
tú	*hubieras*
él, ella, usted	*hubiera*
nosotros, nosotras	*hubiéramos*
vosotros, vosotras	*hubierais*
ellos, ellas, ustedes	*hubieran*

And some examples:

Era posible que ustedes no hubieran sabido la verdad.	**It was possible that you hadn't known the truth.**
Si yo me hubiera escondido, ellos no me habrían encontrado.	**If I had hidden myself, they wouldn't have found me.**

Chapter 17

What You Like to Do

What do you like to do in your "free" time? Of course, you probably have many *deberes* (obligations), but you also entertain yourself with things that you enjoy. This chapter will help you explore your hobbies and pastimes in Spanish.

Likes and Dislikes

The verb that will help you indicate your preferences is *gustar*. To translate, "I like hamburgers," use *gustar*, but switch the subject and object around, so that the subject is what pleases you (hamburgers) and the object is "I": *me gustan las hamburguesas*—literally, "hamburgers please me." Now take a look at some other examples:

Because the subject of these sentences is something that is liked, it can either be singular or plural, but it is always in third person, so you only have *gusta* and *gustan* as verb choices (assume you stay in the present tense). As for the object, it is always an indirect object pronoun: me, you, him, her, it, us, them (for a review of indirect object pronouns, refer back to Chapter 13). Listen to Track 59 and take a look at the following examples.

TRACK 59

Me gusta el café.	**I like coffee.**
Me gustan las flores.	**I like flowers.**
Te gusta el café.	**You like coffee.**
Te gustan las flores.	**You like flowers.**
Le gusta el café.	**He/she likes coffee. /** **You like coffee. (usted)**
Le gustan las flores.	**He/she likes flowers. /** **You like flowers. (usted)**
Nos gusta el café.	**We like coffee.**
Nos gustan las flores.	**We like flowers.**
Os gusta el café.	**You like coffee. (vosotros)**
Os gustan las flores.	**You like flowers. (vosotros)**
Les gusta el café.	**They like coffee. /** **You like coffee. (ustedes)**
Les gustan las flores.	**They like flowers. /** **You like flowers. (ustedes)**

So what if what you like is not a thing, but an action? For example, how would you say "I like to travel"? Think of this phrase as "I like traveling." Since "traveling" may be thought of in the singular, you would say *Me gusta viajar.*

In Combination with Gustar

Keep in mind that as simple as this construction is to use, there are certain combinations of words that may change what you mean to say. For instance, be careful to put the modifier in the right place—generally in back of what you want modified. Compare the following:

Me gusta mucho viajar.	**I really like to travel.**
Me gusta viajar mucho.	**I like to travel a lot/often.**

Untranslatable redundant constructions may also be used to emphasize or clarify the indirect object. Listen to Track 60 and review the following examples.

TRACK 60

A mí me gusta el boxeo.	**I like boxing.**
El boxeo me gusta a mí.	
A ti te gusta la ópera.	**You like the opera.**
La ópera te gusta a ti.	
A él le gusta María.	**He likes Maria.**
María le gusta a él.	
A ella le gustan los perros.	**She likes dogs.**
Los perros le gustan a ella.	
A usted le gusta la pesca. La	**You like fishing.**
pesca le gusta a usted.	
A nosotros nos gusta el vino.	**We like wine.**
El vino nos gusta a nosotros.	
A vosotros os gusta el chocolate.	**You like chocolate.**
El chocolate os gusta a vosotros.	
A nosotras nos gusta el ajo.	**We like garlic.**
El ajo nos gusta a nosotras.	
A ellos les gusta el té.	**They like tea.**
El té les gusta a ellos.	
A ellas les gusta la cerveza.	**They like beer.**
La cerveza les gusta a ellas.	
A ustedes les gusta el actor.	**You like the actor.**
El actor les gusta a ustedes.	

In the Negative

To state these statements in the negative, place *no* before the indirect object. "I don't like boxing" may be translated into Spanish in three ways, as follows:

No me gusta el boxeo.
A mí no me gusta el boxeo.
El boxeo no me gusta a mí.

Not Just in the Present

The verb *gustar* may also appear in other tenses. For instance, take a look at the following sentences. Can you recognize the tense of each one?

Me gustaba el ajedrez.	**I used to like chess.**
Nos ha gustado viajar a Lima	**We have liked to travel to Lima**
desde pequeños.	**since we were little.**
Te gustará mi amiga.	**You will like my (girl) friend.**

¿Qué te gusta?

Translate the following sentences, using the appropriate form of *gustar* and vocabulary learned in the previous section. Use your English-to-Spanish and Spanish-to-English dictionary to look up words you don't already know.

1. You (informal, plural) like talking with my friends.

   _____

2. They like to work.

   _____

3. We like rice and chicken.

   _____

4. You (informal, singular) used to like the Johnsons.

_____

5. You (formal, plural) liked Spain.

_____

Just Saying "No"

As you've seen with *gustar*, the act of negating a positive statement is simply a matter of placing a "no" before the verb. The easiest example is the sentence *No hablo.* (I don't speak.) As you know, however, any language has a multitude of ways to express a single point. This is also the case with saying "no." First, let's review positive and negative words in the following table.

Vocabulary: Positives and Negatives

Positive	Negative
algo (something)	*nada* (nothing)
alguien (someone)	*nadie* (no one)
alguna vez, otra vez (sometimes, another time)	*ninguna vez, nunca* (never)
alguno (some)	*ninguno* (none)
a veces (sometimes)	*jamás* (never)
o (or)	*ni, ni siquiera* (nor, not even)
sí (yes)	*no* (no)
siempre (always)	*nunca* (never)
también (too)	*tampoco* (neither)
todo (all)	*nada* (nothing)
todavía (still)	*ya no* (no longer)
ya (already)	*aún no* (not yet)

Whereas a double negative in English is said to be logically equivalent to a positive statement, it simply confirms the negative in Spanish. For example:

Yo no voy allí nunca.	**I never go there.** (**Literally: I don't go there never.**)
Yo no voy a ningún sitio.	**I don't go anyplace.** (**Literally: I don't go to no place.**)

Yes or No?

Translate the following sentences, using the vocabulary learned in the previous section. Use your English-to-Spanish and Spanish-to-English dictionary to look up words you don't already know.

1. I always eat vegetables.

   _____

2. I never eat vegetables.

   _____

3. Someone waits for you.

   _____

4. No one is here.

   _____

5. At times, Fred and Ginger go out dancing.

   _____

Verbs That Act Like Gustar

There is a whole group of verbs in Spanish that behave similarly to *gustar*. The simplest example is the verb *disgustar* (to dislike):

Me disgusta viajar.	**I dislike to travel.**
Te disgusta el café.	**You dislike coffee.**
Nos disgustan las flores.	**We dislike flowers.**

Other verbs that should be used in the same "inverted" way as *gustar* and *disgustar* are listed in the following table.

Verbs That Act Like Gustar

agradar	to please
doler	to hurt, be in pain
encantar	to delight, charm
faltar	to be lacking
hacer falta	to need
interesar	to interest
parecer	to seem, appear
sobrar	to be left

Now listen to Track 61 as you read the following examples.

TRACK 61

Nos agradan los perros, pero no los gatos.	**We like dogs but not cats.**
Te duele el brazo.	**Your arm hurts.**
Me encantan las flores.	**I love flowers.**
No le falta ni dinero ni poder.	**He doesn't lack money nor power.**
Os hacen falta vuestros padres.	**You need your parents.**
Nos interesa el fútbol americano.	**We are interested in football.**
La camisa me parece muy pequeña.	**It seems to me that the shirt is too small.**
Te sobró comida.	**You had food left over.**

Practice What You've Learned

Translate the following sentences, using the appropriate form of the verbs that behave like *gustar*. Use your English-to-Spanish and Spanish-to-English dictionary to look up words you don't already know.

1. I was lacking courage.

   _____

2. My head hurts.

   _____

3. Do you (informal, singular) miss your automobile?

   _____

4. We are interested in learning Spanish.

   _____

5. Are you (informal, plural) pleased by romantic films?

   _____

What Do You Like to Do?

What do you like to do in your free time? What are some hobbies and activities you are interested in? The following section will help you discuss these hobbies and activities in Spanish.

Going Places

As you remember, the verb "to go" in Spanish is *ir*. Use the expression *ir a* . . . ("to go to . . .") with the words and phrases in the following table.

Ir a . . .

los almacenes	the department stores
un concierto	a concert
las carreras de caballo	the horse races
las carreras de coches	the car races
un casino	a casino
una competencia	a competition
las corridas de toro	the running of bulls
las discotecas	the discotheques, clubs
un parque de diversiones	an amusement park
un partido de . . .	a game of . . .
la playa	the beach
visitar a amigos	visit friends
visitar a parientes	visit relatives

A similar construction is *ir de . . .* ("to go . . ."). This construction generally appears with one of the words listed in the following table.

Ir de . . .

compras	shopping
excursión	on excursions
pesca	fishing
vacaciones	on vacation
viaje	on a trip
visita	visit

Activities do require you to think of not only who does something and when, but also how that activity is described. Some activities are considered ones that you "play" (*jugar*) and others that you "do" (*hacer*).

Sports-related activities are generally expressed with the verb *hacer* (to do). For instance, *hacer natación* is literally "to do swimming." The following table contains a list of activities that you "do."

Hacer . . .

aeróbic	aerobics
alpinismo	mountain climbing
artes marciales	martial arts
deportes de aventura	extreme sports
buceo	scuba diving
ciclismo	cycling
ejercicios	exercise
equitación	horseback riding
surf	surfing
esquí	skiing
levantar pesas	weightlifting
navegación	sailing
patinaje (sobre hielo)	(ice-)skating

With *jugar,* things are easier. The idea of "playing" sports is the same in Spanish as in English. For instance, *jugar al ajedrez* means "to play chess." (Remember that when you put *a* and *el* together, they merge into *al,* as in this case, when you use the construction *jugar a . . .* and *el ajedrez.*) For other sports terms used in this construction, see the following table.

Jugar a . . .

el baloncesto/básquetbol	basketball
el balonvolea/voleibol	volleyball

Jugar a . . .

el béisbol	baseball
el billar	billiards, pool
los bolos	bowling
las cartas	cards
los dardos	darts
el fútbol	soccer
el fútbol americano	American football
el golf	golf
la lotería	the lottery
el póquer	poker
la ruleta	roulette
el solitario	solitaire
el tenis	tennis
el veintiuno	21 (blackjack)

But some of us like more sedentary activities, such as reading. And there is so much to read—just take a look at the following table.

Leer . . .

biografías	biographies
cuentos	stories, short stories
cuentos de hadas	fairy tales
libros	books
las noticias	the news
novelas de ciencia ficción	science fiction novels
novelas policíacas	detective novels
novelas románticas	romance novels
periódicos	newspapers

poesía	poems
recetas	recipes
revistas	magazines

Talk Music

Let's get more specific here. Many people like to listen to music, but their tastes vary—some people listen to CDs and other to records. Some may prefer hip-hop and other listen to country music. First, take inventory of your equipment.

Vocabulary: Musical Equipment

el altavoz	speaker
el amplificador	amplifier
los auriculares	headphones
el disco compacto	compact disc, CD
el reproductor de audio digital (de MP3)	MP3 player
el tocacasetes	cassette player
el reproductor de CD	CD player
el volumen	volume
el Walkman	Walkman

You can use four related verbs with this equipment: *tocar* (to play), *escuchar* (to listen), *grabar* (to record), and *disfrutar* (to enjoy).

Listening to Music

Translate the following sentences using the verbs *tocar* (to play), *escuchar* (to listen), *grabar* (to record), and *disfrutar* (to enjoy) and the vocabulary you have just learned.

1. We like to play CDs.

   _____

2. I listen to the news on the radio.

   _____

3. They enjoy listening to Elvis Crespo and Carlos Vives.

   _____

4. The CD player has headphones and two speakers.

   _____

Sitting Down at the Computer

In Spain, the computer is called _el ordenador_ (programmable ordering machine). In Latin America, it is called _el computador_ or _la computadora_ (the computing machine). For consistency, this book has used la computadora throughout.

FACT

With the technological advances of the past decades, this is a time of great flux in the world of technical Spanish. Words are being created on the spot and discarded just as quickly. Within the computer industry, though, some basic terminology is starting to stick.

Here is some basic terminology related to _la computadora._

Computer-Related Terms

@ _(arroba)_	"at" in e-mail addresses
la barra de herramientas	toolbar
el botón de encendido	on button

el botón de reinicio	reset button
el cable	cable
la computadora/ el ordenador portátil	notebook computer
el disco duro	hard drive
el escáner	scanner
el escritorio	onscreen desktop
el fichero	file (in Spain)
la impresora láser	laser printer
el módem	modem
el monitor	monitor
los motores de búsqueda	search engines
el mouse/ratón	mouse (in Latin America)
el nombre de usuario	user name
la página Web	Web page
la pantalla	screen
el proveedor de Internet	Internet service provider
el ratón	mouse (in Spain)
el sitio Web	Web site
la sobremesa	desktop
el teclado	keyboard
el vínculo	link

Computer-Related Actions

abrir un archivo	to open or start a file
bajar/descargar programas	to download programs
buscar un fichero	to search for a file
cambiar la configuración actual	to change the present configuration
cerrar la ventana de un programa	to close a program's window

Computer-Related Actions

chatear con	to chat with
conectar a la Web	to connect to the Web
correr un programa	to run a program
elegir del menú	to select from the menu
empezar un programa	to start a program
encender la computadora	to turn on the PC
enviar mensajes por correo electrónico	to send messages via e-mail
lanzar un programa	to launch a program
minimizar una ventana	to minimize a window
navegar el/la Web	to surf the Web
prender la computadora	to turn on the PC
presionar la tecla	to press the key
pulsar con el ratón	to tap/click with the mouse
salir de un programa	to exit from a program
seleccionar un icono	to select an icon

Log On in Spanish

Apply the terminology you have just learned by translating the following sentences into Spanish. Use your English-to-Spanish and Spanish-to-English dictionary to look up words you don't already know.

1. I turn on my computer every day.

   _____

2. She connects to the Web to read her e-mail.

   _____

3. Do you also search for intereresting Web sites?

_____

4. They chat with their brother on weekends.

_____

5. Humberto cannot start the computer because his brother changed the configuration.

_____

Chapter 18

Any Questions?

Spanish has various ways for making inquiries, also known as "interrogative statements." You can rely on the intonation (tone of voice), interrogative pronouns and adverbs, subject-verb switch with interrogative intonation patterns, and interrogative tags. Sounds difficult? It's not. This chapter will show you how.

Listen to the Intonation

Everything you say has a "melody." Within phrases, there are points where your vocal chords are at their most relaxed—when you pause. There are points where your vocal chords are at their most tense—when you convey a specific state of mind. And more often your vocal chords are in a medium state of tension—when you simply wish to convey your thoughts as carried by the words that you have chosen.

In short, intonation (or patterns of inflection) allows you to distinguish a statement from a question or from an exclamation, as follows:

- **Statement:** Intonation patterns associated with statements generally start and end with low inflection that modulates regularly in a medium tension of voice.
- **Question:** Intonation patterns associated with statements turned to questions generally end with high inflection of the voice.
- **Exclamation:** Intonation patterns associated with exclamations follow patterns similar to statements but with sharper contrasted inflection within the phrase or sentence.

Learn Your Interrogatives

Most of the questions you have encountered up to this point have begun with an interrogative pronoun or adverb. These interrogatives generally begin the interrogative phrase and identify the object or person about which there is some doubt. It is important to recognize that these pronouns and adverbs are distinguished in writing with an accent mark.

Interrogatives (which sometimes act like pronouns and other times like adjectives, but don't worry about that) are special in the number of different factors that guide their use. Keep in mind that interrogatives work to fill in the blanks of notions requiring more information to be completely understood. Some of them conjugate according to number (singular or plural), while others don't. The same is true for considerations of gender.

Interrogatives Without Gender or Number

Some interrogatives function without being gender- or number-specific.

Interrogatives Without Gender or Number

¿Cómo?	How?
¿Cuándo?	When?
¿Dónde?	Where?
¿Qué?	What?

TRACK 62

¿Cómo está Mauricio?	**How is Mauricio?**
¿Cuándo será abogado Rafico?	**When will Rafico be a lawyer?**
¿Dónde está la iglesia?	**Where is the church?**
¿Qué tenía Gloria en la mano?	**What did Gloria have in her hand?**

¿Cómo?

Though generally used to ask "how," *¿cómo?* is one of those small words that have various situational uses. In a question, you may use it to ask about the condition of a noun or manner of an action. If you didn't hear what somebody said, you can say *¿Cómo?* In English, it translates to something like "Excuse me?" This word is also used to express surprise and to inquire as to how that surprise came to occur. (You may also use *¿cómo?* to form a rhetorical question.) For examples, take a look at the following questions:

TRACK 63

¿Cómo está el tiempo?	**How is the weather?**
¿Cómo es el clima en Vera Cruz?	**How is the climate in Vera Cruz?**
¿Cómo le gusta el café?	**How does he like his coffee?**
¿Cómo debo cocinar el bistec?	**How should I cook the steak?**
¿Cómo? ¿Qué significa ésto?	**Excuse me? What does that mean?**
¿Cómo es que están aquí tus hermanos?	**How is it that your siblings are here?**

¿Cuándo?

The Spanish "when" is much more straightforward. It is used in questions related to time. (To practice telling time, you should refer back to Chapter 9.)

TRACK 64

¿Cuándo estarán en casa los niños?	**When will the children be at home?**
¿Cuándo llegaste a casa?	**When did you get home?**

¿Dónde?

The Spanish "where," though as simple to use as *¿cuándo?* is interesting in that it often needs help to express a question regarding "place." That is, it is often used with prepositions. For the list of prepositions, as well as some examples, take a look at the following table.

¿Dónde? in Combination with Prepositions

Preposition	Question
a (to)	*¿adónde?*
de (from)	*¿de dónde?*
en (in)	*¿en dónde?*
por (by)	*¿por dónde?*

TRACK 65

¿Dónde está Gloria?	**Where is Gloria?**
¿Adónde fue Marco?	**Where did Marco go to?**
¿De dónde es Marisela?	**Where is Marisela from?**
¿En dónde se lastimó?	**Where did he hurt himself?**
¿Por dónde caminó?	**By which way did she walk?**

¿Qué?

¿Qué? is another word with many meanings. Within a question, it generally translates to "what?" It may:

- Stand on its own as a familiar alternative to *¿cómo?*—for example, to ask "What did you say?"
- Precede a noun where the subject is defined within the question, like "What time is it?"
- Precede a verb where the question refers to something in general terms rather than by a specific instance. It may be assumed that the person making the inquiry possesses no knowledge of the possible responses to his or her question. For example, "What's in here?"

Here are some examples of using *qué* in questions:

TRACK 66

¿Qué me dijiste?	**What did you say to me?**
¿Qué hora es?	**What time is it?**
¿Qué día es hoy?	**What day is it?**
¿Qué modelo de coche tiene Pedro?	**What car model does Peter have?**
¿Qué comida hay?	**What food is there?**
¿Qué está en la caja?	**What is in the box?**
¿Qué compraba en el almacén?	**What was he purchasing at the store?**

Add the preposition *por,* and the result is another question, *¿por qué?* This phrase may be used to ask "by what (reason)," "for what (purpose)," and so on, but most often it simply translates to "why?"

¿Por qué no me dices la verdad?	**Why won't you tell me the truth?**
¿Por qué vosotros insistís en esperar?	**Why do you insist on waiting?**

When *por qué* is not used as an interrogative, it changes to *porque* (no accent mark) to mean "because." For instance: *¿Por qué no está Juan en casa?* (Why is Juan not at home?) *Porque está en la escuela.* (Because he is at school.)

Interrogatives with Number but Without Gender

Some interrogatives do possess *número* (number) but not *género* (gender). Interrogatives that comprise this category are listed in the following table.

Interrogatives with Number but Without Gender

Interrogative	English
¿Cuál?	which (singular)
¿Cuáles?	which (plural)
¿Quién?	who (singular)
¿Quiénes?	who (plural)

TRACK 67

¿Cuál de los pasteles quiere Marí?	**Which of the pastries does Mari want?**
¿Cuáles de estos libros prefiere Sebastián?	**Which of these books does Sebastian prefer?**
¿Quién estuvo en la reunión?	**Who was at the gathering/reunion?**
¿Quiénes aquí tienen treinta años?	**Who here are thirty years old?**

¿Cuál? and ¿Cuáles?

Cuál is an interrogative pronoun that causes confusion for many beginners. It may be said that it is the Spanish word for "which." However, you will often see it translated as "what." The cause of the confusion, then, is how to choose between *¿cuál?* and *¿qué?* The rules you should follow are:

1. When preceding a verb, cuál refers to a specific instance rather than a general idea. It implicitly presupposes prior knowledge of instances and asks that the respondent make a selection. Compare:

¿Qué está en la caja?	**What is in the box?**
¿Cuál está en la caja?	**Which one is in the box?**
¿Qué compraba en el almacén?	**What was he purchasing in the store?**
¿Cuáles compraba en el almacén?	**Which ones was she purchasing at the store?**

2. It may establish the selection more explicitly when used within the combination *¿Cuál(es) + de + (noun/pronoun) . . . ?*

¿Cuál de las joyas está en la caja?	**Which one of the jewels is in the box?**
¿Cuáles de estos videos son buenos?	**Which of these videos are good?**

3. When used with a form of *ser* and certain words, *cuál* is always chosen instead of *qué*, despite the vagueness that accompanies these words. Here are some examples:

¿Cuál era la diferencia?	**What was the difference?**
¿Cuáles fueron las dificultades?	**What were the difficulties?**
¿Cuál ha sido el motivo?	**What has been the motive?**
¿Cuáles son los problemas?	**What are the problems?**
¿Cuál será la razón?	**What will the reason be?**
	I wonder what the reason is?
¿Cuál es la solución?	**What is the solution?**

¿Quién? and *¿Quiénes?*

Quién is much less complicated than most interrogative pronouns. It is translated as "who" or "whom"—all you have to be concerned about is the number of people being represented. Furthermore, keep in mind that *quién* and *quiénes* sometimes appear with a preposition, *a* ("to," or personal preposition), *de* ("of" or "from"), or *en* ("in" or "about"). For some examples, see the following sentences:

TRACK 68

¿Quién habló en la recepción?	**Who spoke at the reception?**
¿Quiénes participaron?	**Who participated?**
¿A quién buscas?	**Who are you looking for?**
¿De quién es ese coche?	**Whose automobile is it?**
¿En quiénes pensaba Joaquín?	**About whom was Joaquin thinking?**

Interrogatives with Number and Gender

This section includes only one interrogative, *cuánto*. This interrogative is a little tricky in that it can have two very similar meanings, "how much" and "how many," depending on the number, singular or plural, employed. Compare the following sentences:

TRACK 69

¿Cuánto dinero tiene Javier?	**How much money does Javier have?**
¿Cuánta plata tiene Javier?	**How much money does Javier have? (colloquial)**
¿Cuánto cuesta?	**How much does it cost?**
¿En cuánto está lista?	**In how much time will she be ready?**
¿Cuántos años tiene Jorge?	**How old is Jorge?**
¿Cuántas bufandas tiene Beatriz?	**How many scarves does Beatriz have?**

As you can see, the interrogative *cuánto* acts as an adjective by changing in gender and number according to the noun that it modifies, so that, for example, if you want to ask "how many years?" you take *años* (years) and modify *cuánto* accordingly (to *cuántos*).

A with Interrogative Pronouns

A often plays an important role in determining the nature, subject, or object of the information requested. You've seen it translated as "at" and "to." And, as you remember, it may act as a personal particle placed before objects that designate people. Take a look at how *a* behaves with interrogatives in the following sentences:

TRACK 70

¿A cómo está la gasolina?	**At how much is gasoline?**
¿Adónde viaja Ximena?	**To where does Ximena travel?**
¿A qué se refiere la maestra?	**To what is the teacher referring?**
¿A qué fiesta irá Benjamín?	**To which party will Benjamin go?**
¿A quién vio Jaime en el concierto?	**Whom did Jaime see at the concert?**
¿A cuánto está el agua?	**At how much is the water?**
¿A cuántos kilómetros está el museo?	**At how many kilometers is the museum?**

Subject-Verb Switch and Interrogative Tags

You are probably unconsciously very familiar with the subject-verb switch that often occurs in English to transform a statement into a question. For example: "Mary is a teacher" can switch to "Is Mary a teacher?" in order to act as a question. The same transformations are possible in Spanish.

La cama está contra la pared.	**The bed is against the wall.**
¿Está la cama contra la pared?	**Is the bed against the wall?**

Equally as common in English and in Spanish is the addition of a phrase of doubt to a statement, thereby rendering it, for all intents and purposes, a question. For example:

La cama está contra la pared, ¿no?	**The bed is against the wall, isn't it?**
Paca no trajaba, ¿o sí?	**Paca does not work, or does she?**
Rodrigo no hace ejercicios, ¿verdad?	**Rodrigo doesn't do exercises, right?**

Interjections

The exclamatory phrases that are set off by ¡ . . . ! often use three of the accented words that you have already encountered in the capacity of interrogatives: *¡Qué!*, *¡Cuánto!* and *¡Cómo!* (Note that the accent marks are also present in these words when they act as exclamatory expressions.) With these simple words, the exclamatory possibilities are endless.

¡Qué!

Qué is used within a variety of structures that express surprise or strong emotion:

1. *¡Qué + (sustantivo)!*
   What a (noun)!

2. *¡Qué + (adjetivo)!*
   That's (adjective)! How (adjective)!

3. *¡Qué + (sustantivo) + tan + (adjetivo)!*
   What a(n) (adjective) (noun)!

4. *¡Qué + (sustantivo) + más + (adjetivo)!*
   What a(n) (adjective) (noun)!

5. *¡Qué + (adverbio)!*
   That's (adverb)! How (adverb)!

6. *¡Qué + (adjetivo) + (ser)!*
   How (adjective) + (subject pronoun) am/is/are!

7. *¡Qué + (adjetivo) + (ser) + (sustantivo)!*
   How (adjective) + (noun) am/is/are!

8. *¡Qué + (adjetivo) + (estar)!*
   How (adjective) + (subj. pronoun) am/is/are!

9. *¡Qué + (adjetivo) + (estar) + (sustantivo)!*
   How (adjective) + (noun) am/is/are!

10. *¡Qué + (adverbio) + (verbo)!*
    How (adverb) + (subj. pronoun) + (verb)!

11. *¡Qué + (adverbio) + (verbo) + (sustantivo)!*
    How (adverb) + (subj. pronoun) + (verb) + (noun)!

¡Qué espectáculo!	**What a show!**
¡Qué maravilloso!	**How marvelous!**
¡Qué perrito tan simpático!	**What a charming puppy!**
¡Qué caballo más veloz!	**What a fast horse!**
¡Qué lejos!	**How far!**
¡Qué seria es!	**How serious she is!**
¡Qué rápido es tu coche!	**How fast your car is!**
¡Qué alegre estoy!	**How happy I am!**
¡Qué rudo está Ernesto hoy!	**How rude is Ernest today!**
¡Qué bien baila!	**How well he dances!**
¡Qué bien baila Lisa!	**How well Lisa dances!**

¡Qué fácil!

Translate the following interjections into Spanish. Use your English-to-Spanish and Spanish-to-English dictionary to look up words you don't already know.

1. What a tall young man!

_____

2. What a sad story!

_____

3. How far she swims!

_____

4. How lazy she is!

_____

5. What a car!

_____

¡Cómo! and ¡Cuánto!

The interjections *cómo* and *cuánto* use their own structures to express strong emotion. The possible constructions are listed below:

1. *¡Cómo + (verbo)!*
   How + (subject pronoun) + (verb)!

2. *¡Cómo + (verbo) + (sustantivo)!*
   How + (noun) + (verb)!

3. *¡Cuánto + (verbo) + (sustantivo)!*
   How much + (noun) + (verb)!

4. *¡Cuánto + (sustantivo) + (verbo)!*
   How much/many + (verb) + (noun)!

TRACK 71

¡Cómo canta!	**How she sings!**
¡Cómo lloró!	**How he cried!**
¡Cómo cocina tu mamá!	**How your mother cooks!**
¡Cómo lloraba el niño!	**How the baby was crying!**
¡Cuánto habla Juan!	**How much Juan talks!**
¡Cuánto lloró el niño!	**How much the baby cried!**
¡Cuánta gente está aquí!	**How many people are here!**
¡Cuántos gatos tienes!	**How many cats you have!**

¡Cuánto sabes!

Translate the following interjections into Spanish. Use your English-to-Spanish and Spanish-to-English dictionary to look up words you don't already know.

1. How much they ran!

   _____

2. How I want to be tall!

   _____

3. How Marco and Lucía smoked!

   _____

4. How much I wanted to eat!

   _____

5. How many chores we have!

   _____

What's Better and What's Best?

As you often have to do in English, there will be times when your descriptions of things will require that you make comparisons between two or more items. Comparisons can be made to show equivalency or difference.

Two equal modifiers may be compared by using the construction *tan + adjetivo/adverbio + como* (as + adjective/adverb + as). For example:

Mi coche es tan rápido como el de Raúl.	**My car is as fast as Raul's.**
El niño canta tan bien como su hermana.	**The boy sings as well as his sister.**

Comparison of objects tends to center on quantity. As such, the construction above may be slightly altered: *tanto + noun + como*. For example:

Mi computadora tiene tanta memoria como la tuya.	**My computer has as much memory as yours.**

The general structure for comparison of unequals uses the adjective qualifier + *que* + noun/adjective/adverb. To show that something is more than another, simply use *más* (more) as the qualifier. For example:

Hay más manzanas que naranjas.	**There are more apples than oranges.**
Roberto es más bajo que su hermano.	**Robert is shorter than his brother.**
Ella habla más rápidamente que David.	**She speaks more quickly than David.**

Likewise, to show that something is less than something else, simply use *menos* (less, minus) as the qualifier. For example:

Hay menos asientos que personas.	**There are less seats than people.**
El tango es menos popular en España que en Argentina.	**Tango is less popular in Spain than in Argentina.**

Él hace las cosas menos cuidadosamente que su compañero.	**He does things less carefully than his partner.**

As you would expect, not all comparisons can be made so simply. Some adjectives and adverbs don't get along with *más* and *menos.* Instead, they are modified into the comparative form (this sometimes also occurs in English: compare "well" and "better"). For some examples, check the following table.

Irregular Comparisons

Adjective	Comparative Form
bien (well)	*mejor* (better)
bueno (good)	*mejor* (better)
grande (big, large)	*mayor* (larger, older)
joven (young)	*menor* (younger)
mal (badly)	*peor* (worse)
malo (bad)	*peor* (worse)
mucho (much)	*más* (more)
pequeño (small)	*menor* (smaller)
poco (little)	*menos* (less)
viejo (old)	*mayor* (older)

Following are a few examples of how these irregulars are treated in a sentence:

El trabajo de Sandra es bueno, pero el de Susana es mejor.	**Sandra's work is good, but Susana's is better.**
Jaime es viejo, pero César es mayor.	**Jaime is old, but Cesar is older.**
Ser pobre es peor que ser feo.	**Being poor is worse than being ugly.**

There are many other expressions that allow comparison, including: *de la misma manera* (in the same way); *igual que* (the same as); *inferior a* (inferior to); *superior a* (superior to); and *parecido a* (similar to).

Superlatives

Often you will need to describe things of an exceptional nature or quality. In English, you would add the ending "–est" to a modifier (adjective or adverb) to describe something that is the best—"biggest," "strongest," "smartest," and so on. This form is known as superlative.

In Spanish, the superlative form also relies on the words *más* and *menos*, which appear with a definite article to signify "most" and "least." The superlative construction works as follows: *artículo definido + más/menos + adjetivo/adverbio + de* (definite article "the" + more/less + adjective/adverb + of). For example:

Supermán es el más poderoso de los superhéroes.	**Superman is the most powerful of the superheroes.**
Javier es el menos responsable de los hermanos.	**Javier is the least responsible of the brothers.**
Pepito es el estudiante más vago.	**Pepito is the laziest student.**

¡Cómo comparas!

Translate the following comparisons into Spanish. Use your English-to-Spanish and Spanish-to-English dictionary to look up words you don't already know.

1. You (informal, singular) sing as well as my sister.

_____

2. I have as many coins as you.

_____

3. There is less work than people.

_____

4. Julio has more experience than Pedro.

_____

5. You (formal, singular) are older than Jenny.

_____

Chapter 19

A Day in the Life

The only way to really learn another language is to see it, hear it, and think it—just plain live it on a day-to-day basis. This chapter will help you achieve this by concentrating on what most people do in their daily lives, and will introduce you to the concept of the reflexive verbs.

One Day in the Life of Celso

The following mini essay is written by Celso about his day. See how much you can understand of what he is saying, and listen to Track 72 to hear the pronunciation.

TRACK 72

> *Hola. Yo soy Celso, el hermano de Estefi. La mañana típica para mí comienza a las seis, la hora que me despierto. Soy un poco lento para levantarme, especialmente cuando hace frío afuera. A veces me quedo acostado y miro hacia el techo de mi dormitorio. Me gusta pensar en el día que me espera mientras escucho la radio.*
>
> *Por lo general, me levanto a las seis y cuarto, cuando sé que no hay nadie en el baño. Después de salir de la cama, me cepillo los dientes y me lavo el sueño de la cara. Ya despierto, saludo a mi mami, mi papi, y a mi hermanita. Como todos nos apresuramos a partir, no hay mucho tiempo para hablar.*
>
> *Me ducho, me afeito (¡de veras!) y me visto en treinta minutos. A veces desayuno en casa. Pero cuando no tengo tiempo, espero para hacerlo en la escuela. Salgo para la escuela a las siete de la mañana. Tomo el tren y llego allí con tiempo suficiente para hablar con mis amigos antes de mi primera clase.*

So, how did you do? How much were you able to understand? If you need help, take a look at the translation below.

> Hi. I'm Celso, Estefi's brother. A typical morning for me begins at six, the hour I wake up. I am a little slow to get myself up, especially when it's cold outside. At times I stay in bed and look toward the ceiling of my bedroom. I like thinking about the day that awaits me while I listen to the radio.
>
> I usually get up at 6:15 a.m., when I know that there is no one in the bathroom. After getting myself up from bed, I brush my teeth and wash the sleep from my face. Now awake, I greet my dear mother, father, and sister. Because we are all rushing ourselves to leave, there isn't much time to speak.

I shower, shave (it's true!), and get dressed within thirty minutes. Sometimes I eat breakfast at home. But when I don't have time, I wait to do it at school. I leave for school at 7 a.m. I take the train and arrive there with enough time to speak with my friends before my first class.

What Did You Notice?

In Celso's story, did you notice the following phrases?

la hora que me despierto	**the hour when I wake up**
me quedo acostado	**I stay in bed**
me levanto a las seis y cuarto	**I get up at 6:15 a.m.**
me cepillo los dientes	**I brush my teeth**
me ducho, me afeito, y me visto	**I take a shower, shave, and get dressed**

You might wonder what the pronoun *me* is doing in these sentences. After all, it can't be a direct-object pronoun, right? Well, not exactly. In this case, *me* acts as a reflexive pronoun. That is, it reflects back to the subject. If the subject is *yo* (as it is in this case), the reflexive pronoun will be *me*. Other reflexive pronouns are outlined in the following table.

Reflexive Pronouns

Subject Pronoun	Reflexive Pronoun	English
yo	*me*	myself
tú	*te*	yourself
él, ella	*se*	himself, herself
usted	*se*	yourself (polite)
nosotros, nosotras	*nos*	ourselves
vosotros, vosotras	*os*	yourselves
ellos, ellas	*se*	themselves
ustedes	*se*	yourselves

Introducing Reflexive Verbs

There is a class of verbs (appropriately called reflexive verbs) that relies on reflexive pronouns to convey their meanings correctly. Reflexive verbs may be categorized in various ways. Celso showed you how you might use them to describe your daily routine. Here is a list of items you probably do without even thinking about them (refer to the table that follows). Try to apply them in sentences that describe what you do daily.

Verbs and Their Reflexive Counterparts

acostar (to lay something down)	*acostarse* (to lay down, to go to bed)
afeitar (to shave someone or something)	*afeitarse* (to shave oneself)
bañar (to bathe)	*bañarse* (to bathe oneself)
cepillar (to brush)	*cepillarse* (to brush oneself)
comportar (to involve)	*comportarse* (to behave)
despedir (to dismiss, see someone off)	*despedirse* (to say goodbye)
despertar (to awaken)	*despertarse* (to awaken oneself)
desvestir (to unclothe)	*desvestirse* (to undress oneself)
divertir (to amuse)	*divertirse* (to enjoy oneself)
dormir (to sleep)	*dormirse* (to fall asleep)
duchar (to shower)	*ducharse* (to take a shower)
fregar (to scrub, wash)	*fregarse* (to scrub or wash oneself)
lavar (to wash)	*lavarse* (to wash oneself)
levantar (to lift)	*levantarse* (to get up)
limpiar (to clean)	*limpiarse* (to clean oneself)
llamar (to call)	*llamarse* (to be called, to call oneself)
llevar (to take, carry)	*llevarse* (to carry oneself)
maquillar (to apply makeup to someone)	*maquillarse* (to apply makeup to oneself)

Verbs and Their Reflexive Counterparts

olvidar (to forget)	*olvidarse* (to forget oneself)
parar (to stand, stop)	*pararse* (to stop oneself)
peinar (to comb)	*peinarse* (to comb oneself)
pintar (to paint)	*pintarse* (to paint oneself)
poner (to put, place)	*ponerse* (to put on)
preocupar (to worry)	*preocuparse* (to worry oneself, get worried)
quemar (to burn)	*quemarse* (to burn oneself)
quitar (to remove, take away)	*quitarse* (to get rid of, remove something)
secar (to dry)	*secarse* (to dry oneself off)
sentar (to sit)	*sentarse* (to sit oneself down)
ver (to see)	*verse* (to see oneself, imagine oneself)
vestir (to wear, dress in)	*vestirse* (to dress oneself)

Do keep in mind that even if you perform an action on a part of yourself (let's say, when you wash your hands or brush your hair), you should still use the reflexive form of the verb (*lavarse las manos, cepillarse el pelo*).

One peculiarity in the way parts of the body are treated in Spanish, particularly with the reflexive verbs, involves not expressing possession. So when you wash your hands, the literal translation of what you say in Spanish is not "I wash my hands," but rather "I wash the hands." Since many of the things you do on a daily basis do involve different parts of your body, first look at the table of reflexive verbs and think about how you might describe your routine. Before actually writing down your routine, however, list the various verbs that describe acts that you can perform on the specific body parts listed. Also, don't forget to learn the definite article of each of the words describing parts of your body—it will help you remember the word's gender.

The Human Body

el antebrazo	forearm
la axila	armpit
la barbilla	chin
la boca	mouth
el brazo	arm
la cabeza	head
la cara	face
la ceja	eyebrow
el codo	elbow
el cuello	neck
el dedo	finger
el diente	tooth
la encía	gum
la frente	forehead
el labio	lip
la lengua	tongue
la mano	hand
la mejilla	cheek
la muela	molar
la muñeca	wrist
el músculo	muscle
el muslo	thigh
la nariz	nose
la oreja	outer ear
el pelo	hair
la pestaña	eyelash
el pie	foot
la pierna	leg
la planta del pie	sole of foot

The Human Body

la quijada	jaw
la sien	temple
el talón	heel
el tobillo	ankle

The structure of these reflexive constructions is generally simple: subject + reflexive pronoun + verb. Here's an example of how reflexive verbs work:

Lavo los platos.	**I wash the plates.**
Me lavo las manos.	**I wash my hands.**

In the first sentence, the action is done by the subject toward *los platos* (the direct object). In the second sentence, the direct object is *las manos,* which is part of *yo,* so the sentence is reflexive—the action is done to one's self.

The Daily Routine

Translate the following sentences using the appropriate reflexive verbs and pronouns. Use your English-to-Spanish and Spanish-to-English dictionary to look up words you don't already know.

1. I get up at ten at night.

   _____

2. We wash our hair every morning.

   _____

3. Did you (informal, singular) shave your head?

   _____

4. I rinse my mouth after brushing my teeth.

   _____

5. Leticia applies makeup on her eyes.

Additional Categories of Reflexive Verbs

Not all reflexive verbs are concerned with personal hygiene and the daily routine. Some reflexive verbs are categorized by the standardized manner they are translated into English. One category includes the verbs that may be translated with the words "to get . . ."

Reflexive Verbs That Mean "To Get . . ."

Verb	Reflexive Verb
acercar (to bring near)	*acercarse* (to get closer)
alegrar (to make happy, enliven)	*alegrarse* (to get happy)
alistar (to ready, prepare)	*alistarse* (to get ready)
asustar (to frighten)	*asustarse* (to get frightened)
cansar (to make tired)	*cansarse* (to get tired)
callar (to quiet a person or situation)	*callarse* (to get quiet)
emborrachar (to make drunk)	*emborracharse* (to get drunk)
enfermar (to sicken)	*enfermarse* (to get sick)
enfriar (to make cold)	*enfriarse* (to get cold)
entusiasmar (to excite)	*entusiasmarse* (to get enthusiastic, excited)
inquietar (to incite)	*inquietarse* (to get restless)
marear (to make dizzy)	*marearse* (to get dizzy)
mejorar (to make better)	*mejorarse* (to get better)

Another category contains verbs that change meaning radically with the addition of the reflexive pronoun. You really need to learn these pairs separately, since knowing one won't necessarily help you figure out the meaning of the other.

Other Reflexive Verbs

Verb	Reflexive Verb
acabar (finish, end)	*acabarse* (to run out of, ruin one's condition)
acordar (to agree)	*acordarse* (to remember)
burlar (to trick)	*burlarse* (to make fun of, ridicule)
comportar (to involve)	*comportarse* (to behave)
dar (to give)	*darse a* (to devote oneself to)
dar (to give)	*darse con/contra* (to hit oneself with/against)
	darse por (to consider oneself)
enojar (to make angry)	*enojarse* (to become angry)
fiar (to vouch for, to sell on credit)	*fiarse* (to trust)
fijar (to fix, fasten)	*fijarse* (to settle in, to notice, to put attention to)
ir (to go someplace)	*irse* (to go away, leave)
liar (to tie up)	*liarse con alguien* (to have an affair with someone)
llevar (to take, carry)	*llevarse* (to get, win)
	llevarse bien/mal (to get along well/poorly)
negar (to deny)	*negarse* (to refuse)
parecer (to seem)	*parecerse* (to be alike, look alike)
portar (to carry)	*portarse bien/mal* (to behave oneself/be naughty)
probar (to prove, test, try, taste)	*probarse* (to try on)
quedar (to remain, stay, fit, be left over)	*quedarse con* (to keep)
quemar (to burn)	*quemarse* (to burn oneself out)
quitar (to remove, take away)	*quitarse* (to go away, get rid of something)

Verb	Reflexive Verb
referir (to tell, relate)	*referirse* (to refer to)
saltar (to jump)	*saltarse* (to skip, come off)
sentir (to feel)	*sentirse bien/mal* (to feel well/ill)
reír (to laugh at)	*reírse* (to laugh)

And, finally, there's a category of verbs that can exist only in the reflexive form. Without reflexive pronouns, these verbs don't have any meaning. Refer to the following table for a list of verbs that are always reflexive.

Verbs That Exist Only in the Reflexive Form

arrepentirse	to regret
atenerse	to abide by, conform, comply
atreverse	to dare
atreverse con alguien	to be disrespectful with someone
quejarse	to complain
rebelarse	to rebel
resentirse con/contra	to feel resentment toward/against

Constructions with Ponerse

One word in particular, *ponerse* (which normally means "to put on," as in clothing), adopts a new meaning ("to start to") when placed in a combination with *a* + infinitive.

Ponerse + a + Infinitive

Verb	Ponerse + a + Verb
vestir (to dress)	*ponerse a vestir* (to start to dress someone)
caminar (to walk)	*ponerse a caminar* (to start to walk)
llorar (to cry)	*ponerse a llorar* (to start to cry)
comer (to eat)	*ponerse a comer* (to start to eat)

Reflecting on the Verb

Translate the following sentences, employing reflexive pronouns. Use your English-to-Spanish and Spanish-to-English dictionary to look up words you don't already know.

1. He complained about the noise.

   _____

2. When are you (informal, plural) leaving to Florida?

   _____

3. She dares to steal.

   _____

4. You (formal, singular) sit down.

   _____

5. She is called Nancy.

   _____

Your Home

A big part of your life is a place where you spend at least some of your free time, and where your Spanish zone is—your home! *¿Dónde vive?* (Where do you live?) You might live in an apartment (*un apartamento*), a house (una casa), or a dormitory (*un dormitorio* or *una residencia de estudiante*). The following vocabulary tables will provide you with some words to use in Spanish related to your home, which you can use to answer questions in the next exercise.

Vocabulary: In Your Home

el ático	attic
el balcón	balcony
la cocina	kitchen
el comedor	dining room
el cuarto de baño	bathroom
el dormitorio	bedroom
el garaje	garage
el jardín	garden
la lavandería	laundry room
el patio	patio
el piso	level, floor
la sala	living room
la sala de estar	family room
el sótano	basement
el suelo	floor
el techo	roof

Vocabulary: Furniture

el armario	closet
la alfombra	carpet
la almohada	pillow
el cajón	drawer
la cama	bed
el colchón	mattress
el cuadro	picture
el despertador eléctrico	electric alarm
el espejo	mirror
el estante para libros	bookcase
la lámpara	lamp

Vocabulary: In the Kitchen

la batidora	hand mixer
la cafetera eléctrica	electric coffeemaker
el cajón de cubiertos	cutlery drawer
la cocina de gas	gas stove
el congelador	freezer
el escurridor de platos	dish drainer
el estante de las especias	spice rack
el fregadero	(kitchen) sink
el grifo de agua	water tap
el horno	oven
el lavavajillas	dishwasher
el microondas	microwave
la nevera	refrigerator
el tocador	dresser

Colors

Chances are probably high that most of the things that are in your home are there because they are either functional or pleasing to your eyes. Regardless of function or aesthetics, you probably coordinate much of what you have by color. The colors of the things you choose make you the artist within your home, dabbing a white toaster here and a blue wastebasket there. Take a look at the following table for some vocabulary and start adding color into your descriptions.

Vocabulary: Colors

amarillo	yellow
anaranjado	orange
azul	blue
beige	beige
blanco	white

Vocabulary: Colors

café	brown
claro	light
gris	gray
marrón	brown
morado	purple
negro	black
oscuro	dark
pardo	brown
rojo	red
rosado	pink
verde	green
violeta	violet

ALERT!

As adjectives, colors must agree with the gender and number (singular or plural) of the nouns they describe. Colors ending in *–e* or a consonant cannot be modified by gender. They can only agree with the items they modify in number. For example: *Elisa tiene camisas azules claras* (Elisa has light blue shirts).

What Color Is It?

Describe the items in your home by color, using the vocabulary you have just learned. Use your English-to-Spanish and Spanish-to-English dictionary to look up words you don't already know.

1. *¿De qué color es tu baño?*

2. *¿De qué color son tus chanclas?*

_____

3. *¿De qué color son tus sábanas?*

_____

4. *¿De qué color son tus cortinas?*

_____

5. *¿De qué color es tu coche?*

_____

Dining Out

Dining out for the first time at a Spanish restaurant does not have to be a stressful situation. Don't worry—you don't have to express everything perfectly and in complete sentences. Armed with a smile and a friendly attitude, you should be able to get by on a minimal vocabulary.

Often verbs aren't even needed. Simply read out loud the items you want from *el menú* (the menu) and add a *por favor* (please) at the end of your request. When the food comes, don't forget to say *gracias* (thank you). At the end of the meal, you say *la cuenta, por favor* (check, please). You pay your bill, you say *muchas gracias,* and you are out the door. Here are a few other phrases that might help you along:

TRACK 73

Necesito un poco de mostaza para mi perro caliente.	**I need a little bit of mustard for my hot dog.**
Yo quiero el bistec poco asado.	**I want the steak rare.**
Rocío quería vino tinto con su cena.	**Rocio wanted red wine with her dinner.**
Marcos no quiso conducir después de tomar bebidas alcohólicas.	**Marcos did not want to drive after drinking alcoholic beverages.**
¿Se puede fumar aquí?	**Can one smoke here?**

When looking at a menu, you will see so many dining options that it is impossible to present a complete list. But here are some foods that may interest you.

Vocabulary: Meats and Seafood

la almeja	clam
el atún	tuna
el ave	poultry
el bistec	steak
las camarones	shrimp
la carne de res	beef
el cerdo	pork
la chuleta	chop
el cordero	lamb
el hígado	liver
el jamón	ham
la langosta	lobster
el pescado	fish
el pollo	chicken
la salchicha	sausage
el salmón	salmon
la ternera	veal
el tiburón	shark
el tocino	bacon

FACT

How much you want something cooked is just a matter of degrees and can be communicated by simply adding *poco* (a little), *casi* (almost), and *bien* (well, colloquial) to one of the preparation methods above. You can also say *poco hecho* (rare) or *muy hecho* (very or well done). For example: *Quiero el bistec bien asado. Pero mi esposa lo quiere casi crudo.* (I want the steak well done. But my wife would like it almost raw.)

Vocabulary: Fruits and Vegetables

la berenjena	eggplant
el brócoli	broccoli
la cebolla	onion
la cereza	cherry
el champiñón	mushroom
la ciruela	plum
el durazno	peach
la espinaca	spinach
la fresa	strawberry
los frijoles	beans
la guayaba	guava
la lechuga	lettuce
la lima	lime
el limón	lemon
el mango	mango
la manzana	apple
el melón	melon
la naranja	orange
la papa	potato
el pepino	cucumber
la pera	pear
la piña	pineapple
la uva	grape
la zanahoria	carrot

Vocabulary: Other Foods

el arroz	rice
el arroz con leche	rice pudding
la avena	*oats*
el flan	*caramel custard*

Vocabulary: Other Foods

los huevos	*eggs*
la galleta	*cookie*
la leche	*milk*
el maíz	*corn*
la mantequilla	*butter*
la miel	*honey*
el pan	*bread*
las pasas	*raisins*
el pastel	*cake, pie*
el queso	cheese
el trigo	wheat

In addition to the food, you are more than likely to be interested in how the food is prepared. For some relevant vocabulary, see the following table.

Vocabulary: Food Preparation

ahumado	smoked
a la parilla	grilled
a la romana	deep fried
asado	roasted
crudo	raw
frito	fried
hervido	boiled
salteado	sautéed

Chapter 20

Means of Communication

You are coming to the end of the book. You have learned a great deal—congratulations! Now, it's time to put all you know into practice. In this chapter, you will see how you might use your newly developed skills to communicate with others, *en persona* (in person), *por carta* (by letter), and *por teléfono* (by telephone).

20

In Person

The most basic form of communication is conversation. Whether you are chatting with an old friend or making small talk with the person sitting next to you on the bus, you are communicating. Now that it's time to practice what you learned by speaking Spanish, here are some basics you will find useful. First, let's begin by learning the basics of conversation with people whom you already know.

Familiar Greetings

With familiarity comes a multitude of greetings that are often colloquial and may be used interchangeably. Here is a common exchange among two Spanish speakers who know each other well enough to use the *tú* (informal) address:

Inés:	*Hola, ¡qué gusto verte!*
	Hi, what a pleasure to see you!
Mateo:	*Hola, ¿cómo estás?*
	Hi, how are you?
Inés:	*Bien, gracias. Y, ¿cómo te va?*
	I'm well, thanks. And how is it going?
Mateo:	*Más o menos.*
	So-so.
Inés:	*¿Qué te pasa? ¿Qué hay de nuevo?*
	What's going on? What's new?
Mateo:	*Nada en particular.*
	Nothing in particular.
Inés:	*Adiós.*
	Good-bye.
Mateo:	*Chao.*
	Bye.

At a Social Gathering

What makes learning a new language so much fun is that it affords you opportunities to meet people you would not have met before. Again, keep in mind that formality and familiarity act as catalysts to forming relationships. When it comes to *las presentaciones* (the introductions), you have many options to choose from. Take a look below at what you have available:

Le presento (a usted) al señor Suarez.	**I present to you Mr. Suarez.**
Te presento (a ti) a mi amigo Emilio.	**I present you to my friend Emilio.**
Les presento (a ustedes) a la señora Perez.	**I present you all to Mrs. Perez.**
Les presento (a ustedes) a mi amiga Elena.	**I present you all to my friend Elena.**

Other ways of saying this are:

Me gustaría presentarle al señor Zambrano.	**I would like to present to you Mr. Zambrano.**
Quisiera presentarte a mi hermano Roberto.	**I wanted to present to you my brother Roberto.**
Tengo el gusto de presentarles a María Lorenzo.	**I have the pleasure of introducing to you all Maria Lorenzo.**

For a more casual approach, you can simply say, "This is [name]."

Éste es mi hijo, Paco.	**This is my son, Paco.**
Ésta es mi esposa, Rosa.	**This is my wife, Rose.**

The response to an introduction is generally the same for formal and familiar situations. When somebody has just been introduced to you, you might respond as follows:

Mucho gusto en conocerle, señor Cardoza.	**It is a pleasure to meet you, Mr. Cardoza.**
Mucho gusto, Rita.	**It's a pleasure, Rita.**
Es un placer.	**It's a pleasure.**
Encantado. Encantada.	**I am charmed. (masculine and feminine)**

In response, you will get something like:

Igualmente.	**Likewise.**
El gusto es mío.	**The pleasure is mine.**

Making Conversation in Spanish

Once introduced, the host would most certainly "welcome" you with a *bienvenido* (if you are male) or a *bienvenida* (if you are female), as well as a smile. It's just that simple. Of course, once the introductions are done, it's time for real conversations to begin.

Once you have met or have been introduced to someone, courtesy extends past the initial meeting and into your entire dealing with the person. Since you are just starting out with Spanish, there will be times when you will need to ask for some clarification. To better understand what the person is trying to communicate to you, you might have to resort to the following strategies.

First, "get the floor" with a polite interruption:

Perdón. Perdóneme.	**Pardon. (informal and formal versions)**
Disculpe, por favor.	**Please excuse me.**

Next, indicate that you are experiencing some confusion because of various circumstances.

No entiendo. No comprendo.	**I don't understand.**

No la oí. No lo escuché.	**I didn't hear you. I wasn't listening to you.**
No sé. Me olvidé.	**I don't know. I forgot.**

Try to remedy the situation by expressing your confusion in the form of a question.

¿Cómo?¿Qué dijo (usted)?	**What? What did you say?**
¿Qué dijiste (tú)?	
¿Qué significa . . . ?	**What does . . . mean?**
¿Cuándo se dice . . . ?	**When does one say . . . ?**
¿Por qué dice (usted) que . . . ?	**Why do you say that . . . ?**
¿Por qué dices (tú) que . . . ?	

Politely request that the speaker repeat what was said.

Por favor, repítalo (usted).	**Please repeat it.**
Por favor, repítelo (tú).	
¿Puede (usted) repetirlo?	**Can you repeat it?**
¿Puedes (tú) repetirlo?	
Por favor, dígalo (usted) otra vez.	**Please say it again.**
Por favor, dilo (tú) otra vez.	
¿Me lo puede (usted) repetir?	**Can you repeat it for me?**
¿Me lo puedes (tú) repetir?	
Hágame (usted) el favor de hablar más despacio. Hazme el favor de hablar más despacio.	**Do me the favor of speaking more slowly.**

To see how you might use these strategies, take a look at the following dialogue between a teacher, Mr. Franco, and his student, Mateo:

Señor Franco:	*Los jeroglíficos eran . . .*
	Hieroglyphics were . . .
Mateo:	*Perdón, Señor Franco. No entiendo.*
	Pardon me, Mr. Franco. I don't understand.

Señor Franco:	*¿No entiendes qué?* **What don't you understand?**
Mateo:	*¿Qué significa jeroglífico?* **What does jeroglífico mean?**
Señor Franco:	*Disculpa. Jeroglífico significa "hieroglyphic."* **Forgive me. Jeroglífico means "hieroglyphic."**

When you are learning a language, it might seem that everyone is speaking too fast, and you want them to slow down so that you can hear every word they are saying. To ask a person you are speaking with to speak slower, you can say:

| *Estás hablando muy rápido.* | **You are speaking too quickly.** |
| *Por favor,¿me lo repites más despacio?* | **Will you repeat it more slowly, please?** |

Here are some other phrases that you might find useful:

- When you are passing through a crowd, you can say *con permiso* (excuse me).
- If you need to apologize, you can say *¡Lo siento mucho!* (I am so sorry!)
- When you leave the dining table, and would like to excuse yourself, you can say *con su permiso* (could you excuse me).

Conversation Starters

Suppose you are ready to start communicating, but you don't know how to begin. Here are some conversation topics for you to consider:

- *El tiempo* (the weather)
- *La situación económica* (the current economic situation)
- *La situación internacional* (the current international situation)

- *Las películas que están estrenando en el cine* (the films they are showing at the movies)

The easiest way to get a discussion going is to ask questions. Here are a few—can you think of any others?

TRACK 74

¡Qué buen tiempo hace!	**What good weather it is.**
¿No lo cree?	**Don't you agree?**
¡Qué mal tiempo hace afuera!	**What bad weather it is outside.**
¿No lo cree?	**Don't you agree?**
¿Qué le gusta hacer?	**What do you like to do?**
¿Cuál es su comida favorita?	**What is your favorite food?**
¿Qué piensa?	**What do you think?**

Farewells

All conversations eventually come to an end. Ways of saying good-bye *(despedidas)* may be placed into three general categories:

1. Short-term separations that last between several minutes to a day or two. In such a case, you can say:

Hasta luego. Te veo mas tarde.	**I'll see you later.**
Hasta pronto.	**See you soon.**

2. Separations with a determined length (when you know when you'll see each other again). In such a situation, you could say:

Hasta la próxima.	**Until the next time.**
Hasta otro día.	**Until another day.**
Hasta mañana.	**Until tomorrow.**

3. Separations of indeterminate length. When you don't know when you'll see each other again, you might say:

Adiós.	**Good-bye.**
Hasta la vista.	**Until I see you again.**

As with greetings, *despedidas* may also be classified as formal or familiar. Take a look at what you might say when you end a formal conversation:

Bueno, ha sido un placer.	**Well, it's been a pleasure.**
Que le vaya bien.	**May things go well for you.**
Que tenga un buen día.	**Have a good day.**
Que pase un buen día.	**I hope you go through a good day.**
Que duerma bien.	**I hope you sleep well.**

Most casual good-byes follow a similar structure, but in the *tú* form:

Que te vaya bien.	**I hope things go well for you.**
Que tengas un buen día.	**I hope you have a good day.**
Que pases un buen día.	**I hope you go through a good day.**
Que duermas bien.	**Sleep well.**
Dulces sueños.	**Sweet dreams**.

Communication by Mail

Although e-mail is quickly supplanting the physical letter as the most frequent means of written communication, the features and disciplines required by traditional letter writing are as important as ever and do apply to e-mail. Regardless of the means of transfer (whether it's on paper or in an electronic message), the amount of time you spend on crafting a letter or memorandum shows others how seriously you take the subject matter and at what level of consideration you hold the reader.

In general, written Spanish is considered highly stylized, more formal, and less forgiving. The reason for this is because of the permanence of the "record." Any *faltas* (mistakes) will appear on the page or in the file for as long as the recipient holds on to it.

To a certain extent, conversations allow and may even encourage you to make mistakes. Since most people would rather not correct small errors and/or may speak in a nonstandard way, you may go on for weeks saying *el mano*, when you know perfectly well that it should be *la mano* (the hand). The exercises in this book and others rely on the written word out of necessity, but also as a means of making concrete whatever topic is up for discussion. Every time you write in Spanish, you make it and the subject matter you write about more concrete within your mind. This is why, regardless of whether you actually send them or not, writing letters is so important. Keeping a daily journal written in Spanish only can also help achieve the same objectives.

ALERT!

You already know all about the formality associated with the *tú* and *usted* and the Spanish verbs. Given the facilities the language does provide, not to use them correctly will reflect badly on you. While this may convince you to avoid writing in Spanish as much as possible, it is actually the reason why you must write more—to practice.

As with any correspondence, you must consider your audience and the level of familiarity you may use in writing. Remember never to send out any written communication without checking it first for grammar, spelling, and, particularly, colloquial expressions. The reasons for checking grammar and spelling are obvious. Sounding foolish or uneducated is never fun. But more importantly, writing to perfect your Spanish will help you to focus on grammatical concepts that may have seemed esoteric when you first learned them.

The Fundamentals of Good Letter Writing

There are six fundamental parts to every letter, discussed in the following sections.

La fecha (the Date)

As in English, the date is a standard part of the letter. In Spanish, however, it is not simply a question of the month, date, and year, but also of the place from which the letter originates. Unless this region is incorporated in the letterhead (*el membrete*), it generally accompanies and precedes the date near the upper right-hand corner (*la parte superior derecha*) of the paper. Take a look at the date variations you may find in Spanish letters (all referring to June 12, 2002):

- 12 de junio de 2002
- Chicago, 12 de junio de 2002
- Chicago, 12 junio 2002
- 12/6/2002

When referring to dates, keep in mind that the actual date (number) is always written before the month. If the friendly letter is brief, the date can also be found at the end of the letter, near *la parte inferior derecha* (the lower right-hand corner).

El encabezamiento (the Heading)

As in English, the form that the heading takes depends on the purpose of the letter and the intended recipient. It is located below the date, but on the opposing side. In a business letter, the heading takes the form of a block of information describing the destination. The information in the heading begins with the following:

- *Nombre de la empresa* (name of the firm)
- *Calle* (street address)
- *Código postal, ciudad* (postal/zip code, city)
- *País* (country)

FACT

Many addresses in Latin America and Spain are not of the form that employs a directional reference point in addition to numerals associated with buildings on a street. That is, you will rarely find anything similar to 1029 NE 23rd Place. You will simply find numbers and streets, like *calle Ochoa 29.*

In more formal business letters, the heading also includes the name and title of the recipient. If the title is not based on position or is unknown, simply use *distinguido(a) señor(a)* (distinguished Mr./Mrs.). Notice that in a Spanish greeting to the recipient, abbreviations are seldom used. For example:

- *Distinguido Señor Arellano*
- *Distinguida Señora Méndez*

For personal or informal letters, the recipient's address is often skipped, with the salutation being the next printed item. The most common salutations coincide with their English counterparts. Here are a few examples:

- *Querido Miguel* (dear Miguel)
- *Queridísima Marta* (dearest Martha)
- *Mis queridos Mario y Fernanda* (my dear Mario y Fernanda)

La introducción (the Introduction)

As in English, it is always good form to provide an introduction to your correspondence. Whereas common courtesy requires it in friendly letters, this is not the case with business letters, where efficiency is at a premium. Here are a few common introductions, running from the most casual to the more formal:

Hola, Fabián, ¿cómo estás?	**Hi, Fabian, how are you?**
Le escribo para . . .	**I am writing to you to . . .**
Deseo comunicarle que . . .	**I wish to communicate to you . . .**
Deseo hacerle saber . . .	**I would like to inform you . . .**

El cuerpo (the Body)

The body of the letter is what will give you the chance to show off your Spanish knowledge! There are no hard-and-fast rules here, but remember to stick to your point and make sure that the tone of your letter is consistent with your message.

La despedida (the Farewell)

Although the body of the letter doesn't fit into a formula, the farewell does. Friendly letters often exhibit one of the following closing lines:

- *Besos y abrazos* (kisses and hugs)
- *Con un abrazo para ti* (with an embrace for you)
- *Con todo mi cariño* (with all my affection)

- *Te saludo muy cordialmente* (greeting you very cordially)
- *Un cordial saludo* (a cordial greeting)

La firma (the Signature)

This one's easy: Signatures are the same in Spanish and English!

A Sample Letter

Take a look at the following sample letter. See how much of it you can understand. To see the translation, refer to Appendix E.

Querida amiga:

No sabes la alegría que me ha causado recibir tu nueva dirección. Ha pasado demasiado tiempo desde la última vez que hablamos. ¿Cómo están todos?, ¿tu mamá y tu papá? Espero que bien. ¿Qué hay de nuevo? Ojalá que los vea a ustedes la próxima vez que viaje hacia allá.

Yo también recuerdo todas las veces que charlamos. Espero hacerlo otra vez, pronto.

Con todo mi cariño,
Lisa

Making Phone Calls

Communicating by phone is very similar to communicating in person, but you may need to know some telephone vocabulary. First, you might learn a few words that can be used to talk about telephone sets and phone usage.

Vocabulary: Using the Phone

el auricular/la bocina	the handset
la cabina de teléfono	telephone booth
colgar el teléfono	to hang up the phone
dejar un recado	to leave a message
descolgar el auricular	to pick up the handset
hacer una llamada	to make a phone call

llamar	to call
marcar, oprimir	to dial, press
telefonear, llamar por teléfono	to phone
el teléfono de botones	push-button telephone
el teléfono inalámbrico	cordless telephone
el tono (la señal)	dial tone

Next, identify the components of your phone number and how to place a phone call.

Vocabulary: Placing a Phone Call

la asistencia de operador	operator assistance
la clave de área, el código	area code
con tarjeta de crédito	with a credit card
de larga distancia	long distance
de persona a persona	person to person
la guía de teléfono	the phone guide
el número de teléfono	phone number
por cobrar	collect call
el prefijo del país	country code

Speaking on the Phone

As in English, Spanish offers general useful phrases to facilitate the social interaction that may take place during a phone call. When initiating a conversation by phone, be prepared to receive:

1. A standard formal salutation. For example:

Buenos días.	**Good morning.**
Buenas tardes.	**Good afternoon/evening.**
Buenas noches.	**Good night.**

2. A direct acknowledgment of your call. For example:

Diga.	**Used primarily in Spain and literally translates to "Say!"**
Dígame.	**Tell me.**
¡Bueno!	**Used primarily in Latin American countries, literally translates as "Well!"**
¡Aló!	**Hello!**

After the initial greeting, you will want to introduce yourself. Here are a few examples:

Me llamo César Peñaherrera.	**My name is Cesar Peñaherrera.**
Soy el Sr. Ríos.	**It's Mr. Rios. / I am Mr. Rios.**
Soy la Sra. Velázquez.	**It's Mrs. Velazquez. / I am Mrs. Velazquez.**
Soy la Srta. Roldós.	**It's Miss Roldos. / I am Miss Roldos.**
Mi nombre es Jaime Moreno.	**My name is Jaime Moreno.**

If the call is to someone whom you don't know and the connection is not clear, you may be asked one of the following questions:

¿Cómo se escribe (su nombre)?	**How do you spell it/your name?**
¿Quiere deletreármelo, por favor?	**Could you please spell it for me?**

Remember to go slow when spelling out your name. When distinguishing a specific characteristic of a letter, its description follows the letter. (For a review of how to pronounce each letter in the Spanish alphabet, refer back to Chapter 2.) For example, to spell *María,* you may say *"M mayúscula* (capital M), *a, r, i acentuada* (accented i), *a."*

After the initial greeting, you may want to ask to speak with someone. Listen to Track 75 to hear the following examples:

TRACK 75

¿Puedo hablar con el Sr. Salgado, por favor?	**Can I please speak with Mr. Salgado?**

Quisiera hablar con la Sra. Guzmán, por favor.	**I would like to speak with Mrs. Guzman.**
¿Podría ponerme con el Departamento de Servicio de Agua?	**Could you connect me to the Water Service Department?**
¿Podría hacerme el favor de informarle a la Srta. Acevedo que su hermana la llama, por favor?	**Could you please do me the kind act of informing Miss Acevedo that her sister is calling?**
¿Puede pasarme al Sr. Estevez?	**Can you transfer me to Mr. Estevez?**

Responses to your request may include:

¿De parte de quién?	**Who is calling?**
Sí, por supuesto. No cuelgue.	**Yes, of course. Don't hang up.**
Un momento, por favor, mientras lo/la busco.	**One moment, please, while I look for him/her.**
Lamento hacerlo/hacerla esperar.	**I'm sorry for making you wait.**
Se lo/la paso.	**I'll transfer you.**
Lo siento, pero no está.	**I'm sorry, but he/she is not in.**
Lo siento, pero está hablando por la otra línea.	**I'm sorry, but he/she is on the other line.**
Lo siento, pero está con un cliente.	**I'm sorry, but he/she is with a client.**
¿Desea dejar un recado?	**Would you like to leave a message?**
¿Puede llamar más tarde?	**Can you call later?**
¿Quiere esperar?	**Do you want to wait?**
¿Quiere hablar con otra persona?	**Would you like to speak with someone else?**

At this point you may either leave your information for a callback or proceed with a conversation with your intended party. *¡Buena suerte!* (Good luck!)

Appendix A

Spanish-to-English Glossary

Spanish English
a to, personal pronoun
a la derecha de . . . to the right of . . .
a la izquierda de . . . to the left of . . .
a la vez at the same time
a mano derecha on the right side
a mano izquierda on the left side
a menudo often
a tiempo on time
a veces at times
abajo downstairs
abarcar to take on
abdominal abdominal
abierto open, opened
el abogado attorney, lawyer
abrazar to embrace
abreviar to abbreviate
abril April
abrir to open
la abstinencia abstinency
abstraer to make abstract
la absurdidad absurdity
la abuela (abuelita) grandmother (grandma)
la abuelita grandma
el abuelito grandpa
el abuelo (abuelito) grandfather (grandpa)
la abundancia abundancy
abundante abundant
aburrido boring
aburrir to bore
abusivo abusive
acá over here
acabar to finish

acariciar to caress, pet
accesible accessible
accidentar to produce an unexpected event
accidente accident
acciones actions
acecinar to dry-cure
aceituna olive
aceptable acceptable
acomodable adaptable
acompañar to accompany
acondicionar to condition
acostado reclined
la actividad activity
el actor/la actriz actor/actress
actuar to act
acudir to frequent a place
adentro inside
el adjetivo adjective
la admiración admiration
admisible admissible
el adolescente adolescent
adorable adorable
adorar to adore
la aduana customs
el adulto adult
el adversario adversary
advertir to warn
aéreo aerial
aeróbicos aerobics
el aeropuerto airport
afable affable
afectuoso affectionate
afeitar to shave
Afganistán Afghanistan
afgano Afghani
la afluencia affluence
afortunadamente fortunately
África Africa
africano African

afuera outside
el agente agent
la agilidad agility
agosto August
agotado exhausted
agradable pleasant weather
agradecer to thank (for)
la agricultura agriculture
el agua water
las aguas waters
el águila eagle
la ahijada goddaughter
el ahijado godson
ahijar to adopt
ahora now
ahuyentar to drive away
el aire air
aislar to isolate
el ajedrez chess
el ajo garlic
al fondo de at/in the back of
al lado de to the side of, next to
la extensión extension cord
alarmante alarming
albanés Albanian
Albania Albania
el alcohol alcohol
el alcoholismo alcoholism
alegórico alegoric
alemán German
Alemania Germany
el alfabeto alphabet
el álgebra algebra
algunas veces sometimes
el alma, el soul
el almacén store, warehouse
las almas souls
almorzar to lunch
el alpinismo mountain climbing

altar altar
el altavoz speaker
el altavoz de sonidos agudos tweeter
el altavoz de sonidos graves woofer
el altavoz de sonidos medios mid-range speaker
alto tall
la altura height
aludir to allude (to)
amable kind, amiable
amanecer to grow light (at dawn)
amar to love
amarillo yellow
ambicioso ambitious
ambos both
la ambulancia ambulance
América America
americano American
el amigo friend
amistoso friendly
el amo (de casa) househusband (male)
el amor love
las ampliaciones expansions
el amplificador amplifier
el analista de inventario inventory analyst
el análisis, el analysis
ancho wide, broad
el anciano elderly
andar to walk
animado animated
el animal animal
aniñado childish
el aniversario anniversary
el año year
el año pasado last year

el año próximo/el próximo año next year

anochecer to grow dark (at night)

ansioso anxious

anteayer day before yesterday

la anticipación anticipation

la antigüedad antiquity

antiguo old

antipático unpleasant

anual annual

apacible pleasant, gentle

apagar to turn off

aparecer to appear

aparentemente apparently

el apellido last name

apetecer to desire, crave

aplaudir to applaud, to approve

aplicar to apply

apostar to bet, to post

el apoyo support

apretar to tighten

aquel that (at a distance)

aquí here

Arabia Saudita Saudi Arabia

el árbol tree

el ardor ardor

las armas arms

la arquería archery

el arquitecto architect

arrendar to rent, lease

arriba upstairs

la arrogancia arrogance

las artes marciales martial arts

el artista artist

ascender to ascend

asesinar to murder

así así so-so

asir to seize

el asistente ejecutivo executive assistant

asistir attend

la asociación association

astral astral

el astronauta astronaut

asustado frightened

el ataúd coffin

la atención attention

atender to attend to

Atlántico Atlantic

el atleta athlete

el atletismo athletics

atontado stunned

atractivo attractive

atraer to attract

atragantar to choke

atrás back

atrasado late

la atrocidad atrocity

audaz bold

el auditor auditor

aullar to howl, shriek

el aumento increase

aun even

aún yet, still

auspiciar to sponsor

Australia Australia

australiano Australian

Austria Austria

austriaco Austrian

auténtico authentic

el auto automobile

el autobús bus

la autoestima self-esteem

el automóvil car

el automovilismo car racing

el autor author

autoritario domineering

el ave bird

la avenida avenue

la aventura adventure

avergonzado embarrassed

avergonzar to shame

averiguar to inquire

ayer yesterday

la ayuda help

ayudar(se) to help (oneself)

el bádminton badminton

bagaje cargo, military baggage

bailar to dance

el baile dance

bajo short

el baloncesto basketball

el balonmano handball

el balonvolea volley ball

el banquero hipotecario mortgage banker

el barón baron

el básquetbol basketball

el baúl chest

beber to drink

la bebida a drink

el béisbol baseball

belga Belgian

Bélgica Belgium

bello beautiful

beneficial beneficial

la bicicleta bicycle

bien educado well mannered

bienvivir to live well

bilingüe bilingual

el billar billiards

el billón trillion

biodegradable biodegradable

la biografía biography

Birmania Burma

birmano Burmese

el bistec (beef) steak

blanco white

blasfemable capable of being blasphemed

la blusa blouse

la boda wedding

el boleto ticket

el bolígrafo pen

el bombero fireman

la bondad goodness

bondadoso good, kind

bonito, a pretty

borracho drunk

el botón de encendido on button

el botón de reinicio reset button

boxear to box

la bravura bravery

el brazo arm

la brevedad brevity

brillante brilliant

británico British

la broma practical joke

brusco blunt, rude

la brutalidad brutality

bucear to scuba dive

el buceo scuba diving

el buen tiempo nice weather

bueno good

bueno para good for

buscar to look (for)

el caballo horse

el cabello hair

caber to fit (into)

la cabeza head

el cable cable

cada each, every

caer to fall

la caída fall

el cajero cashier

el cajón drawer

la calabaza pumpkin

el calambre cramp

calculable calculable

calcular to calculate

calentar to heat (up)

la calificación grade

californiano Californian

el calor heat

caluroso hot

calvo bald

el camarero waiter

Cambodia Cambodia

camboyano Cambodian

caminar walk

la camisa shirt

Canadá Canada

canadiense Canadian

la canción song

cansado tired

el cantante singer

cantar to sing

el caos chaos

la capacidad capacity

capaz capable

el capital the capital (business money)

la capital the capital of a city

el capitalismo capitalism

el capitalista capitalist

caprichoso capricious

el caradura disrespectful person

la cárcel jail

el cardiólogo cardiologist

cariñoso loving
la carne flesh, meat
la carrera race
la carta letter
las cartas cards
la cartelera listing
la casa house, home
casado married
el castellano Spanish from Castille
la cata de vino wine tasting
la catástrofe catastrophe
la catedral cathedral
catorce fourteen
ceder to submit, surrender
celoso jealous
la cena dinner
el censor censor
el centeno rye
central central
cerca near
cerca de . . . close to . . .
el cereal cereal
cernir to sieve
cero zero
cerrado closed
cerrar to close
el césped lawn
las chanclas slippers
la chanza joke
el chaquete backgammon
checo Czech
el chicle chewing gum
China China
chino Chinese
el chiste joke
el choclo overshoe, corn
el chocolate chocolate
la chuleta (pork) chop
la cicatriz scar
el ciclismo cycling
el ciclista cyclist
ciego blind
el cielo sky
el científico scientist
cierto certain, true
la cigüeña stork
cinco five
cincuenta fifty

cínico cynical
la cintura waist
la circunstancia circumstance
la ciruela plum
la cita appointment
la ciudad city
el ciudadano citizen
la claridad clarity
clarificar to clarify
claro clear
la clase class
clavar to nail
el clavo nail
cocer to cook, boil
el coche car
la cocina gastronómica gourmet cooking
el coco coconut, head
coger to grasp, grab
cohibir to inhibit
coincidir to coincide
coincidir (con) to coincide (with a person)
el colchón mattress
el cólera cholera
la cólera anger
colgar to hang
color color
el coma the coma
la coma the comma
combatir to combat
el comentario commentary
comenzar to begin
comer to eat
comercial commercial
el cometa the comet
la cometa the kite
cometer un error to make a mistake
cómico funny
el compañero companion
la compañía company
el competidor competitor
competir to compete
comprar to purchase
comprender to understand
comprensible comprehensible

comprobar to verify, check
la computadora portátil notebook computer
la comunidad community
con with
el concierto concert
la concuñada brother-in-law's spouse
concurrir to concur
conducir drive
el conductor conductor, driver
el conector de altavoces speaker jack
el conector de auriculares headphone jack
el conector de micrófono microphone jack
confesar to confess
el confesor confessor
confundir to confuse
la confusión confusion
congelado frozen
conocer to be acquainted
la consciencia conscience
consecutivo consecutive
conseguir to obtain
el consejero de inversiones investment advisor
el conservadorismo conservatism
la consola console
la consonante consonant
constante constant
constipado congested, has a head cold
constipar to stop up nasal passages as in a cold
construir to construct
el consultor de mercadeo marketing consultant
consumir to consume, to use up
contadas veces seldom
el contable accountant
el contador accountant
contagioso contagious
contento satisfied
contestar to respond (to)

continuar to continue
contradictorio contradictory
contraer to contract
contrario contrary
contribuir to contribute
convertible convertible
convertir to convert
cordial cordial
Corea Korea
coreano Korean
la correa leather strap
corregir to correct
correr run
corresponder to reciprocate, to belong to
el corte the cut
la corte the court
cortés courteous
la cortina curtain
la cosa thing
coser to sew/stitch
la costumbre custom
crear to create
crecer to grow
creer to believe
criar to breed and rear
la criatura young child
el crimen crime
criminal criminal
el criquet cricket
la crisis crisis
cristiano Christian
crudo raw
cruel cruel
cruzar to cross
el cuadro picture
cuál which
cuándo when
cuarenta forty
cuarto fourth
cuatro four
cubierto covered, cloudy
cubrir to cover
el cuchillo knife
el cuello neck
la cuenta account, bill, check
el cuento story
el cuento de hadas fairy tale
el cuerpo body

cuidar to care for
culinario culinary
la cultura culture
cultural cultural
cumplir to carry out
la cuñada sister-in-law
el cuñado brother-in-law
el cura the priest
la cura the cure
curable curable
la curiosidad curiosity
curioso curious
cursi pretentious
el curso course
danés, danesa Danish
dar to give
dar clases en . . . to teach . . .
dar paseo en barco to take a trip on a boat
dar paseo en bicicleta to tour on bicycle
de of, from
de acuerdo in agreement
de día during the day
de espaldas lying on one's back
de guardia on duty
de la mañana of the morning
de la noche of the night (after sunset)
de la tarde of the afternoon/of the evening
de moda in fashion
de paseo am walking by, on a short trip
de pie standing
de regreso on one's way back
de rodillas kneeling
de vacaciones on vacation
de vez en cuando once in a while
de viaje on a trip
de vuelta back
debajo under(neath)
debajo de . . . under . . .
debatir to debate, to argue
deber duty, must, to owe, to ought to
débil weak

decidir to decide
décimo tenth
decir to say
la decisión decision
el decorado decorated
el dedo finger
deducir to deduce
defender to defend
defensivo defensive
definir to define
del of the
delante de . . . in front of . . .
delgado thin
delicioso delicious
el delito crime
demasiado too, overly
democrático democratic
demostrar to demonstrate
el dentista dentist
depender to depend
el dependiente clerk
el despotismo despotism
desagradecer to be ungrateful (for)
el desagüe drain
el desahogo emotional relief
el desahucio eviction
desaparecer to disappear
el descargue an unloading
desconocer not to recognize
desde since
desde hace for (a time frame)
el deseo desire/wish
desnudo undressed
desobedecer to disobey
despedir to see off, fire
despejado without clouds
desperdiciar to waste
despierto awake
después later
el destructor destroyer
destruir to destroy
el detector detector
detrás de . . . behind . . .
la deuda debt
devolver to return
el día day
el dialecto dialect
el diario daily

dibujar to draw
el diccionario dictionary
diciembre December
diecinueve nineteen
dieciocho eighteen
dieciséis sixteen
diecisiete seventeen
diez ten
la diferencia difference
diferente different
difícil difficult
digestible digestible
dignatario dignitary
la dignidad dignity
Dinamarca Denmark
el director director
discernir to discern
el disco record
el disco compacto compact disc
discutir to discuss
el diseñador de software software developer
el diseñador designer
disfrutar to enjoy
la disquetera diskette drive
distraer to distract
doce twelve
docto learned, expert
el doctor a person with a doctorate, doctor
el dogmatismo dogmatism
el dólar dollar
el dolor pain
dolorido aching
domingo Sunday
el dominó dominoes
dormido asleep
dos two
drástico drastic
el duelo sorrow
dulce sweet
durable durable
durante during
ebrio drunk
echar to throw out
la edad age
el editor editor
educacional educational

EE. UU. U.S.A.
egipcio Egyptian
Egipto Egypt
el egoismo selfishness
egoísta selfish
el ejecutivo executive
el ejemplo example
ejercer to practice (a trade)
el ejercicio exercise
el the (masc.)
él he
el elefante elephant
la elegancia elegance
elegante elegant
elegir to choose decisively
ella she
ellas they (fem.)
ellos they (masc.)
embarazada pregnant
embarazar to impregnate, to hinder
embellecer to embellish, adorn
emerger to emerge
emigrado emigrated
el emisario emissary
emitir to emit or give off
emocionado moved, touched
emocional emotional
empezar to begin
el empleo employment
empobrecer to impoverish
la empresa firm, company
enamorado in love
encantado delighted
encender to light, turn on
el enchufe de corriente electrical outlets
encontrar to encounter
enero January
enfadado disgusted, angered at someone
el énfasis emphasis
la enfermedad sickness
enfermizo sickly
enfermo sick
enfrente in front
enojado angry
enriquecer to enrich

entender to understand
enterrar to bury
entrar to enter
entregar to hand over
entretenido amusing
envejecer to grow old
enviar to send
envolver to wrap
el episodio episode
la época time, epoch
el equipaje baggage
el equipo equipment
el equipo de alta fidelidad Hi-fi system
el equipo estereofónico stereo system
la equitación horseback riding
el error error
esbelto proportioned
esbozo first draft, outline
la escala scale
el escáner scanner
escocés, escocesa Scottish
Escocia Scotland
escoger to choose
escribir to write
escuchar to listen (to)
la escuela school
la escultura sculpture
esencia essence
esencial essential
el esfuerzo effort
la esgrima fencing
eslavo Slav
esnob snob
eso that
especial special
el especialista specialist
el espectáculo performance, show
esperar to hope, to wait (for)
el espíritu spirit
el esposo spouse
el esquí skiing
el esquí acuático water skiing
esta vez this time
establecer to establish
estacionar to park

el estado state
Estados Unidos United States
estadounidense American (from the United States)
el estanque pond
estar to be
la estatura height
la estatura mediana medium height
este año this year
el estilo style
el estudiante student
estudiar to study
estupendamente stupendously
la eternidad eternity
etíope Ethiopian
Etiopía Ethiopia
la euforia euphoria
Europa Europe
europeo European
el evangelismo evangelism
la evidencia evidence
evitable avoidable
exactamente exactly
examen exam
excelente excellent
exhalar to exhale
exhibir to exhibit
la exigencia demand
exigir to demand, require
la existencia existence
explicable explicable
explicar to explain
el explosivo explosive
exportar to export
el éxtasis ecstasy
extender to extend
extinguir to extinguish
el extranjero foreigner
extraño strange
extraordinario extraordinary
la fachada façade
fácil easy
fácilmente easily
falseable falsifiable
la fama fame
famoso famous
fatal fatal

el favor favor
favorecer to favor
febrero February
febril feverish
federal federal
feliz happy
el fénix phoenix
feo ugly
la ferocidad fierceness
el ferrocarril railway
el fervor fervor
fiar to trust, lend
la fiebre fever
fijar to fasten
Filipinas Philippines
filipino Filippino
el filtro protector surge protector
el fin de semana weekend
finalmente finally
fingir to fake
finlandés, finlandesa Finnish
Finlandia Finland
la física physics
físico physical, physicist
el fisiculturismo bodybuilding
flaco thin, skinny
florecer to flower, flourish
el fonógrafo phonograph
la fractura fracture
la fragilidad fragility
francés French
Francia France
frecuente frequent
frecuentemente frequently
fregar to rub
freír to fry
frenar to brake
frente, el the front line in battle
la frente forehead
fresco fresh
el frío cold/I fry
la fruta fruit
fuerte strong
fundamental fundamental
fundir to fuse, to cast
el fútbol soccer

el fútbol americano football
el futuro future
galés, galesa Welsh
el garaje garage
el gato cat
generalmente generally
generoso generous
genial pleasant
la gente people
gentil courteous
el gerente manager (masc. and fem.)
el gesto facial gesture
la gimnasia gymnastics
el girasol sunflower
la gloria glory
el glosario glossary
el golf golf
el golpe blow, hit
golpeado bruised
gordo fat
el gorrión sparrow
gozar to enjoy
la grabadora de casete cassette recorder
grabar to record
gracioso amusing
gran grand, great
Gran Bretaña Great Britain
grande big, large
granizar to hail
Grecia Greece
griego Greek
el gringo a person from a non-Spanish country
la gripe influenza
la grúa crane
grueso thick, stout
guapo handsome
guardar to store
la guedeja lion's mane
la guerra war
el guía the person who guides
la guía the book, booklet
guiñar to wink
el guisado stew
la guitarra guitar
el gusano worm, caterpillar

gustar to please
el gusto pleasure
haber to have (aux. verb)
hábil skillful
el hábito habit
hablar to speak
hacer to do, to be, to make
hacia toward
Haití Haiti
haitiano Haitian
halagüeño attractive, flattering
hallar to find
la halterofilia y la potencia weightlifting and strength
el hambre hunger
la hamburguesa hamburger
hay there is, there are
el hecho fact, deed
helado freezing
helar to freeze
hereditario hereditary
herir to injure
la hermana (hermanita) sister
la hermana mayor older sister
la hermana menor younger sister
la hermanastra stepsister
el hermanastro stepbrother
el hermano (hermanito) brother
hermoso beautiful, handsome
hervir to boil
el hierro iron
la hija (hijita) daughter
la hija política daughter-in-law
la hija única only child
la hijastra stepdaughter
el hijastro stepson, stepchild
el hijo (hijito) child, son
el hijo político son-in-law
el hipo hiccup
hipocorístico affectionate form of a name
hola hi
holandés, holandesa Dutch
Holanda Holland

honorable honorable
honrado honorable
la horticultura horticulture
hospedar to receive the needy
el hospital hospital
el hotel hotel
hoy today
la huella a trace
el hueso bone
el huésped guest
el huevo egg
la huída escape
huir to flee
húmedo humid
la humildad humility
el humor humor
la idea idea
ideal ideal
el idealismo idealism
idealista idealist
el idioma language
igual equal
la igualdad equality
ilegal illegal
ileso unharmed
la impaciencia impatience
impaciente impatient
impedir to hinder
importante important
importar to import, to cause to matter
el impresionismo impressionism
la impresora láser laser printer
inactivo sedentary
el incendiario incendiary
el incentivo incentive
incomparable incomparable
la independencia independence
India India
indio Indian
el individualismo individualism
inevitable inevitable
la infancia infancy
inferior inferior
la información information

informar to inform
el ingeniero químico chemical engineer
Inglaterra England
inglés, inglesa English
la inocencia innocence
la insistencia insistence
el inspector inspector
la institución de beneficencia charity
el instructor instructor
el internista internist
interrumpir to interrupt
el interruptor power switch
la intolerancia intolerance
introducir to introduce
inventar to invent
el inventor inventor
la inversión inversion
el invierno winter
la invitación invitation
invitado invited
ir to go
Irán Iran
iraní Iran (masc. and fem.)
Iraq Iraq
iraquí Iraqi (masc. and fem.)
Irlanda Ireland
irlandés, irlandesa Irish
irritable irritable
Israel Israel
israelí Israeli (masc. and fem.)
Italia Italy
italiano Italian
el jabón soap
Jamaica Jamaica
jamaicano Jamaican
Japón Japan
japonés, japonesa Japanese
jerosolimitano Jerusalemite
joven young
jovial jovial, jolly
la joya jewel
jueves Thursday
el juez judge
jugar to play
juguetón playful
julio July
junio June

la justicia justice
la juventud youth
el kárate karate
el keroseno kerosene
el kilo, kilogramo kilogram
el kilómetro kilometer
el kilovatio kilowatt
la kinesiología kinesiology
kurdo Kurd, Kurdish
la the (fem.)
menor smallest, youngest
el lago lake
lamentable lamentable
lastimado hurt
el laúd lute
el lector de DVDs DVD player
leer to read
legítimo legitimate
lejos far
lejos de . . . far from . . .
el lenguaje language
la letra letter (of the alphabet)
el levantamiento de pesas weightlifting
la ley law
el liberalismo liberalism
la libra pound (weight)
el libro book
limpio clean
el linaje lineage
la lingüística linguistics
el lío mess
listo prepared
literario literary
la literatura literature
llamar(se) to call (oneself)
llamar por teléfono to telephone
llegar to arrive
lleno full
lleno de vida full of life
llevar to carry, to wear
llover to rain
la llovizna drizzling
lloviznar to drizzle
la lluvia rain
lluvioso rainy
local local
loco crazy, outgoing

lógico logical
los auriculares headphones
la lotería lottery
el luchador fighter, wrestler
lucir to shine, brighten
la luna moon
lunes Monday
luterano Lutheran
la luz (luces) light(s)
la luz del disco duro hard drive light
la madera wood
la madrastra stepmother
la madre mother
la madrina godmother
madrugar to rise early
maduro mature, ripe, wise
el maestro teacher
el magnetismo magnetism
el maíz corn
mal educado ill-mannered
la maleta suitcase
malhablado potty mouth
la mamá mom
la mami mommy
mañana tomorrow
la mano hand
la manzana apple, city block
el mapa map
la máquina machine
mareado dizzy
el marido husband
marino marine
martes Tuesday
marzo March
más more
más allá de . . . beyond . . .
el masaje massage
la mascota pet
el materialismo materialism
mayo May
mayor older
mayor de edad of the age of maturity
me llamo I am called
el mecánico mechanic(al)
mecer to sway, rock
mediano medium
el médico doctor, physician

el mediodía noon
medir to measure
mejor better
mejor dicho rather, said more accurately
melancólico melancholic
mentalmente mentally
mentir to lie, deceive
el mentor mentor
el menú menu
el mercader merchant
la merced mercy
merecer to deserve
merendar to snack in the afternoon
el mesero waiter
meter to put (in)
meticuloso meticulous
el metro meter
mexicano Mexican
México Mexico
mi(s) my
mía(s), mío(s) mine
el miembro member
mientras while
miércoles Wednesday
mil a thousand
millón million
el millonario millionaire
mínimo minimum
mirar to look (at), watch
mirar to look at, to watch
mirar la televisión watch television
miserable miserable
el misionario missionary
el módem modem
el modista dressmaker
molesto annoyed
molestoso a bothersome person
la moneda coin
el monitor monitor
la montaña mountain
el montañismo mountain sports
moralista moralist
moreno dark-haired, dark-complexioned

mortal fatal
el mosquito mosquito
mostrar to show, exhibit
el motor motor
el mozo waiter
muchas veces many times
mucho much, a lot
los muebles furniture
muerto dead
la mujer woman, wife
el multicine movie multiplex
el mundo world
la música music, woman musician
musical musical
el músico musician
musulmán, musulmana Moslem
muy very
nacer to be born
nacional national
la nacionalidad nationality
el nacionalismo nationalism
nadar swimming
nadie no one
naranja orange
la natación swimming
natural natural
naturalmente naturally
la navegación sailing
navegar sailing
necesariamente necessarily
necesario necessary
necesitar to need
negar to deny, refuse
negativo negative
negociable negotiable
el negocio business
negro black
nervioso nervous
el neumático tire
neutral neutral
nevado snowy
el nieto, la nieta grandson, granddaughter
la nieve snow
el niño, la niña child, boy, girl
la niñez childhood
no no

el nombre name
normalmente normally
norteamericano North American
Noruega Norway
noruego Norwegian
nosotros, nosotras us
la nota grade, note
las noticias news
la novela de ciencia ficción science fiction novel
la novela histórica historical novel
la novela policiaca detective novel
la novela romántica romance novel
el novelista novelist
noveno ninth
noventa ninety
noviembre November
la nube cloud
nublado cloudy
la nuera daughter-in-law
nuestro(s) our
nueve nine
nunca never
o sea that is
el oasis oasis
obedecer to obey
la obligación duty, obligation
la obra work, product
oscuro dark, obscure
el obsequio gift
obstruir to block
obviamente obviously
ochenta eighty
ocho eight
octavo eighth
octubre October
ocupado busy
ofender to offend
oficial official
ofrecer to offer
el oído internal ear
oír to hear
el ojo eye
oler to smell
el olor smell

olvidar   to forget
la omisión   omission
once   eleven
operar   to operate
la opinión   opinion
oponer   to oppose
la oportunidad   opportunity
el opositor   opponent
optar   to choose
optimista   optimist
el orden   order (as opposed to chaos)
la orden   command, request
el ordenador portátil   notebook computer
ordinario   ordinary
la oreja   exterior ear
orgánico   organic
organizable   organizable
original   original
el oro   gold
ostensible   ostensible
el otoño   autumn, fall
otro   other, another
el paciente   patient
pacífico   pacifist
padecer   to suffer
el padrastro   stepfather
el padre   father
el padrino   godfather to one's child, friend
la paella   Spanish rice dish
pagar   to pay (for)
el país   country
país de Gales   Wales
el paisaje   landscape
el pájaro   bird
pálido   pale
la panadería   bakery
la pantalla   screen
los pantalones   trousers
el papá   father
Papá Noel   Santa Claus
el papel   paper
las paperas   mumps
el papi   daddy
Paquistán   Pakistan
paquistaní   Pakistani (masc. and fem.)

para   for, to
el paracaidismo   parachuting
la parada   stop, parade
el parapente   paragliding
parcial   partial
parecer   to seem, to appear
la pared   wall
el parentesco   kinship
el parque   a park
la parra   grapevine
participar   to participate
pasable   passable
pasado mañana   day after tomorrow
pasear   stroll through
pasear en barco   boating
el pastor   pastor
paterno   paternal
patético   pathetic
el patinaje   skating
el patinaje sobre hielo   ice-skating
el patriotismo   patriotism
el peaje   toll
el pedazo   piece
el pediatra   pediatrician
la pelea   fight
el peligro   danger
pelirrojo   redhead
el peluquero   barber
pensar   to think
peor   worse
pequeño   small
perder   to lose
la pereza   laziness
perfectamente   perfectly
el periódico   newspaper
la periodista   journalist
permitir   to permit
pero   but
el perro   dog
perseguir   to pursue
la persona   person
personalmente   personally
la pesca   fishing
el peso   weight
el pez   fish (swimming in water)
la pez   tar

el pianista   pianist
el piano   piano
el pie   foot
la piedad   pity/mercy
la piel   skin
el piloto   pilot
el pingüino   penguin
pintar   to paint
pintura al óleo   oil painting
el piragüismo   sailing by light canoe
el piso   floor
la pista   trail, hint
la placa   license plate
el plan   plan
la plancha   iron (for ironing)
el plantaje   planting
platicar   to chat
la pletina   cassette deck
el plomo   lead
el plumaje   plumage
pobre   poor
poco   little
poder   to be able to do; power
el poema   poem
la poesía   poetry
polaco   Polish
el, la policía   the police officer (masc. and fem.)
la policía   police force
Polonia   Poland
el poncho   poncho, cape
poner   to place, to put
popular   popular
el póquer   poker
el porcentaje   percentage
porque   because
la porra   stick
la posesión   possession
la posibilidad   possibility
posible   possible
posiblemente   possibly
la postura   posture
potente   potent
practicar   to practice
precisamente   precisely
la preferencia   preference
preferible   preferable
preferir   to prefer

preguntar   to ask
la preocupación   worry
preocupado   worried
preparar   to prepare
presbiteriano   Presbyterian
presentable   presentable
el presidente   president
presidir   to hold a group's most important post
el primo, la prima   cousin
el primo hermano   first cousin
el primo segundo   second cousin
primario   primary
la primavera   spring
primero   first
el primogénito   first born
principalmente   principally
probablemente   probably
el problema   problem
proceder   to proceed
producir   to produce
el profesor   professor
el profesor de música   music teacher
el programador   programmer
progresivo   progressive
prometer   to promise
pronto   soon
propio   own
el protector   protector
proteger   to protect
próximo   next
prudente   prudent
púa   barb
el pueblo   town/village
la puerta   door
pulir   to polish
el puño   fist
que   that
qué   what
quebrar   to break
quedar   to remain
la queja   complaint
quejarse   to complain
quemar   to burn
querer   to want, or love
querido   beloved
el queso   cheese

quien   who
la quijada   jaw
quince   fifteen
quinto   fifth
quitar   to take away
quizás   perhaps
el rabo   tail
racional   rational
el radicalismo   radicalism
el radio   the radius, the physical radio
la radio   the radio programming
el radiocasete portátil   portable stereo
la radiografía   X-ray picture
la raíz   root, origin
la ranura de la disquetera   diskette drive slot
el ratón   mouse
la raya   line
la razón   reason
reaccionar   to react
reanudar   to renew
rebatir   to refute
la receta   recipe
recibir   to receive
recoger   to gather
recomendar   to recommend
recordar   to remember
redactar   to compose, edit
redondo   round
reembolsar   to reimburse
reexaminar   to re-examine
el reflector   reflector
el régimen   regimen
la región   region
la regla   rule
la regrabadora de CDs   CD-RW drive
regular   regular
rehusar   to refuse
el reino   kingdom
reír(se)   to laugh
la rejilla de ventilación   ventilation grill
el relámpago   lightning
relampaguear   to flash with lightning

el relampagueo   lightning flash
relativamente   relatively
rellenar   to fill out
remitir   to send
rendir   to hand over
reñir   to quarrel
renunciar   to quit
el reo   criminal
repetidas veces   repeatedly
repetir   to repeat
la repisa   shelf
el repostero   pastry maker
el reproductor de discos compactos   CD player
República Checa   Czech Republic
republicano   republican
el requisito   requirement
el resfriado   cold (as in sick with a cold)
la residencia   residence
resistir   to resist, to tolerate
resolver   to resolve
respetable   respectable
el resto de mi vida   the rest of my life
restringir   to limit
resumir   to sum up
retirado   retired person
el reto   challenge
el retrato   portrait
retroceder   to turn back
la reunión   gathering
revisar   to check
la revista   magazine
el rey   king
rezar   to pray
el riesgo   risk
el rincón   corner
robado   stolen
robusto   robust
el roedor   rodent
rogar   to beg, to plead
romper   to break
la roña   scab
la ropa   clothes
la rosa   rose

rosado   rosy, pink
rubio   blond(e)
la rueda   wheel
el ruido   noise
la ruleta   roulette
rumiar   to ruminate
el rumor   rumor
sábado   Saturday
saber   to know
sacar   to draw, take out
el sacerdote   priest
sahumar   to perfume with incense
la sala   living room
el salario   salary
salir   to leave, go out
salpicar   to sprinkle
la salud   health
el santo   saint
el sarampión   measles
el sastre, la sastra   tailor
satisfacer   to satisfy
saudita   Saudi Arabian
secundario   secondary
la sed   thirst
sediento   thirsty
el seductor   seducer
seguir   to follow
segundo   second
seis   six
la semana pasada   last week
la semana próxima/la próxima semana   next week
sensacional   sensational
sentado   seated
sentir   to feel
septiembre   September
séptimo   seventh
ser   to be
la serie   series
serio   serious
serpiente   serpent
servir   to serve
sesenta   sixty
setenta   seventy
sexto   sixth
si   if
sí   yes
siempre   always

siete   seven
siguiente   following
la sílaba   syllable
simpático   agreeable
simple   simple
la síntesis   synthesis
el sintonizador   tuner
sintonizar   to tune
sinvergüenza   shameless
siquiera   at least
Siria   Syria
sirio   Syrian
el sistema hidráulico   hydraulic system
sobre . . .   over, on top of . . .
la sobremesa   desktop
sobrevivir   to overcome
la sobrina   niece
el sobrino   nephew
sobrio   sober
el socialismo   socialism
el socio   associate
el sol   sun
la soledad   solitude
solitario   solitaire
solo   alone, only
sólo   only
soltar   to release
soltero   single
soñar   to dream
sonreír   to smile
sorprender   to surprise
sosegado   calmed
su(s)   your (polite), his, her, their
subir   to ascend
Sudáfrica   South Africa
sudafricano   South African
sudar   to sweat
Suecia   Sweden
sueco   Swedish
la suegra   mother-in-law
el suegro   father-in-law
la suela   sole
el sueldo   salary
el sueño   dream, sleep, sleepiness
la suerte   luck
sufrir   to suffer

Suiza Switzerland

suizo Swiss

superior superior

supervisor supervisor

el surf surfing

surgir to surge, appear

el sustantivo noun

suya(s), suyo(s) yours (polite), his, hers, theirs

el tabernero barkeeper

tailandés, tailandesa Thailandese

Tailandia Thailand

talentoso talented

también also

tampoco neither

tantas veces so many times

tanto so much

la tapa cover, lid

la tarde afternoon, evening

la tarjeta de navidad Christmas card

la tasa measure

el tasador de bienes inmuebles realty appraiser

el taxi taxi

la taza cup, bowl

el techo roof

el teclado keyboard

tejer to knit

la tela fabric

telefonear to telephone

el teléfono telephone

temer to fear

temeroso fearful

la temperatura a temperature

el tenedor fork

tener to have (to be)

el tenis tennis

el tenis de mesa table tennis

el tenor tenor

tercer third

el terciopelo velvet

el terreno land, field

el terrorismo terrorism

texano Texan

la tez complexion, skin

el tío, la tía uncle, aunt

el tigre tiger

la tinta tint, dye

tinto tinged, red (wine)

el tiro con arco archery

el tiro a fusil shooting

la toalla towel

el tocacasete cassette player

el tocadiscos (analógico) turntable

el tocadiscos CD CD player

tocar to touch, to play

toda la vida the whole life, all the time

todo all, every

la tolerancia tolerance

tomar to take

el tomate tomato

el tornado tornado

la torre tower, tower console

la tos cough

el trabajo work

el trabalenguas tongue twister

tradicional traditional

traducir to translate

traer to bring

tragantón gluttonous

tragar to swallow

tranquilo calm

transcurrir to pass, to elapse

trasmitir to transmit

travieso mischievous

trece thirteen

treinta thirty

tres three

el trigo wheat

triste sad

la tristeza sadness

tronar to thunder

trotear jog

tú you (familiar)

tu(s) your (familiar)

el tubo tube

turco Turk, Turkish

el turista tourist

Turquía Turkey

tutear treat informally

tuya(s), tuyo(s) yours (familiar)

último last

uña fingernail

unir to unite

universal universal

uno one, a

usar to use

usted you (polite)

ustedes you all

usual usual

usualmente usually

útil useful

la vaca cow

vaciar to empty

valer to be valued

el valor valor

el vandalismo vandalism

varias veces several times

varios various

varón male

el vaso glass

el vecino neighbor

vegetariano vegetarian

veinte twenty

veintiuno 21 (blackjack)

la vela sailing

la velocidad velocity

vencer to conquer

el vendedor salesperson

vender to sell

venir to come

ver to see

ver televisión to watch television

el verano summer

el verbo verb

la verdad truth

las verduras vegetables

la vergüenza shame

el vestido dress

vestir to dress

vez, veces time(s)

viajar to travel

el vicepresidente vice president

la vida life

la videocámara video camera

viejo old

viento wind

viernes Friday

el vigor vigor

visible visible

la viuda widow

la vocal vowel

el volante badminton, steering wheel

volar to fly

el voleibol volleyball

el volumen volume

la voluntad will

el voluntario voluntary

volver to return

el vuelo en ala delta hang gliding

Washington Washington

el xilófono xylophone

y and

el yanqui an American (person)

la yegüita small mare

el yerno son-in-law

yo I

Yemen Yemen

yemení Yemeni

zambullir to dive

el zapato shoe

la zarzamora blackberry

el zoológico zoo

Appendix B

English-to-Spanish Glossary

21 (blackjack) **veintiúno**
abbreviate, to **abreviar**
abdominal **abdominal**
abstinency **la abstinencia**
absurdity **la absurdidad**
abundancy **la abundancia**
abundant **abundante**
abusive **abusivo**
acceptable **aceptable**
accessible **accesible**
accident **el accidente**
accompany, to **acompañar**
account, bill **la cuenta**
accountant **el contador, el contable**
aching **dolorido**
act, to **actuar**
action **la acción**
activity **la actividad**
actor, actress **el actor, la actriz**
adaptable **acomodable, adaptable**
adjective **el adjetivo**
admiration **la admiración**
admissible **admisible**
adolescent **el adolescente**
adopt, to **ahijar**
adorable **adorable**
adore, to **adorar**
adult **el adulto**
adversary **el adversario**
aerial **aéreo**
aerobics **aeróbics**
affable **afable**
affectionate **afectuoso**
affectionate form of a name **hipocorístico**
affluence **la afluencia**
Afghan **afgano**
Afghanistan **Afganistán**

Africa **África**
African **africano**
afternoon/evening **la tarde**
age **la edad**
agent **el agente**
agility **la agilidad**
agreeable **simpático**
agriculture **la agricultura**
August **agosto**
air **el aire**
airport **el aeropuerto**
Albania **Albania**
Albanian **albanés, albanesa**
alcohol **el alcohol**
alcoholism **el alcoholismo**
algebra **el álgebra**
all, every **todo**
allude (to), to **aludir**
alone, only **solo, sólo**
alphabet **el alfabeto**
alphabetic letter **la letra**
also **también**
altar **el altar**
always **siempre**
ambitious **ambicioso**
ambulance **la ambulancia**
America **América**
American **americano**
American (person), an **el yanqui**
amplifier **el amplificador**
amusing **entretenido**
amusing **gracioso**
analysis **análisis**
and **y**
anger **la cólera**
angry **enojado**
animal **el animal**
animated **animado**
anniversary **el aniversario**
annoyed **molesto**

annual **anual**
anticipation **la anticipación**
antiquity **la antigüedad**
anxious **ansioso**
apparently **aparentemente**
appear, to **aparecer**
applaud (to), to **aplaudir**
approve **aplaudir**
apple, city block **la manzana**
apply, to **aplicar**
appointment **la cita**
April **abril**
archery **la arquería**
archery **el tiro con arco**
architect **el arquitecto**
ardor **el ardor**
arm **el brazo**
arms **las armas**
arrive, to **llegar**
arrogance **la arrogancia**
artist **el artista**
ascend, to **ascender**
ascend, to **subir**
ask, to **preguntar**
asleep **dormido**
associate **el socio**
association **la asociación**
astral **astral**
astronaut **el astronauta**
at least **siquiera**
athlete **el atleta**
Atlantic **Atlántico**
atrocity **la atrocidad**
attend to **atender, asistir**
attention **la atención**
attorney, lawyer **el abogado**
attract, to **atraer**
attractive **atractivo**
attractive, flattering **halagüeño**
auditor **el auditor**

aunt **la tía**
Australia **Australia**
Australian **australiano**
Austria **Austria**
Austrian **austriaco**
authentic **auténtico**
author **el autor**
automobile **el auto**
autumn, fall **el otoño**
avenue **la avenida**
avoidable **evitable**
awake **despierto**
back **atrás, de vuelta**
back of . . . (at/in the) **al fondo de(l) . . .**
backgammon **el chaquete**
badminton **el bádminton**
badminton, steering wheel **el volante**
baggage **el equipaje**
bakery **la panadería**
bald **calvo**
barb **la púa**
barber **el peluquero**
barkeeper **el tabernero**
baron **el barón**
baseball **el béisbol**
basketball **el baloncesto**
basketball **el básquetbol**
be able (to) **poder**
be acquainted, to **conocer**
be born, to **nacer**
be ungrateful (for) **desagradecer**
be valued **valer**
be, to **estar, ser**
beating, (a) **el vapuleo**
beautiful **bello**
beautiful, handsome **hermoso**
because **porque**
beef steak **el bistec**

beg, to plead **rogar**

begin, to **comenzar**

begin, to **empezar**

behind . . . **detrás de . . .**

Belgian **belga (masc. y fem.)**

Belgium **Bélgica**

believe, to **creer**

beloved **querido**

beneficial **beneficial**

bet, to; post, to **apostar**

better **mejor**

beverage **la bebida**

beyond . . . **más allá de . . .**

bicycle **la bicicleta**

big, large **grande**

bilingual **bilingüe**

billiards **el billar**

billion **mil millones**

biodegradable **biodegra-dable**

biography **la biografía**

bird **el pájaro; el ave**

black **negro**

blackberry **la zarzamora**

blind **ciego**

block, to **obstruir**

blond(e) **rubio**

blouse **la blusa**

blow/hit **el golpe**

blunt, rude **brusco**

boating **pasear en barco**

body **el cuerpo**

bodybuilding **el fisicultu-rismo**

boil, to **hervir, cocer**

bold **audaz**

bone **el hueso**

book **el libro**

booklet **la guía**

bore, to **aburrir**

boring **aburrido**

both **ambos**

bothersome person **molestoso**

bowling **los bolos**

box, to **boxear**

boy, child **el niño**

boyfriend **el novio, el enamo-rado**

brake, to **frenar**

bravery **la bravura**

break, to **quebrar**

break, to **romper**

breed and rear, to **criar**

brevity **la brevedad**

brilliant **brillante**

bring, to **traer**

British **británico**

brother **el hermano**

brother-in-law **el cuñado**

brother-in-law's spouse **la concuñada**

bruised **golpeado**

brutality **la brutalidad**

Burma **Birmania**

Burmese **birmano**

burn **quemar**

bury, to **enterrar**

bus **el autobús**

business **el negocio**

busy **ocupado**

but **pero**

cable **el cable**

calculable **calculable**

calculate, to **calcular**

Californian **californiano**

call (oneself), to **llamar(se)**

calm **tranquilo**

calmed **sosegado**

Cambodia **Cambodia**

Cambodian **camboyano**

Canada **Canadá**

Canadian **canadiense**

capable **capaz**

capacity **la capacidad**

capital of a city **la capital**

capitalism **el capitalismo**

capitalist **el capitalista**

capricious **caprichoso**

car **el automóvil, el coche, el carro**

car racing **el automo-vilismo**

cards **las cartas**

care for **cuidar**

caress, to **acariciar**

cargo **el bagaje**

carry out **cumplir**

carry, to wear **llevar**

cashier **el cajero**

cassette deck **la pletina**

cassette player **el tocacasete**

cassette recorder **la graba-dora de casete**

cat **el gato**

catastrophe **la catástrofe**

cathedral **la catedral**

CD player **el reproductor de discos compactos**

CD player **el tocadiscos de CDs**

CD-RW drive **la regrabadora de CDs**

celebrity **la celebridad**

censor **el censor**

central **central**

cereal **el cereal**

certain, true **cierto**

challenge **el reto**

chaos **el caos**

charity **la institución de beneficencia**

chat, to **platicar**

check **la cuenta**

check, to **revisar**

checkers **las damas**

cheese **el queso**

chemical engineer **el in-geniero químico**

chess **el ajedrez**

chest **el baúl**

chewing gum **el chicle**

child, son **el hijo**

childhood **la niñez**

childish **aniñado**

China **China**

Chinese **chino**

chocolate **el chocolate**

choke, to **atragantar**

cholera **el cólera**

choose, to **escoger, optar**

choose decisively, to **elegir**

chop (pork) **la chuleta**

Christian **cristiano**

Christmas card **la tarjeta de Navidad**

circumstance **la circuns-tancia**

citizen **el ciudadano**

city **la ciudad**

clarify, to **clarificar**

clarity **la claridad**

class **la clase**

clean **limpio**

clear **claro**

clerk **dependiente**

close to . . . **cerca de . . .**

close, to **cerrar**

closed **cerrado**

clothes **la ropa**

cloud **la nube**

cloudy **nublado**

coconut **el coco**

coffin **el ataúd**

coin **la moneda**

coincide, to **coincidir**

cold **el frío**

color **el color**

coma **el coma**

combat, to **combatir**

come, to **venir**

comet **el cometa**

comma **la coma**

command, request **la orden**

commentary **el comentario**

commercial **comercial**

community **la comunidad**

compact disc **el disco com-pacto**

companion **el compañero**

company **la compañía**

compete, to **competir**

competitor **el competidor**

complain, to **quejarse**

complaint **la queja**

complexion, skin **la tez**

compose/edit (to) **redactar**

comprehensible **comprensible**

concert **el concierto**

concur, to **concurrir**

condition, to **acondicionar**

conductor, driver **el conductor**

confess, to **confesar**

confessor **confesor**

confuse, to **confundir**

confusion **la confusión**

congested, head cold **cons-tipado**

conquer, to **vencer**

conscience **la consciencia**

consecutive **consecutivo**

conservatism **el conserva-dorismo**

console **la consola**

consonant **la consonante**

constant **constante**

construct, to **construir**

consume, to **consumir**

contagious **contagioso**

continue, to **continuar**

contract, to **contraer**

contradictory **contradictorio**

contrary **contrario**

contribute, to **contribuir**

convert, to **convertir**

convertible **convertible**

cordial **cordial**

corn **el maíz**

corner **el rincón**

correct, to **corregir**

cough **la tos**

country **el país**

course **el curso**

court **la corte**

courteous **cortés, gentil**

cousin **primo, la prima**

cover, lid **la tapa**

cover, to **cubrir**

covered (with clouds) **cubierto**

cow **la vaca**

cramp **el calambre**

crane **la grúa**

crazy, outgoing **loco**

create, to **crear**

cricket **el criquet**

crime **el crimen**

crime **el delito**

criminal **criminal, reo**

crisis **la crisis**

cross, to **cruzar**

CD-ROM player **la unidad de CD-ROM**

cruel **cruel**

culinary **culinario**

cultural **cultural**

culture **la cultura**

cup, bowl **la taza**

curable **curable**

cure, the **la cura**

curiosity **la curiosidad**

curious **curioso**

curtain **la cortina**

custom **la costumbre**

customs **la aduana**

cut, the **el corte**

cycling **el ciclismo**

cyclist **el ciclista**

cynical **cínico**

Czech **checo**

Czech Republic **República Checa**

daddy **el papi**

daily **el diario**

dance **el baile**

dance, to **bailar**

Dane, Danish **danés, danesa**

danger **el peligro**

dark, obscure **oscuro**

dark-haired **moreno**

darts **los dardos**

DAT recorder **la pletina digi-tal**

daughter **la hija**

daughter-in-law **la hija política, la nuera**

day **el día**

day after tomorrow **pasado mañana**

day before yesterday **anteayer**

dead **muerto**

debate, to **debatir**

debt **la deuda**

December **diciembre**

decide, to **decidir**

decision **la decisión**

decorated **decorado**

defend, to **defender**

defensive **defensivo**

define, to **definir**

delegated **delegado**

delicious **delicioso**

delighted **encantado**

demand **la exigencia**

demand, to **exigir**

democratic **democrático**

demonstrate, to **demostrar**

Denmark **Dinamarca**

dentist **el dentista**

deny, refuse **negar**

depend, to **depender**

despotism **el despotismo**

deserve, to **merecer**

designer **el diseñador**

desire, crave **apetecer**

desire, to crave **introducir**

desire/wish **el deseo**

desktop **la sobremesa**

destroy, to **destruir**

destroyer **el destructor**

detective novel **la novela policiaca**

detector **el detector**

dialect **el dialecto**

dice **los dados**

dictionary **el diccionario**

difference **la diferencia**

different **diferente**

difficult **difícil**

digestible **digestible**

dignitary **dignatario**

dignity **la dignidad**

dinner **la cena**

director **el director**

disappear, to **desaparecer**

discern, to **discernir**

discuss, to **discutir**

disgusted, angered at some-one **enfadado**

diskette drive **la disquetera**

diskette drive slot **la ranura de la disquetera**

disobey, to **desobedecer**

disrespectful **caradura**

distract, to **distraer**

dive, to **zambullir**

diving **el buceo**

dizzy **mareado**

do, to be, to make **hacer**

doctor **el médico**

dog **el perro**

dogmatism **dogmatismo**

dollar **el dólar**

domineering **autoritario**

dominoes **el dominó**

door **la puerta**

downstairs **abajo**

drain **el desagüe**

drastic **drástico**

draw or take out, to **sacar**

draw, to **dibujar**

drawer **el cajón**

dream, sleep, sleepiness **el sueño**

dream, to **soñar**

dress **el vestido**

dress, to **vestir**

dressmaker **el modista**

drink, to **beber**

drive, to **conducir**

drive away, to **ahuyentar**

drizzle, to **lloviznar**

drizzling **la llovizna**

drunk **ebrio, borracho**

dry-cure, to **acecinar**

durable **durable**

during **durante**

during the day **de día**

Dutch **holandés, holandesa**

duty **la obligación, el deber**

DVD player **el lector de DVDs**

each, every **cada**

each one **cada uno, cada una**

eagle **el águila**

easily **fácilmente**

easy **fácil**

eat, to **comer**

ecstasy **el éxtasis**

editor **el editor**

educational **educacional**

effort **el esfuerzo**

egg **el huevo**

egotism **el egoísmo**

Egypt **Egipto**

Egyptian **egipcio**

eight **ocho**

eighteen **dieciocho**

eighth **octavo**

eighty **ochenta**

elderly **el anciano**

electrical outlet **el enchufe de corriente**

elegance **la elegancia**

elegant **elegante**
elephant **el elefante**
eleven **once**
embarrassed **avergonzado**
embellish, to **embellecer**
embrace, to **abrazar**
emerge, to **emerger**
emigrated **emigrado**
emissary **el emisario**
emit or give off, to **emitir**
emotional **emocional**
emotional relief **el desahogo**
emphasis **el énfasis**
employment **el empleo**
empty, to **vaciar**
enamored **enamorado**
encounter, to **encontrar**
England **Inglaterra**
English **inglés, inglesa**
enjoy, to **disfrutar**
enjoy, to **gozar**
enrich, to **enriquecer**
enter, to **entrar**
episode **el episodio**
equal **igual**
equality **la igualdad**
equipment **el equipo**
error **el error**
escape **la huída**
essence **la esencia**
essential **esencial**
establish, to **establecer**
eternity **la eternidad**
Ethiopia **Etiopía**
Ethiopian **etiope**
euphoria **la euforia**
Europe **Europa**
European **europeo**
evangelism **evangelismo**
even **aun**
eviction **desahucio**
evidence **la evidencia**
exactly **exactamente**
exam **el examen**
example **el ejemplo**
excellent **excelente**
executive **el ejecutivo**
executive assistant **el asistente ejecutivo**

exercise **el ejercicio**
exhale, to **exhalar**
exhausted **agotado**
exhibit, to **exhibir**
existence **la existencia**
expansion **la ampliación**
explain, to **explicar**
explainable **explicable**
explosive **explosivo**
export, to **exportar**
extend, to **extender**
extension cord **la extensión**
exterior ear **la oreja**
extinguish, to **extinguir**
extraordinary **extraordinario**
extreme sports **la aventura**
eye **el ojo**
fabric **la tela**
façade **la fachada**
facial gesture **el gesto**
fact, deed **el hecho**
fairy tale **el cuento de hadas**
fake, to **fingir**
fall **la caída**
fall, to **caer**
falsifiable **falseable**
fame **la fama**
famous **famoso**
far **lejos**
far from . . . **lejos de . . .**
fasten, to **fijar**
fat **gordo**
fatal **fatal, mortal**
father **el padre, el papá**
father-in-law **el suegro**
favor **el favor**
favor, to **favorecer**
fear **temer**
fearful **temeroso**
February **febrero**
federal **federal**
feel, to **sentir**
fencing **la esgrima**
fervor **el fervor**
fever **la fiebre**
feverish **febril**
fierceness **la ferocidad**
fifteen **quince**
fifth **quinto**

fifty **cincuenta**
fight **la pelea**
fighter, wrestler **el luchador**
Filipino **Filipino**
fill out, to **rellenar**
finally **finalmente**
find, to **hallar**
finger **el dedo**
fingernail **la uña**
finish, to **acabar**
Finland **Finlandia**
Finlander **finlandés, finlandesa**
fireman **el bombero**
firm, company **la empresa**
first **primer**
first born **el primogénito, la primogénita**
first cousin **el primo hermano, la prima hermana**
first draft, outline **el esbozo**
fish **el pez**
fishing **la pesca**
fist **el puño**
fit (into), to **caber**
five **cinco**
flash with lightning, to **relampaguear**
flee, to **huir**
flesh, meat **la carne**
floor **el piso**
flower or flourish, to **florecer**
fly, to **volar**
follow, to **seguir**
following **siguiente**
foot **el pie**
football **el fútbol americano**
for (time frame) **desde hace**
for, to **para**
forehead **la frente**
foreigner **el extranjero**
forget, to **olvidar**
fork **tenedor**
fortunately **afortunadamente**
forty **cuarenta**
four **cuatro**
fourteen **catorce**
fourth **cuarto**
fracture **la fractura**

fragility **la fragilidad**
frame **el marco**
France **Francia**
freeze, to **helar**
freezing **el helado**
French **francés, francesa**
frequent **frecuente**
frequent a place, to **acudir**
frequently **frecuentemente**
fresh **fresco**
Friday **viernes**
friend **el amigo**
friendly **amistoso**
frightened **asustado**
front, in **enfrente**
front line (in battle) **el frente**
frozen **congelado**
fruit **la fruta**
fry, to **freír**
full **lleno**
full of life **lleno de vida**
fundamental **fundamental**
funny **cómico**
furniture **los muebles**
fuse, to cast **fundir**
future **el futuro**
garage **el garaje**
garlic **el ajo**
gather, to **recoger**
gathering **la reunión**
generally **generalmente**
generous **generoso**
German **alemán, alemana**
Germany **Alemania**
gift **el obsequio, el regalo**
girl **la niña**
girlfriend **la novia, la enamorada**
give, to **dar**
glass **el vaso**
glory **la gloria**
glossary **el glosario**
gluttonous **tragantón**
go, to **ir**
goddaughter **la ahijada**
godfather to one's child, friend **el padrino**
godmother to one's child, friend **la madrina**

godson **el ahijado**

gold **el oro**

golf **el golf**

good **bueno**

good for **bueno para**

good, kind **bondadoso**

goodness **la bondad**

gourmet cooking **la cocina gastronómica**

grade **la calificación, la nota**

grand, great **gran, grande**

granddaughter **la nieta**

grandfather, grandpa **el abuelo, el abuelito**

grandmother, grandma **la abuela, la abuelita**

grandson **el nieto**

grapevine **la parra**

grasp or grab, to **coger**

Great Britain **Gran Bretaña**

Greece **Grecia**

Greek **griego**

grow, to **crecer**

grow dark (at night), to **anochecer**

grow light (at dawn), to **amanecer**

grow old, to **envejecer**

guest **el huésped**

guitar **la guitarra**

gymnastics **la gimnasia**

habit **el hábito**

hail, to **granizar**

hair **el cabello, el pelo**

Haiti **Haití**

Haitian **haitiano**

hamburger **la hamburguesa**

hand **la mano**

hand over, to **entregar**

hand over, to **rendir**

handball **el balonmano**

hang gliding **el vuelo en ala delta**

handsome **guapo**

hang, to **colgar**

happy **feliz**

hard drive light **la luz del disco duro**

have, to **tener, haber (aux.)**

he **él**

head **la cabeza**

headphone jack **el conector de auriculares**

headphones **los auriculares**

health **la salud**

hear, to **oír**

heat (up), to **calentar**

heat **el calor**

height **la altura**

height **la estatura**

help **la ayuda**

help oneself, to **ayudar(se)**

here **aquí**

hereditary **hereditario**

hi **hola**

hiccup **el hipo**

Hi-fi system **el equipo de alta fidelidad**

hinder, to **impedir**

historical novel **la novela histórica**

Holland **Holanda**

homeowner **el dueño (de casa)**

honorable **honorable**

honorable **honrado**

hope or wait for, to **esperar**

horse **el caballo**

horseback riding **la equitación**

horticulture **la horticultura**

hospital **el hospital**

hot **caluroso**

hotel **el hotel**

house, home **la casa**

how **cómo**

howl or shriek, to **aullar**

humid **húmedo**

humility **la humildad**

humor **el humor**

hunger **el hambre**

hurt **lastimado**

husband **el esposo**

husband **el marido**

hydraulic system **el sistema hidráulico**

I **yo**

ice-skating **el patinaje sobre hielo**

idea **la idea**

ideal **ideal**

idealism **el idealismo**

idealist **idealista**

if **si**

illegal **ilegal**

ill-mannered **mal educado**

impatience **la impaciencia**

impatient **impaciente**

import, to, or to cause to matter **importar**

important **importante**

impoverish, to **empobrecer**

impregnate, to **embarazar**

impressionism **el impresionismo**

in agreement **de acuerdo**

in fashion **de moda**

in front of . . . **delante de . . .**

incendiary **el incendiario**

incentive **el incentivo**

incomparable **incomparable**

increase **el aumento**

independence **la independencia**

India **India**

Indian **indio**

individualism **el individualismo**

inevitable **inevitable**

infancy **la infancia**

inferior **inferior**

influenza **la gripe**

inform, to **informar**

information **la información**

inhibit, to **cohibir**

injure, to **herir**

innocence **la inocencia**

inquire, to **averiguar**

inside **adentro**

insistence **la insistencia**

inspector **el inspector**

instructor **el instructor**

internal ear **el oído**

internist **internista**

interrupt, to **interrumpir**

intolerance **la intolerancia**

invent, to **inventar**

inventor **el inventor**

inventory analyst **el analista de inventario**

inversion **la inversión**

investment advisor **el consejero de inversiones**

invitation **la invitación**

invited **invitado**

Iran **Irán**

Iranian **iraní (masc. y fem.)**

Iraq **Iraq**

Iraqi **iraquí (masc. y fem.)**

Ireland **Irlanda**

Irish **irlandés, irlandesa**

iron (metal) **el hierro**

iron (appliance) **la plancha**

irritable **irritable**

isolate, to **aislar**

Israel **Israel**

Israeli **israelí (masc. y fem.)**

Italian **italiano**

Italy **Italia**

jail **la cárcel**

Jamaica **Jamaica**

Jamaican **jamaicano**

January **enero**

Japan **Japón**

Japanese **japonés, japonesa**

jaw **la quijada**

jealous **celoso**

Jerusalemite **jerosolimitano**

jewel **la joya**

jog **trotear**

joke **la chanza, el chiste**

journalist **el periodista**

jovial, jolly **jovial**

judge **el juez**

July **julio**

June **junio**

justice **la justicia**

karate **el kárate**

kerosene **el keroseno**

keyboard **el teclado**

kilogram **el kilo, el kilógramo**

kilometer **el kilómetro**

kind, amiable **amable**

kinesiology **la kinesiología**

king **el rey**
kingdom **el reino**
kinship **el parentesco**
kite **la cometa**
kneeling **de rodillas**
knife **el cuchillo**
knit, to **tejer**
know, to **saber**
Korea **Corea**
Korean **coreano**
Kurd, Kurdish **kurdo**
lake **el lago**
lamentable **lamentable**
land/field **el terreno**
landscape **el paisaje**
language **el idioma, el lenguaje**
laser printer **la impresora láser**
last **último**
last name **el apellido**
last week **la semana pasada**
last year **el año pasado**
late **atrasado**
later **después**
laugh **reír(se)**
law **la ley**
lawn **el césped**
laziness **la pereza**
lead **el plomo**
learned/expert **el docto**
leather strap **la correa**
leave or go out, to **salir**
left of . . . (to the) **a la izquierda de . . .**
left side, on the **a mano izquierda**
legitimate **legítimo**
letter **la carta**
liberalism **el liberalismo**
license plate **la placa [or "la matrícula" for car]**
lie, deceive, to **mentir**
life **la vida**
light (adj.) **claro**
light(s) **la luz, las luces**
light or turn on, to **encender**
lightning **el relámpago**

lightning flash **el relampagueo**
limit, to **restringir**
line **la raya**
lineage **linaje**
linguistics **la lingüística**
lion's mane **la guedeja**
listen (to), to **escuchar**
listing **la cartelera**
literary **literario**
literature **la literatura**
little **poco**
live well, to **bienvivir**
living room **la sala**
local **local**
logical **lógico**
look (for), to **buscar**
look at, to watch **mirar**
lose, to **perder**
lottery **la lotería**
love **el amor**
love, to **amar**
loving **cariñoso**
luck **la suerte**
lunch **el almuerzo**
lunch, to **almorzar**
lute **el laúd**
Lutheran **luterano**
lying on the back **de espaldas**
machine **la máquina**
magazine **la revista**
magnetism **el magnetismo**
make a mistake, to **cometer un error**
make abstract, to **abstraer**
male **varón**
manager **el gerente**
many times **muchas veces**
map **el mapa**
March **marzo**
marine **el marino**
marketing consultant **el consultor de mercadeo**
married **casado**
marry, to **casar(se)**
martial arts **las artes marciales**
massage **el masaje**

materialism **el materialismo**
mattress **el colchón**
mature, ripe, wise **maduro**
May **mayo**
measles **el sarampión**
measure **la tasa**
measure, to **medir**
mechanic(al) **el mecánico**
medium **mediano**
medium height **la estatura mediana**
melancholic **melancólico**
member **el miembro**
mentally **mentalmente**
mentor **el mentor**
menu **el menú**
merchant **el mercader**
mercy **la merced**
mess **el lío**
meter **el metro**
meticulous **meticuloso**
Mexican **mexicano**
Mexico **México**
microphone jack **el conector de micrófono**
mid-range speaker **el altavoz de sonidos medios**
million **el millón**
millionaire **el millonario**
mine **mío(s), mía(s)**
minimum **mínimo**
mischievous **travieso**
miserable **miserable**
missionary **el misionario**
modem **el módem**
mom **la mamá**
mommy **la mami**
Monday **lunes**
monitor **el monitor**
moon **la luna**
moralist **moralista**
more **más**
morning **la mañana**
mortgage banker **el banquero hipotecario**
mosquito **el mosquito**
mother **la madre**
mother-in-law **la suegra**

motor **el motor**
mountain **la montaña**
mountain climbing **el alpinismo**
mountain sports **el montañismo**
mouse **el ratón**
moved, touched **emocionado**
movie multiplex **el multicine**
much, a lot **mucho**
mumps **las paperas**
murder, to **asesinar**
music teacher **el profesor de música**
music **la música**
musical **musical**
musician **el músico**
my **mi(s)**
nail **el clavo**
nail, to **clavar**
name **el nombre**
national **nacional**
nationalism **el nacionalismo**
nationality **la nacionalidad**
natural **natural**
naturally **naturalmente**
near **cerca**
necessarily **necesariamente**
necessary **necesario**
neck **el cuello**
need, to **necesitar**
negative **negativo**
negotiable **negociable**
neighbor **el vecino**
neither **tampoco**
nephew **el sobrino**
nervous **nervioso**
neutral **neutral**
never **nunca**
news **las noticias**
newspaper **el periódico**
next **próximo**
next week **la próxima semana**
next year **el próximo año**
nice weather **el buen tiempo**
niece **la sobrina**
night (after sunset) **la noche**
nine **nueve**

nineteen **diecinueve**
ninety **noventa**
ninth **noveno**
no **no**
no one **nadie**
noise **el ruido**
noon **el mediodía**
normally **normalmente**
North
American **norteamericano**
Norway **Noruega**
Norwegian **noruego**
noun **el sustantivo**
not to recognize **desconocer**
notebook computer **el ordenador/la computadora portátil**
novelist **el novelista**
November **noviembre**
now **ahora**
oasis **el oasis**
obey, to **obedecer**
obtain, to **conseguir**
obviously **obviamente**
October **octubre**
of, from **de**
of the **del**
of the age of maturity **mayor de edad**
offend, to **ofender**
offer, to **ofrecer**
official **oficial**
often **a menudo**
oil painting **la pintura al óleo**
old **antiguo, viejo**
older **mayor**
olive **la aceituna**
omission **la omisión**
on button **botón de encendido**
on duty **de guardia**
on one's way back **de regreso**
on top **sobre**
once in a while **de vez en cuando**
one **uno**
only **solo (adv.), único (adj.)**
open, to **abrir**

opened **abierto**
operate, to **operar**
opinion **la opinión**
opponent **el opositor**
opportunity **la oportunidad**
oppose, to **oponer**
optimist **optimista**
orange **la naranja**
order **la orden**
ordinary **ordinario**
organic **orgánico**
organizable **organizable**
original **original**
ostensible **ostensible**
other, another **otro**
our **nuestro(s)**
outside **afuera**
over, on top of . . . **sobre . . .**
over here **acá**
overcome, to **sobrevivir**
overshoe, corn **el choclo**
own **propio**
pacifist **el pacífico**
pain **el dolor**
paint, to **pintar**
Pakistan **Paquistán**
Pakistani **paquistaní (masc. y fem.)**
pale **pálido**
paper **el papel**
parachuting **el paracaidismo**
paragliding **el parapente**
park **el parque**
park, to **estacionar**
partial **parcial**
participate, to **participar**
pass, to elapse **transcurrir**
passable **pasable**
pastor **el pastor**
pastry maker **el repostero**
paternal **paterno**
pathetic **patético**
patient **el paciente**
patriotism **el patriotismo**
pay (for), to **pagar**
pediatrician **el pediatra**
pen **el bolígrafo**
penguin **el pingüino**

people **la gente**
percentage **el porcentaje**
perfectly **perfectamente**
performance, show **el espectáculo**
perfume with incense, to **sahumar**
perhaps **quizás**
permit, to **permitir**
person **la persona**
person from a non-Spanish country **el gringo**
person who guides **el guía**
person with doctorate, Ph.D. **el doctor**
personally **personalmente**
pet **la mascota**
Philippines **Filipinas**
phoenix **el fénix**
phonograph **el fonógrafo**
physical, physicist **físico**
physician **el médico**
physics **la física**
pianist **el pianista**
piano **el piano**
piece **el pedazo**
pilot **el piloto**
pity/mercy **la piedad**
place, to put **poner**
plan **el plan**
planting **el plantaje**
play a sport or game, to **jugar**
playful **juguetón**
pleasant **genial**
pleasant, gentle **apacible**
pleasant weather **agradable**
please, to **gustar**
pleasure **gusto**
plum **la ciruela**
plumage **el plumaje**
poem **el poema**
poetry **la poesía**
poker **el póquer**
Poland **Polonia**
police force **la policía**
police officer **el, la policía**
Polish **polaco**
polish, to **pulir**

poncho, cape **el poncho**
pond **el estanque**
poor **pobre**
popular **popular**
portable stereo **el radiocasete portátil**
portrait **el retrato**
possession **la posesión**
possibility **la posibilidad**
possible **posible**
possibly **posiblemente**
posture **la postura**
potent **potente**
potty mouth **malhablado**
pound **la libra**
power **poder**
power switch **el interruptor**
practical joke **la broma**
practice (a trade), to **ejercer**
practice, to **practicar**
pray, to **rezar**
precisely **precisamente**
prefer, to **preferir**
preferable **preferible**
preference **la preferencia**
pregnant **embarazada**
prepare, to **preparar**
prepared **listo**
Presbyterian **presbiteriano**
presentable **presentable**
president **el presidente**
pretentious **cursi, pretencioso**
pretty **bonito**
priest **el sacerdote; el cura**
primary **primario**
principally **principalmente**
probably **probablemente**
problem **el problema**
proceed, to **proceder**
produce, to **producir**
produce an unexpected event, to **accidentar**
professor **el profesor**
programmer **el programador**
progressive **progresivo**
promise, to **prometer**
proportioned **esbelto**
protect, to **proteger**

protector **el protector**
prudent **prudente**
pumpkin **la calabaza**
purchase, to **comprar**
pursue, to **perseguir**
put (in), to **meter**
quarrel, to **reñir**
quit, to **renunciar**
race **la carrera**
radicalism **el radicalismo**
radio programming **el/la radio**
radius, the physical radio **el radio**
railway **el ferrocarril**
rain **la lluvia**
rain, to **llover**
rainy **lluvioso**
rather, said more accurately **mejor dicho**
rational **racional**
raw **crudo**
react, to **reaccionar**
read, to **leer**
ready for **listo para**
realty appraiser **el tasador de bienes inmuebles**
reason **la razón**
receive, to **recibir**
receive the needy, to **hospedar**
recipe **la receta**
reciprocate, to belong to **corresponder**
reclined **acostado**
recommend, to **recomendar**
record **el disco**
record, to **grabar**
redheaded **pelirrojo**
re-examine, to **reexaminar**
reflector **el reflector**
refuse to **rehusar**
refute, to **rebatir**
regimen **el régimen**
region **la región**
regular **regular**
reimburse, to **reembolsar**
relatively **relativamente**
release, to **soltar**
remain, to **quedar**

remember, to **recordar**
renew, to **reanudar**
rent, lease, to **arrendar**
repeat, to **repetir**
repeatedly **repetidas veces**
republican **republicano**
requirement **el requisito**
reset button **el botón de reinicio**
residence **la residencia**
resist, to tolerate **resistir**
resolve, to **resolver**
respectable **respetable**
respond (to) **contestar**
rest of my life **el resto de mi vida**
retired person **retirado**
return, to **devolver**
return, to **volver**
right of . . . (to the) **a la derecha de . . .**
right side, on the **a mano derecha**
rise early, to **madrugar**
risk **riesgo**
robust **robusto**
rodent **el roedor**
romance novel **la novela romántica**
roof **el techo**
root, origin **la raíz**
rosy **rosado**
roulette **la ruleta**
round **redondo**
rowing **el remo**
rub, to **fregar**
ruby **el rugby**
rule **la regla**
ruminate, to **rumiar**
rummy **rumiante**
rumor **el rumor**
run **correr**
rye **el centeno**
sad **triste**
sadness **la tristeza**
sailing **la navegación**
sailing **la vela**
sail, to **navegar**

sailing by light canoe **el piragüismo**
saint **el santo**
salary **el salario**
salary **el sueldo**
salesperson **el vendedor**
same time, at the **a la vez**
Santa Claus **Papá Noel**
satisfied **contento**
satisfy, to **satisfacer**
Saturday **sábado**
Saudi Arabia **Arabia Saudita**
Saudi Arabian **saudita**
say, to **decir**
scab **la roña**
scale **la escala**
scanner **el escáner**
scar **la cicatriz**
school **la escuela**
science fiction novel **la novela de ciencia ficción**
scientific **científico**
Scotland **Escocia**
Scottish **escocés, escocesa**
screen **la pantalla**
scuba dive, to **bucear**
scuba diving **el buceo**
sculpture **la escultura**
seated **sentado**
second **segundo**
second cousin **primo segundo**
secondary **secundario**
sedentary **inactivo**
seducer **el seductor**
see, to **ver**
see off or fire, to **despedir**
seem, to appear **parecer**
seize, to **asir**
seldom **contadas veces**
self-esteem **la autoestima**
selfish **egoísta**
sell **vender**
send, to **enviar**
send, to **remitir**
sensational **sensacional**
September **septiembre**
series **la serie**
serious **serio**
serpent **la serpiente**

serve, to **servir**
seven **siete**
seventeen **diecisiete**
seventh **séptimo**
seventy **sesenta**
several times **varias veces**
sew, to **coser**
sew or stitch, to **coser**
shame **la vergüenza**
shame, to **avergonzar**
shameless person **sinvergüenza**
shave, to **afeitar**
she **ella**
shelf **la repisa**
shine, to brighten **lucir**
shirt **la camisa**
shoe **el zapato**
shooting **el tiro a fusil**
short **bajo**
show, to exhibit **mostrar**
sick **enfermo**
sick with a cold **tener un resfriado**
sickly **enfermizo**
sickness **la enfermedad**
side of (to the), next to **al lado de(l) . . .**
sieve, to **cernir**
simple **simple**
since **desde**
sing, to **cantar**
singer **el cantante**
single **soltero**
sister **la hermana**
sister-in-law **la cuñada**
sister-in-law's spouse **el concuñado**
six **seis**
sixteen **dieciséis**
sixth **sexto**
sixty **setenta**
skate (over ice), to **patinar (sobre el hielo)**
skating **patinaje**
skiing **el esquí**
skillful **hábil**
skin **la piel**
sky **el cielo**

Slav **eslavo**
slippers **las chanclas**
small **pequeño**
small mare **la yegüita**
smell **el olor**
smell, to **oler**
smile, to **sonreír**
snack, to **merendar**
snob **esnob**
snowing **la nieve**
snowy **nevado**
so many times **tantas veces**
so much **tanto**
soap **el jabón**
sober **sobrio**
soccer **el fútbol**
socialism **el socialismo**
software developer **el diseñador de software**
sole **la suela**
solitaire **solitario**
solitude **la soledad**
sometimes **algunas veces**
song **la canción**
son-in-law **el hijo político, el yerno**
soon **pronto**
sorrow **el duelo**
so-so **así así**
soul **el alma**
South Africa **Sudáfrica**
South African **sudafricano**
Spanish (from Castille) **castellano**
sparrow **el gorrión**
speak, to **hablar**
speaker **el altavoz**
speaker jack **el conector de altavoces**
special **especial**
specialist **el especialista**
spirit **el espíritu**
sponsor, to **auspiciar**
spring **la primavera**
sprinkle, to **salpicar**
standing **de pie**
standing **parado**
state **el estado**

stepbrother **el hermanastro**
stepdaughter **la hijastra**
stepfather **el padrastro**
stepmother **la madrastra**
stepsister **la hermanastra**
stepson, stepchild **el hijastro**
stereo system **el equipo estereofónico**
stew **el guisado**
stick **la porra, el palo**
stolen **robado**
stop, parade **la parada**
store, to **guardar**
store, warehouse **el almacén**
stork **la cigüeña**
story **el cuento**
strange **extraño**
stroll through, to **pasear**
strong **fuerte**
student **el estudiante**
study, to **estudiar**
stunned **atontado**
stupendously **estupendamente**
style **el estilo**
submit or surrender, to **ceder**
suffer, to **padecer, sufrir**
suitcase **la maleta**
sum of money (business) **el capital**
sum up, to **resumir**
summer **el verano**
Sunday **domingo**
sunflower **el girasol**
sunny **sol**
superior **superior**
supervisor **el supervisor**
support **el apoyo**
surfing **el surf**
surge protector **el filtro protector**
surprise, to **sorprender**
swallow, to **tragar**
sway, to rock **mecer**
sweat, to **sudar**
Sweden **Suecia**
Swedish **sueco**
sweet **dulce**

swim, to **nadar**
swimming **la natación**
Swiss **suizo**
Switzerland **Suiza**
syllable **la sílaba**
synthesis **la síntesis**
Syria **Siria**
Syrian **sirio**
table tennis **el tenis de mesa**
tail **el rabo**
tailor **el sastre**
take, to **tomar**
take a trip on a boat **dar paseo en barco**
take away, to **quitar**
take on, to **abarcar**
talented **talentoso**
tall **alto**
tar **la pez**
taxi **el taxi**
teach, to **enseñar**
teacher **el maestro**
telephone **el teléfono**
telephone, to **telefonear, llamar por teléfono**
temperature **la temperatura**
ten **diez**
tennis **el tenis**
tenor **el tenor**
tenth **décimo**
terrorism **el terrorismo**
Texan **texano**
Thailand **Tailandia**
Thailandese **tailandés, tailandesa**
thank (for), to **agradecer**
that **eso**
that **que**
that (at a distance) **aquel**
that is **o sea**
the **el, la**
there is/are **hay**
they **ellos, ellas**
thick, stout **grueso**
thin **delgado**
thin, skinny **flaco**
thing **la cosa**
think, to **pensar**
third **tercero**

thirst **la sed**
thirsty **sediento**
thirteen **trece**
thirty **treinta**
this time **esta vez**
this week **esta semana**
this year **este año**
three **tres**
throw out, to **echar**
thunder, to **tronar**
Thursday **jueves**
ticket **el boleto**
tiger **el tigre**
tighten, to **apretar**
time(s) **vez, veces**
time, epoch **la época**
time, on **a tiempo**
tinged **el tinto**
tired **cansado**
to **a**
today **hoy**
tolerance **la tolerancia**
toll **el peaje**
tomato **el tomate**
tomorrow **mañana**
tongue-twister **el trabalenguas**
too, overly **demasiado**
tornado **el tornado**
touch or play, to **tocar**
tour on bicycle, to **dar paseo en bicicleta**
tourist **el turista**
toward **hacia**
towel **la toalla**
tower, tower console **la torre**
town, village **el pueblo**
trace **la huella**
track and field **el atletismo**
traditional **tradicional**
trail, hint **la pista**
translate, to **traducir**
transmit, to **trasmitir**
travel, to **viajar**
treat informally, to **tutear**
tree **el árbol**
trillion **el billón**
trip, on a **de viaje**
trousers **los pantalones**

trust, or to lend **fiar**
truth **la verdad**
tube **el tubo**
Tuesday **martes**
tune, to **sintonizar**
tuner **sintonizador**
Turk, Turkish **turco**
Turkey **Turquía**
turn back, to **retroceder**
turn off, to **apagar**
turntable **el tocadiscos (analógico)**
tweeter **el altavoz de sonidos agudos**
twelve **doce**
twenty **veinte**
two **dos**
U.S. citizen **estadounidense**
U.S.A. **EE. UU.**
ugly **feo**
under(neath) **debajo**
under... **debajo de ...**
understand, to **comprender, entender**
undressed **desnudo**
unharmed **ileso**
unite, to **unir**
United States **Estados Unidos**
universal **universal**
unload, to **descargar**
unpleasant **antipático**
upstairs **arriba**
use, to **usar**
useful **útil**
usual **usual**
usually **usualmente**
vacation, on **de vacaciones**
valor **el valor**
vandalism **el vandalismo**
various **varios**
vegetables **las verduras**
vegetarian **vegetariano**
velocity **la velocidad**
velvet **el terciopelo**
ventilation grill **la rejilla de ventilación**
verbo **verb**

verify or check, (to) **comprobar**
very **muy**
vice president **el vicepresidente**
video camera **la videocámara**
vigor **vigor**
visible **visible**
volleyball **el balonvolea, el voleibol**
volume **el volumen**
voluntary **el voluntario**
vowel **la vocal**
waist **la cintura**
waiter **el mesero, el mozo, el camarero**
Wales **país de Gales**
walk, to **caminar, andar**
wall **la pared**
want, or love **querer**
war **la guerra**
warn, to **advertir**
Washington **Washington**
waste, to **desperdiciar**
watch **el reloj**
watch television, to **mirar la televisión**
water **el agua**
water skiing **el esquí acuático**
weak **débil**
wedding **la boda**
Wednesday **miércoles**
weekend **el fin de semana**
weight **el peso**
weightlifting **el levantamiento de pesas**
weightlifting and strength **la halterofilia y la potencia**
well mannered **bien educado**
Welsh **galés, galesa**
what **qué**
wheat **el trigo**
wheel **la rueda**
when **cuándo**
where **dónde**

which **cuál**
while **mientras**
white **blanco**
who **quién**
whole life **toda la vida**
wide, broad **ancho**
widow **la viuda**
wife **la esposa, la mujer**
will **la voluntad**
wind **el viento**
windsurfer **el windsurfista**
windsurfing **el windsurf**
wine tasting **la cata de vino**
wink, to **guiñar**
winter **el invierno**
with **con**
without clouds **despejado**
woman **la mujer**
wood **la madera**
woofer **el altavoz de sonidos graves**
work **el trabajo**
work, product **la obra**
work, to **trabajar**
world **el mundo**
worm, caterpillar **el gusano**
worried **preocupado**
worry **la preocupación**
worse **peor**
wrap, to **envolver**
write, to **escribir**
X-ray picture **la radiografía**
xylophone **el xilófono**
year **el año**
yellow **amarillo**
yes **sí**
yesterday **ayer**
yet, still **aún**
you (familiar) **tú**
you (polite) **usted**
you all **ustedes**
young **joven**
young child **la criatura**
youngest **menor**
your (familiar) **tu(s)**
your (polite) **su(s)**

yours (familiar) **tuya(s), tuyo(s)**
yours (polite) **suya(s), suyo(s)**
youth **la juventud**
Yemen **Yemen**
Yemeni **yemení**
zero **cero**
zoo **el zoológico**

Appendix C

Spanish Idioms

Just like any other language, Spanish has phrases that, literally translated, will leave you in a state of quandary. This appendix lists some of the idioms, expressions, and common phrases found in everyday Spanish—you might be surprised to find out that many have a direct counterpart in English. Where appropriate, a sample sentence has been provided for better understanding.

A buen hambre no hay pan duro.
Literally: For good hunger there is no hard bread.
Meaning: Anything tastes good when you're hungry.

No te gustó la cena, pero te comiste todo; a buen hambre no hay pan duro.

You didn't like the meal, but ate everything; anything tastes good when you're hungry.

A causa de
Literally: As a cause of
Meaning: On account of

La fiesta se canceló a causa de un inesperado viaje.

The party was canceled on account of an unexpected trip.

A ciegas
Literally: At blind
Meaning: Blindly

Caminar en una noche tan oscura es igual que caminar a ciegas.

Walking on such a dark night is the same as walking blindly.

A ciencia cierta
Literally: At certain science
Meaning: With certainty

El maestro presenta la materia a ciencia cierta.

The teacher presents the topic with certainty.

A crédito
Literally: At credit
Meaning: On credit

Voy a comprar a crédito mi coche nuevo.

I'm going to buy my new car on credit.

A donde fueras, haz lo que vieras.
Literally: Wherever you go, do what you see.
Meaning: When in Rome, do as the Romans do.

Que tengas un buen viaje, y recuerda que donde fueras haz lo que vieras.

Have a good trip, and remember: When in Rome, do as the Romans do.

A escondidas de
Literally: Hiding from
Meaning: Without the knowledge of

Los novios se veían a escondidas de sus padres.

The couple saw each other without the knowledge of their parents.

A espaldas
Literally: At backs
Meaning: Behind one's back
El joven habló muy mal a espaldas de su amigo.
The young man spoke ill of his best friend behind his back.

A la carrera
Literally: To the race
Meaning: In haste, or hastily
Estoy de prisa y voy a tener que comer a la carrera.
I'm in a hurry and will have to eat hastily.

A la moda
Literally: At the fashion
Meaning: In the latest fashion
Ella siempre está a la moda.
She is always dressed at the latest fashion.

Al lado de
Literally: Next to
Meaning: Beside
Las dos jóvenes siempre se sientan una a lado de la otra.
The two young girls always sit beside each other.

A menudo
Literally: At often
Meaning: Often, frequently
Hay gente que viene a este restaurante muy a menudo.
There are people who come to this restaurant very frequently.

A mi entender
Literally: To my understanding
Meaning: As I understand
A mi entender, la crisis fue solamente una exageración.
As I understand, the crisis was just an exaggeration.

A mi modo de ver
Literally: To my way of seeing
Meaning: In my opinion
A mi modo de ver, la comedia no fue muy buena.
In my opinion, the comedy was not very good.

A ojos cerrados
Literally: At closed eyes
Meaning: Blindly
Ella se dejó llevar por sus amigas a ojos cerrados.
She allowed her friends to guide her blindly.

A ojos vistos
Literally: At seeing eyes
Meaning: Visibly, clearly
En la noche las estrellas se ven a ojos vistos.
At night you can see the stars clearly.

A otro perro con ese hueso.
Literally: To another dog with that bone.
Meaning: You're pulling my leg; I'm not that naïve.
No creo en tu excusa por haber llegado tarde. A otro perro con ese hueso.
I don't believe your excuse for being late. I am not that naïve.

A perder
Literally: To lose
Meaning: To spoil
La cena se va echar a perder si se queda mucho tiempo fuera.
The meal will spoil if it's left out for too long.

A pesar de que
Literally: Despite that
Meaning: In spite of the fact that, despite, even though
A pesar de que salí una hora antes de casa, todavía llegué tarde al trabajo.
Even though I left the house an hour earlier, I still arrived at work late.

A punto fijo
Literally: At a fixed point
Meaning: With certainty
El reportero habló a punto fijo.
The reporter spoke with certainty.

A ratos
Literally: At small periods of time
Meaning: From time to time, at times
A ratos se siente bien, a ratos no.
At times she feels fine, at other times she does not.

A toda hora
Literally: At all hours
Meaning: At all times
La farmacia está abierta a toda hora.
The pharmacy is open at all times.

A todo correr
Literally: At all run
Meaning: At full speed
Salió a todo correr para alcanzar al autobús.
He left at full speed to catch the bus.

A vistas
Literally: At sights
Meaning: On approval, with approval
Fue recibido a vistas buenas.
He was greeted with approval.

A vuelta de correo
Literally: At turn of mail
Meaning: By return mail
Su respuesta vendrá a vuelta de correo.
His response will arrive by return mail.

Ahora mismo
Literally: Now itself
Meaning: Right now
Necesito salir ahora mismo.
I need to leave right now.

Ahora que hay modo.
Literally: Now that there is a way or mood.
Meaning: Make hay while the sun shines.
Trabajo fuerte ahora que hay modo.
I work hard, seizing the opportunity.

Al contrario
Literally: To the contrary
Meaning: To the contrary
Al contrario, yo gané la apuesta.
To the contrary, I won the bet.

Al escape
Literally: At escape
Meaning: Rapidly or quickly
Tuve que salir al escape de la casa.
I had to leave the house quickly.

Al fin
Literally: At the end
Meaning: At last
Al fin se compró un carro nuevo.
At last he bought himself a new car.

Al final de
Literally: At the end of
Meaning: Finally, at the end of
Viene cansado al final de una jornada muy larga.
He arrives tired at the end of a long day's journey.

Al hierro caliente batir de repente.
Literally: The hot iron must be beaten at once.
Meaning: Strike while the iron's hot.
Pide un buen aumento, al hierro caliente batir de repente.
Ask for a good raise, strike while the iron is hot.

Al menos
Literally: At less
Meaning: At least
Al menos pide un nuevo uniforme.
At least ask for a new uniform.

Al pie de la letra
Literally: At the foot of the letter
Meaning: literally, to the letter
El juez aplica la ley al pie de la letra.
The judge applies the law literally to the letter.

Al sereno
Literally: At serene
Meaning: In the night air
Me gusta caminar al sereno.
I like to walk in the night air.

Algunas veces
Literally: Some times
Meaning: Sometimes
Algunas veces desayuno en ese restaurante.
Sometimes I have breakfast in that restaurant.

Ante todo
Literally: Before all
Meaning: Above all
Ante todo, sigo creyendo que ella no es culpable.
Above all, I continue to believe that she is not guilty.

Antes de que
Literally: Before of that
Meaning: Before
Antes de que vengan los invitados, me voy a cambiar de ropa.
I'm going to change clothes before the guests arrive.

Antes de que te cases, mira lo que haces.
Literally: Before you marry, look what you're doing.
Meaning: Look before you leap.
No seas muy impulsivo, antes de que te cases mira lo que haces.
Don't be so impulsive, look before you leap.

Así así
Literally: Thus-thus
Meaning: So-so
Estoy así así.
I am just so-so.

A pesar de
Literally: On the weight of
Meaning: In spite of, even so, anyhow

A pesar de los problemas seguimos luchando diariamente.

In spite of all the problems, we continue our daily struggles.

Atrás de
Literally: Behind the
Meaning: Behind

Siempre se queda atrás de los demás.

She always falls behind the rest.

Incluso cuando
Literally: Even when
Meaning: Even though

Incluso cuando tenía un paraguas me mojé.

Even though I had an umbrella, I still got wet.

Baja el/la radio.
Literally: Lower the radio.
Meaning: Turn the radio down.

Baja el/la radio, que me estás poniendo sordo.

Turn the radio down, you're making me deaf.

Beben agua en el mismo jarrito.
Literally: They drink water from the same little jug.
Meaning: They're as thick as thieves.

No te confíes de esos individuos, ellos beben agua en el mismo jarrito.

Don't trust those individuals, they are as thick as thieves.

Beber a pulso
Literally: To drink at pulse
Meaning: To gulp down

Estaba tan sediento que se bebió a pulso la botella entera de cerveza.

He was so thirsty that he gulped down the entire bottle of beer.

Cada perico a su estaca, cada changa a su mecate.
Literally: Each parrot on its perch, each monkey on its rope.
Meaning: To each his own.

No me gusta la gente con la que anda, pero cada perico a su estaca, cada changa a su mecate.

I don't like the company he keeps, but to each his own.

Cada quien tiene su manera de matar pulgas.
Literally: Each has his way to kill fleas.
Meaning: There's more than one way to skin a cat.

Yo no lo haría así, pero sí, cada quien tiene su manera de matar pulgas.

I wouldn't do it that way, but, yes, there's more than one way to skin a cat.

Cada uno
Literally: Every one
Meaning: Apiece, each one

La recompensa será de cien dólares cada uno.

The reward will be one hundred dollars apiece.

Caer en cama
Literally: To fall in bed
Meaning: To fall ill, to get sick

Me dieron escalofríos y caí en cama.

I had chills and ended up ill.

¡Cállate la boca!
Literally: Shut your mouth!
Meaning: Shut up!

¡Cállate la boca si no sabes lo que dices!

If you don't know what you are saying, shut up!

Camarón que se duerme, se lo lleva la corriente.
Literally: The shrimp that falls asleep will be carried away by the current.
Meaning: You snooze, you lose.

¡Despierta ya! Camarón que se duerme, se lo lleva la corriente.

Wake up already! You snooze, you lose.

Caras vemos, corazones no sabemos.
Literally: Faces we see, hearts we don't know.
Meaning: You can't judge a book by its cover.

No te dejes llevar por las apariencias. Caras vemos, corazones no sabemos.

Don't go by appearances, you can't judge a book by its cover.

Carne de gallina
Literally: Flesh of a hen
Meaning: Goose bumps

De pronto sentí tanto frío que la piel se me pusó como carne de gallina.

Suddenly it became so cold that I got goose bumps.

Casa de locos
Literally: House of crazy people
Meaning: Insane asylum, nut house

¿Por qué hay tanto desorden? Parece una casa de locos.

Why is there such disarray? It looks like a nut house.

Claro como el agua de Xochimilco
Literally: Clear as the water of Xochimilco
Meaning: Clear as mud
Veo todo tan claro como el agua de Xochimilco.
I see everything clear as mud.

Comer frijoles y repetir pollo
Literally: To eat beans and belch chicken
Meaning: His bark is mightier than his bite.
Grita fuerte, pero come frijoles y repite pollo.
He screams loud, but his bark is mightier than his bite.

Como el burro que tocó la flauta
Literally: Like the donkey that played the flute
Meaning: By a stroke of luck
Como el burro que tocó la flauta, nadie sufrió una herida en el accidente.
By a stroke of luck no one was injured in the accident.

Como quitarle un pelo a un gato
Literally: Like pulling a hair from a cat
Meaning: Like a drop in the bucket
Encontrar un nuevo trabajo se le hizo como quitarle un pelo a un gato.
Finding a new job became like catching a drop in the bucket.

Como si
Literally: As if
Meaning: As if
Salió como si fuera perseguido por alguien.
He left as if someone was following him.

Como último recurso
Literally: As a last resort
Meaning: As a last resort
Como último recurso, acudió a las autoridades.
She went to the authorities as a last resort.

Con anticipación
Literally: With anticipation
Meaning: In advance
Pagó su cuenta con anticipación a la fecha en la que tenía que ser pagada.
She paid her bill in advance to the due date.

Con estos bueyes hay que arar.
Literally: With these oxen one must plough.
Meaning: One must make do with what one has.
Si no tienes más, con estos bueyes hay que arar.
If you have nothing else, make do with what you have.

¡Con razón!
Literally: With reason!
Meaning: No wonder!
¡Con razón que no tengo dinero, tengo un agujero en el bolsillo!
No wonder I don't have any money, there is a hole in my pocket!

Cumplir su palabra
Literally: To fulfill one's word
Meaning: To keep one's word
Ella hace lo que sea con tal de cumplir su palabra.
She does whatever it takes to keep her word.

Dar la suave a uno
Literally: To give the smooth to someone
Meaning: To polish the apple
Algún motivo trae para dar la suave a uno.
He must have a motive to try to polish the apple.

Darle lástima
Literally: To give him/herserf pity
Meaning: To pity
A todo el mundo le da lástima ver niños abandonados.
Everyone has pity on seeing abandoned children.

Darle un beso a la botella
Literally: To give the bottle a kiss
Meaning: To take a swig
Olvida las penas y dale un beso a la botella.
Forget your sorrows and take a swig.

De la subida más alta es la caída más lastimosa.
Literally: Of the highest rise, the shortest fall.
Meaning: The bigger they are, the harder they fall.
No tengas miedo. Recuerda que de la subida más alta es la caída más lastimosa.
Don't be afraid. Remember that the bigger they are, the harder they fall.

De sol a sol
Literally: From sun to sun
Meaning: Sunrise to sunset
El campesino trabaja de sol a sol para alimentar a su familia.
The farmer works from sunrise to sunset to feed his family.

De lo suyo; lo suyo
Literally: Of his
Meaning: By nature, his thing
Andar en bicicleta es lo suyo.
Riding bicycles is his nature.

De tal palo, tal astilla
Literally: From such a log such chips
Meaning: A chip off the old block
Se ve que va a ser muy famoso; de tal palo tal astilla.
You can see that he will be very famous; a chip off the old block.

De todos modos
Literally: Of all ways
Meaning: At any rate
De todos modos, ella no quería ir.
At any rate, she did not want to go.

De un golpe
Literally: Of one blow
Meaning: All at once
Robaron el banco de un golpe.
They robbed the bank all at once.

Dentro de poco
Literally: Inside of little
Meaning: In a little while
Dentro de poco tengo que ir al trabajo.
I have to go to work in a little while.

Desayunar con la noticia
Literally: To have breakfast with the news
Meaning: To get the scoop
No le importó quedarse todo el día con tal de desayunar con la noticia.
In order to get the scoop, she didn't mind staying the whole day.

Desde entonces
Literally: Since then
Meaning: Ever since
Ganó la lotería hace tres meses. No trabaja desde entonces.
He won the lottery three months ago. He has not worked since then.

Desnudar a un santo para vestir al otro.
Literally: To strip bare one saint to clothe another.
Meaning: To rob Peter to pay Paul.
La nueva ley no cambió nada. Desnuda a un santo para vestir al otro.
The new law didn't change anything. It's like robbing Peter to pay Paul.

Después de atole
Literally: After the atole (cornmeal drink)
Meaning: Hindsight is better than foresight.
Después de atole, debería haber manejado mejor la situación.
Hindsight is better than foresight; I should have handled the situation better.

Día de campo
Literally: Countryside day
Meaning: Picnic
Estamos planeando un día de campo con toda la familia.
We're planning a picnic with the entire family.

Día de raya
Literally: Day of stripe
Meaning: Payday
El próximo día de raya me voy de fiesta con todos mis amigos.
Next payday, I'm going out with all my friends.

Donde no (colloquial)
Literally: Where no
Meaning: Otherwise
Ven conmigo, donde no, me iré solo.
Come with me, otherwise, I'll go alone.

Echar al olvido
Literally: To throw to forgetfulness
Meaning: To purposefully forget
Echó al olvido su cita y se fue con sus amigos.
He purposefully forgot his date and went with his friends.

Echar de menos
Literally: To throw less
Meaning: To long for
Ahora que ya no están juntos, él la echa de menos muchísimo.
Now that they are no longer together, he longs for her a lot.

Echar la casa por la ventana
Literally: To throw the house through the window
Meaning: To spare no expense
Ganaremos, aunque tengamos que echar la casa por la ventana.
We will spare no expense in order to win.

Echar la llave
Literally: To throw the key
Meaning: To lock the door
No te olvides de echar la llave cuando salgas.
Don't forget to lock the door when you leave.

Echar una mano
Literally: To throw your hand
Meaning: To seize, to give a helping hand
Échame una mano con la tarea.
Help me with my homework.

Echar un sueño
Literally: To throw a dream
Meaning: To take a nap
Estoy muy cansado; me voy a echar un sueño.
I'm too tired; I'm going to take a nap.

En venta
Literally: Of sale
Meaning: On sale
Tuvieron suerte al encontrar la máquina de lavar en venta.
They were lucky to find the washing machine on sale.

Echar un terno
Literally: To throw a curse
Meaning: To swear, curse
Cuando se enoja, comienza a echar ternos.
When he is mad, he begins to swear.

Echar un trago
Literally: To throw a drink
Meaning: To take a drink
Tanto calor merece echarse un buen trago.
Such heat deserves a good drink.

Echar una siesta
Literally: To throw a siesta
Meaning: To take a siesta or nap
Después de ese gran almuerzo, me dan ganas de echarme una siesta.
After that good lunch, I feel like taking a nap.

El agua es para los bueyes, el vino para los hombres.
Literally: Water is for oxen, wine is for men.
Meaning: Let the fish drink water.
Bebe vino, que el agua es para los bueyes, el vino para los hombres.
Drink wine—let the fish drink water.

El campo fértil no descansado tórnase estéril.
Literally: The unrested fertile field turns sterile.
Meaning: All work and no play makes Jack a dull boy.
No trabajes tanto, que el campo fértil no descansado tórnase estéril.
Don't work so much. All work and no play makes Jack a dull boy.

El día menos pensado
Literally: The day less thought about
Meaning: When least expected
El día menos pensado vengo a visitarte.
I'll come to visit you when it's least expected.

El hijo de la gata ratones mata.
Literally: The son of a cat kills mice.
Meaning: Like father, like son.
No confío en ninguno de ellos. Recuerden que el hijo de la gata ratones mata.
I don't trust any of them, remember—like father, like son.

El perico dice lo que sabe, pero no sabe lo que dice.
Literally: The parrot says what he knows, but doesn't know what he says.
Meaning: To learn something parrot-fashion.
No lo escuches. Recuerda que el perico dice lo que sabe, pero no sabe lo que dice.
Don't listen to him. Remember that he only learns something in parrot fashion.

La puesta de sol
Literally: The setting of sun
Meaning: The setting sun
La puesta de sol se luce en la playa.
The setting sun looks great on the beach.

En caliente y de repente
Literally: In heat and suddenly
Meaning: Strike while the iron's hot.
Ahora que tienes su atención, pide en caliente y de repente.
Now that you have their attention, go ahead and ask—strike while the iron's hot.

En cueros
Literally: In leather
Meaning: Naked, stark naked

Traía el traje de baño tan suelto que se quedó en cueros en la piscina.

Her swimming suit was so loose that she ended up naked in the pool.

En grueso
Literally: In wide
Meaning: In bulk, wholesale

Me gusta comprar las cosas en grueso.

I like to buy things wholesale.

En lo más crudo del invierno
Literally: In the rawest of winter
Meaning: In the dead of winter

En lo más crudo del invierno se me perdieron los guantes.

In the dead of winter I lost my gloves.

En marcha
Literally: In march
Meaning: In progress

Todo está en marcha para la fiesta sorpresa.

Everything is in progress for the surprise party.

En menos de lo que canta un gallo.
Literally: In less time than the rooster crows.
Meaning: In the shake of a lamb's tail.

Yo termino la tarea en menos de lo que canta un gallo.

I'll finish my homework in the shake of a lamb's tail.

En otras palabras
Literally: In other words
Meaning: In other words

En otras palabras, no quiero volver a verte aquí.

In other words, I don't want to see you here anymore.

En pleno día
Literally: In full day
Meaning: In broad daylight

El secuestro ocurrió en pleno día.

The kidnapping took place in broad daylight.

En poder de
Literally: In power of
Meaning: In the hands of

El caso está en poder de los abogados.

The case is in the hands of the lawyers.

En realidad
Literally: In reality
Meaning: As a matter of fact

En realidad, todavía soy menor de edad.

As a matter of fact, I'm still underaged.

En un soplo
Literally: In one blow
Meaning: In a jiffy

El carro me lo reparó en un soplo.

He repaired my car in a jiffy.

En vez de
Literally: In time of
Meaning: Instead of

En vez de un trago me tomé un café.

Instead of a drink I had a cup of coffee.

En voz alta
Literally: In high voice
Meaning: Aloud

La única forma de hablar en el estadio fue en voz alta.

The only way to talk in the stadium was aloud.

Enajenamiento de los sentidos
Literally: Alienation of the senses
Meaning: Loss of consciousness

El choque de los dos futbolistas resultó en un enajenamiento de los sentidos.

The collision between the two soccer players resulted in a loss of consciousness.

Entrada de caballo y salida de burro
Literally: Entering on horseback, exiting on a donkey
Meaning: To go off with a bang and out like a light

El boxeador tuvo una entrada de caballo y salida de burro.

The boxer had an entrance that went off with a bang and out like a light.

Entre paréntesis
Literally: Between parentheses
Meaning: By the way

El juego estuvo tremendo. Entre paréntesis, perdiste la apuesta.

The game was great. By the way, you lost the bet.

Entre tanto
Literally: Between so much
Meaning: Meanwhile, in the meantime

El carro está en la mecánica; entre tanto voy a caminar.

The car is in the shop; in the meantime I'm going to walk.

Es como llevar piedras al cerro.
Literally: It's like carrying rocks up the hill.
Meaning: Like carrying coals to Newcastle.

Tratar de que cambien de pensar es como llevar piedras al cerro.

Trying to change their minds is like carrying coals to Newcastle.

Escribir a máquina
Literally: Write at typewriter
Meaning: To typewrite

En todas mis clases, las tareas tienen que escribirse a máquina.

In all my classes, the homework must be typewritten.

Eso es
Literally: That is
Meaning: That's right

Eso es, no hay nada más que decir.

That's right; there is nothing else to say.

Es el colmo
Literally: It is the overflow
Meaning: That's the limit

Es el colmo; no vuelvo a hablar con ellos.

That's the limit; I will not talk to them again.

Eso es harina de otro costal.
Literally: That's flour from another sack.
Meaning: That's a different story.

Cambiaste de tema. Eso es harina de otro costal.

You changed the subject. That's a different story.

Espuma de jabón
Literally: Suds of soap
Meaning: Suds

No te escondas en la espuma de jabón.

Don't hide in the suds.

Está pensando en las musarañas.
Literally: He or she is thinking about the creepy crawlies.
Meaning: He or she is daydreaming.

¿Qué haces? ¿Estás pensando en las musarañas?

What are you doing? Are you daydreaming?

Estar a la mira de
Literally: Being at the lookout of
Meaning: To be on the lookout for

Estamos a la mira del primer caballo en la carrera.

We're on the lookout for the first horse in the race.

Estar al cabo de
Literally: To be at the end of
Meaning: To be well informed

Estamos al cabo de todos los antecedentes.

We are well informed of the antecedents.

Estar como perro en barrio ajeno
Literally: To be like a dog in a foreign neighborhood
Meaning: To feel like a fish out of water

Él no sabe bailar y se siente como perro en barrio ajeno.

He does not know how to dance and it makes him feel like a fish out of water.

Estar de goma
Literally: To be of rubber
Meaning: To have a hangover

Bebió tanto que está de goma.

He drank so much that he has a hangover.

Estar de malas
Literally: To be of bad
Meaning: To be out of luck

Toda la semana ella ha estado de malas.

She's been unlucky all week.

Estar en camino
Literally: To be on the road
Meaning: To be on the way to something

Está en camino a la grandeza.

He´s on his way to greatness.

Falta de conocimientos
Literally: Lack of knowledge
Meaning: Lack of instructions

Se nota tu falta de conocimientos sobre el tema.

Your lack of knowledge is evident.

Falta lo mero bueno.
Literally: The true good is lacking.
Meaning: We are not out of the woods yet.

Hasta que no veamos tierra falta lo mero bueno.

Until we see land, we are not out of the woods yet.

Fuegos artificiales
Literally: Artificial fires
Meaning: Fireworks

Cada cuatro de julio echamos fuegos artificiales.

Every Fourth of July we light fireworks.

Fuera de propósito
Literally: Out of purpose
Meaning: Irrelevant

El contrato nuevo está fuera de propósito. No estamos hablando de eso.

The new contract is irrelevant. We are not discussing that.

Ganar el gordo
Literally: To win the fat one
Meaning: To hit the jackpot

Tuvo tanta suerte que se ganó el gordo.

She had such good luck that she won the jackpot.

Ganar para comer
Literally: To earn to eat
Meaning: To earn a living

¿Qué piensas hacer para ganar para comer?

How do you plan to earn a living?

Ganar tiempo
Literally: To earn time
Meaning: To save time

Voy a usar la autopista nueva para ganar tiempo.

I'm planning to use the new freeway to save time.

Gato escaldado del agua fría huye.
Literally: The scalded cat flees cold water.
Meaning: Once bitten, twice shy.

No creo que vuelva. Gato escaldado del agua fría huye.

I don't think that he will come back—once bitten, twice shy.

Hace aire.
Literally: It makes air.
Meaning: It is windy.

Hace aire fuerte. Parece que viene una tormenta.

It is very windy; a storm seems to be approaching.

Hace buen tiempo.
Literally: It makes good weather.
Meaning: It is good weather.

Estos últimos días ha hecho buen tiempo.

We've had good weather during these last few days.

Hace frío.
Literally: It makes cold.
Meaning: It is cold.

Hace mucho frío para ser solamente septiembre.

It is too cold for being only September.

Hace mal tiempo.
Literally: It makes bad weather.
Meaning: Weather is bad.

No sé por qué hace mal tiempo.

I don't know why the weather is bad.

Hace mucho tiempo.
Literally: It makes a lot of time
Meaning: A long time ago

Hace mucho tiempo vivió aquí un gran héroe.

A long time ago a great hero lived here.

Hacer cocos
Literally: To make coconuts
Meaning: To make eyes at

Todas las muchachas en la escena le hacen cocos a ese actor.

All the girls on the stage make eyes at the actor.

Hacer cola
Literally: To make a tail
Meaning: To form a line

Tuvimos que hacer cola para conseguir las entradas de la nueva película.

We had to form a line to get tickets to the new movie.

Hacer cuco a
Literally: To do sly things to
Meaning: To make a fool of

Los amigos se reunieron para hacerle cuco al extraño.

The friends got together to make a fool of the stranger.

Hacer falta
Literally: To make want
Meaning: To lack, to be needed, to miss

Me hace falta un dólar.

I need a dollar.

Hacer por escrito
Literally: To make for writing
Meaning: To put into writing
Lo hizo por escrito.
He put it in writing.

Hacer una mala jugada
Literally: To make a bad play
Meaning: To play a bad trick
No se llevan bien desde que el uno le hizo una mala jugada al otro.
They don't get along ever since one played a bad trick on the other.

Haz bien y no mires con quién.
Literally: Do right and don't look with whom.
Meaning: Mind your own business.
Tú solo haz tu trabajo. Haz bien y no mires con quién.
You just do your job and mind your own business.

Huellas digitales
Literally: Digital clues
Meaning: Fingerprints
Encontraron huellas digitales en el arma que estaba cerca del difunto.
They found fingerprints on the firearm found next to the dead man.

Huevos revueltos
Literally: Scrambled eggs
Meaning: Scrambled eggs
Me encantan los huevos revueltos de desayuno.
I love scrambled eggs for breakfast.

Ida y vuelta
Literally: Going and turning
Meaning: Round trip
El viaje de ida y vuelta me costó mil dólares.
The round trip cost me a thousand dollars.

Ímpetu de ira
Literally: Haste of anger
Meaning: Fit of rage
En un ímpetu de ira, golpeó al policía.
He struck the police officer in a fit of rage.

Ir de compras
Literally: To go shopping
Meaning: To go shopping
Hoy tengo que ir de compras.
I need to go shopping today.

Ir para atrás
Literally: To go to the back
Meaning: To back up
Para sacar el carro, tuvo que ir para atrás y para adelante.
He had to back up and pull forward in order to take the car out.

Juego de té
Literally: Game of tea
Meaning: Tea set
Ese juego de té es muy caro.
That tea set is very expensive.

Juego limpio
Literally: A clean game
Meaning: Fair play
Los dos equipos jugaron un juego limpio.
Both teams played a fair game.

Juego sucio
Literally: A dirty game
Meaning: Foul play
No son amigos porque uno de ellos juega sucio.
They are not friends because one of them foul-plays.

Jugador de manos
Literally: Player of hands
Meaning: Juggler
Ese jugador de manos es un artista de calidad.
That juggler is an artist of quality.

Junto a
Literally: Near
Meaning: Near to
Junto a su cuerpo encontraron mucho dinero.
They found a lot of money next to his body.

La carne de burro no es transparente.
Literally: The flesh of the donkey is not transparent.
Meaning: I can't see through you.
No veo. La carne de burro no es transparente.
I can't see, I can't see through you.

La mera idea de
Literally: The very idea of
Meaning: The very idea of
La mera idea de salir de viaje no me agrada.
The very idea of traveling does not appeal to me.

La rutina diaria
Literally: The daily routine
Meaning: The daily grind, the daily routine
> *Ya me cansé de la rutina diaria.*
> I'm tired of the daily grind.

La semana pasada
Literally: Last week
Meaning: Last week
> *Fui de vacaciones la semana pasada.*
> I went on vacation last week.

La semana que viene
Literally: The week that will come
Meaning: Next week
> *La semana que viene tengo otra semana de vacaciones.*
> I have another week of vacation next week.

La verdad clara y desnuda
Literally: The clear and naked truth
Meaning: The whole truth
> *Dime la verdad clara y desnuda.*
> Tell me the whole truth.

Le patina el coco.
Literally: His coconut (head) slips.
Meaning: He has a screw loose, he's crazy.
> *No le escuchen. Le patina el coco.*
> Don't listen to him; he has a screw loose.

Más loco que una cabra
Literally: Crazier than a goat
Meaning: As mad as a hatter
> *Tengan cuidado. Está más loco que una cabra.*
> Be careful, he is as mad as a hatter.

Más vale llegar a tiempo que en convidado.
Literally: It's better to arrive on time than to be invited.
Meaning: First come, first served.
> *Tenemos que apresurarnos, recuerda: más vale llegar a tiempo que en convidado.*
> We need to hurry up, remember: first come, first served.

Más vale pájaro en mano que cien volando.
Literally: A bird in the hand is worth more than a hundred flying.
Meaning: A bird in the hand is worth two in the bush.
> *Dame este pollo flacucho. Más vale pájaro en mano que cien volando.*
> Give me the weak-looking chicken, a bird in the hand is worth two in the bush.

Meter la cuchara
Literally: To put the spoon in
Meaning: To stick one's oar in
> *No metas la cuchara donde no te importa.*
> Don't stick your oar where it doesn't belong.

Entre las patas de los caballos
Literally: Amidst the horses' feet
Meaning: To get out of one's depth
> *Con tantos problemas, me sentí como entre las patas de los caballos.*
> I felt out of depth with all those problems.

Mientras que en mi casa estoy, rey soy.
Literally: While in my house, I am king.
Meaning: A man's house is his castle.
> *Trátenme bien. Mientras que en mi casa estoy, rey soy.*
> Treat me well. A man's house is his castle.

No hay nada tan atrevido como la ignorancia.
Literally: There is nothing bolder than ignorance.
Meaning: Fools rush in where angels fear to tread.
> *Recapacita; no hay nada tan atrevido como la ignorancia.*
> Reflect on it; only fools rush in where angels fear to tread.

Otro gallo nos cantará.
Literally: Another rooster will sing for us.
Meaning: That's a horse of a different color.
> *Acepta la segunda propuesta. Otro gallo nos cantará.*
> Take the second offer. It's a horse of a different color.

Pena de muerte
Literally: Penalty of death
Meaning: Capital punishment
> *Ese crimen merece la pena de muerte.*
> That crime deserves capital punishment.

Perder el juicio
Literally: To lose one's judgment
Meaning: To lose one's mind
> *El joven perdió el juicio al ver a su chica con otro.*

The young man lost his mind when he saw his girlfriend with another man.

Por lo tanto
Literally: For the many
Meaning: Therefore
Ya dijimos todo lo que queríamos. Por lo tanto, no hay nada más que hablar.
We said all that we wanted to say. Therefore, there is nothing else to say.

Por mi parte
Literally: For my part
Meaning: As far as I'm concerned
Por mi parte todo ha terminado.
As far as I'm concerned, everything is finished.

Por su cuenta
Literally: By his account
Meaning: All by himself
Él pagará el coche por su cuenta.
He will pay for the car all by himself.

Por un pelito de rana
Literally: By a little hair of a frog
Meaning: It was a close call.
Se salvó de un accidente por un pelito de rana.
He avoided an accident, but it was a very close call.

Prietitos del mismo arroz
Literally: Little dark things from the same rice
Meaning: It's all in a day's work.
Ayudaremos a nuestros amigos. Son prietitos del mismo arroz.
We will help our friends. It's all in a day's work.

Primeros auxilios
Literally: First helps
Meaning: First aid
Los paramédicos llegaron justo a tiempo para darle primeros auxilios.
The paramedics arrived just in time to provide first aid.

Prohibida la entrada
Literally: Prohibited entrance
Meaning: No trespassing
Está prohibida la entrada al parque al anochecer.
There is no trespassing inside the park after dark.

Pues bien (colloquial)
Literally: Well, good
Meaning: Well, then
Pues bien, me voy a casa.
Well, then, I am going home.

Puesto que
Literally: Then what
Meaning: Since, inasmuch as
Puesto que ya no me necesitan, me voy.
Since they no longer need me, I'm leaving.

Punto de inspección
Literally: Point of inspection
Meaning: Checkpoint
Ese punto de inspección está bien situado.
That checkpoint is well placed.

Quedarse como el que chifló en la loma
Literally: To remain like the one who whistled on the hill
Meaning: To be left holding the bag
Todos se fueron y se quedó como el que chifló en la loma.

Everyone left, and he was left holding the bag.

Quedarse con un pie en el estribo
Literally: To remain with a foot in the stirrup
Meaning: To be left standing
La muchacha no acudió y el muchacho se quedó con un pie en el estribo.
The girl never showed up, and the boy was left standing.

Quien ríe de último, ríe mejor.
Literally: Who laughs the last, laughs best.
Meaning: He who laughs last, laughs best.
No importa. Quien ríe de último, ríe mejor.
It doesn't matter. He who laughs last, laughs best.

Rara vez
Literally: Rare time
Meaning: Seldom
El doctor viene a estos lugares muy rara vez.
The doctor comes here very seldom.

Reírse a carcajadas
Literally: To laugh in a burst
Meaning: To laugh one's head off
La muchacha se rió a carcajadas.
The girl roared with laughter.

Saberlo de buena fuente
Literally: To know it from a good source
Meaning: To hear it straight from the horse's mouth
La secretaria llegó a saberlo de buena fuente que habría un ascenso.
The secretary heard that there would be a promotion straight from the horse's mouth.

Saltarse un semáforo
Literally: To jump the traffic light
Meaning: To run a red light
Recibió una multa porque se saltó un semáforo.
He received a fine because he ran a red light.

Ser más listo que un coyote
Literally: To be more intelligent than a coyote
Meaning: As sharp as a tack
Ese tipo es más listo que un coyote.
That guy is as sharp as a tack.

Ser puente
Literally: To be a bridge
Meaning: To be a long weekend
El viernes es puente. Tenemos cuatro días de fiesta: jueves, viernes, sábado y domingo.
Friday is a holiday. We have four days off: Thursday, Friday, Saturday and Sunday.

Si esta víbora te pica, no hay remedio en la botica.
Literally: If this snake bites you, there's no remedy in the pharmacy.
Meaning: You're playing with fire.
Cuidado que no se entere. Si esa víbora te pica, no hay remedio en la botica.
Be careful that she does not find out. You are playing with fire.

Si mi tía tuviera ruedas, sería una bicicleta.
Literally: If my aunt had wheels, she would be a bicycle.
Meaning: If wishes were horses, beggars would ride.
Tú todavía no sabes de la vida. Si mi tía tuviera ruedas, sería bicicleta.
You still don't know about life. If wishes were horses, beggars would ride.

Tener buena cara
Literally: To have a good face
Meaning: To look well
Debes sentirte mejor. Tienes buena cara.
You must feel better. You look well.

Tener calor
Literally: To have heat
Meaning: To be hot
Tengo calor con tanta ropa.
I'm hot with all these clothes.

Tener celos
Literally: To have jealously
Meaning: To be jealous
Tiene muchos celos de verme con otras muchachas.
She is very jealous to see me with other girls.

Tener el pico de oro
Literally: Have the beak of gold
Meaning: To be eloquent
Todos reconocen que tiene el pico de oro.
Everyone is aware of his eloquence.

Tener en la mente
Literally: To have in the mind
Meaning: To have in mind, to have a thought
¿Tú sabes lo que tengo en la mente?
Do you know what I have in mind?

Tener en poco
Literally: To have in little
Meaning: To hold in low esteem
Él tiene en poco su aspecto físico.
He holds in low esteem his physical appearance.

Tener éxito
Literally: To have success
Meaning: To be successful
Trabajó muy duro para tener éxito.
He worked very hard to be successful.

Tener lugar
Literally: To have place
Meaning: To take place
Esa presentación va a tener lugar en un mes.
That show will take place in a month.

Tener más lana que un borrego
Literally: To have more wool than a lamb
Meaning: To have money to burn
Le fue tan bien en los negocios que tiene más lana que un borrego.
He did so well in his business that he now has money to burn.

Tener vergüenza
Literally: To have shame
Meaning: To be ashamed, to be shy
Ella tiene mucha vergüenza de hablar en público.
She is very shy about speaking in public.

Tirar las riendas
Literally: Throw the reins
Meaning: To tighten the reins
Su madre tira las riendas en su casa.
His mother tightens the reins at home.

Todas las veces
Literally: All the times
Meaning: Whenever
Todas las veces que voy a ese restaurante, salgo demasiado lleno.
Whenever I go inside to that restaurant, I come out too full.

Todo el mundo
Literally: All of the world
Meaning: Everyone
Todo el mundo sabe un poco de español.
Everyone knows a little bit of Spanish.

Todo el tiempo
Literally: All the time
Meaning: All the time
Yo voy de compras todo el tiempo.
I go shopping all the time.

Tomar a pecho
Literally: To take to chest
Meaning: To take to heart, to take it personally
Cuidado con lo que le digas, no vaya a tomarlo a pecho.
Be careful with what you say to him, he might take it to heart.

Un día sí y otro no
Literally: One day yes, and another no
Meaning: Every other day
Tengo un trabajo flexible. Trabajo un día sí y otro no.
My job is very flexible. I work every other day.

Un par de
Literally: A pair of
Meaning: A couple of
Son un par de gemelos.
They are a couple of twins.

Una negativa rotunda
Literally: A negative round
Meaning: A flat denial
No le dieron el préstamo. Fue una negativa rotunda.
They did not give him the loan. It was a flat denial.

Una y otra vez
Literally: One and other time
Meaning: Over and over again
Hace lo mismo una y otra vez.
He does the same thing over and over again.

Uno por uno
Literally: One for one
Meaning: One by one
Repartió los regalos de Navidad uno por uno.
He distributed the Christmas gifts one by one.

Unos pocos
Literally: Some few
Meaning: A few
Tan sólo fueron unos pocos los que fueron escogidos.
Only a few were selected.

Valer la pena
Literally: To be worth the pain
Meaning: To be worthwhile
Valió la pena ir a la playa. porque conocimos a muchas chicas guapas.
Going to the beach was worthwhile, because we met a lot of pretty girls.

Valer más
Literally: To be worth more
Meaning: To be worth more
Algunos objetos antiguos valen más hoy que antes.
Some antiques are worth more today than before.

Varias veces
Literally: Several times
Meaning: Several times
Te llamé por teléfono varias veces.
I called you on the phone several times.

Venta pública
Literally: Public sale
Meaning: Auction
Algunas obras de arte están a la venta pública.
Some works of art are up for auction.

Visto que

Literally: Seeing that
Meaning: Seeing that

Visto que no llegó, me fui sola a la fiesta.

Seeing that he did not arrive, I went to the party on my own.

Vivito y coleando

Literally: Alive and wagging tail
Meaning: Alive and kicking

El otro día vi a Miguel. Él está vivito y coleando.

The other day I saw Miguel. He is alive and kicking.

Volver loco

Literally: To become crazy
Meaning: To drive crazy

Este desorden me vuelve loco.

This mess is driving me crazy.

Yo te conozco bacalao, aunque vengas disfrazado.

Literally: I know you codfish, even though you wear a disguise.
Meaning: I know your game.

No me engañes, que yo te conozco bacalao, aunque vengas disfrazado.

You do not fool me, I know your game.

Appendix D

Verb Tables

hablar—regular AR verb
vender—regular ER verb
vivir—regular IR verb
haber—compound tense verb
almorzar
aparecer
apretar
caber
cerrar
conducir
conocer
continuar
dar
decir
dirigir
dormir
enviar
estar
hacer
ir
huir
oír
oler
reír
saber
seguir
ser
tener
venir
ver

HABLAR (TO SPEAK)
Regular –AR verb

	Present	Subjunctive
yo	hablo	hable
tú	hablas	hables
él	habla	hable
nosotros	hablamos	hablemos
vosotros	habláis	habléis
ellos	hablan	hablen

	Preterite	Imperfect
yo	hablé	hablaba
tú	hablaste	hablabas
él	habló	hablaba
nosotros	hablamos	hablábamos
vosotros	hablasteis	hablabais
ellos	hablaron	hablaban

	Future	Conditional
yo	hablaré	hablaría
tú	hablarás	hablarías
él	hablará	hablaría
nosotros	hablaremos	hablaríamos
vosotros	hablaréis	hablaríais
ellos	hablarán	hablarían

Imperfect Subjunctive	Form 1	Form 2
yo	hablara	hablase
tú	hablaras	hablases
él	hablara	hablase
nosotros	habláramos	hablásemos
vosotros	hablarais	hablaseis
ellos	hablaran	hablasen

	Command	Present Participle
(tú)	habla	hablando
	no hables	
(Ud.)	hable	
(nosotros)	hablemos	Past Participle
(vosotros)	hablad	hablado
	no habléis	
(Uds.)	hablen	

VENDER (TO SELL)
Regular –ER verb

	Present	Subjunctive
yo	vendo	venda
tú	vendes	vendas
él	vende	venda
nosotros	vendemos	vendamos
vosotros	vendéis	vendáis
ellos	venden	vendan

	Preterite	Imperfect
yo	vendí	vendía
tú	vendiste	vendías
él	vendió	vendía
nosotros	vendimos	vendíamos
vosotros	vendisteis	vendíais
ellos	vendieron	vendían

	Future	Conditional
yo	venderé	vendería
tú	venderás	venderías
él	venderá	vendería
nosotros	venderemos	venderíamos
vosotros	venderéis	venderíais
ellos	venderán	venderían

Imperfect Subjunctive	Form 1	Form 2
yo	vendiera	vendiese
tú	vendieras	vendieses
él	vendiera	vendiese
nosotros	vendiéramos	vendiésemos
vosotros	vendierais	vendieseis
ellos	vendieran	vendiesen

	Command	Present Participle
(tú)	vende	vendiendo
	no vendas	
(Ud.)	venda	
(nosotros)	vendamos	Past Participle
(vosotros)	vended	vendido
	no vendáis	
(Uds.)	vendan	

VIVIR (TO LIVE)
Regular –IR verb

	Present	Subjunctive
yo	vivo	viva
tú	vives	vivas
él	vive	viva
nosotros	vivimos	vivamos
vosotros	vivís	viváis
ellos	viven	vivan

	Preterite	Imperfect
yo	viví	vivía
tú	viviste	vivías
él	vivió	vivía
nosotros	vivimos	vivíamos
vosotros	vivisteis	vivíais
ellos	vivieron	vivían

	Future	Conditional
yo	viviré	viviría
tú	vivirás	vivirías
él	vivirá	viviría
nosotros	viviremos	viviríamos
vosotros	viviréis	viviríais
ellos	vivirán	vivirían

Imperfect Subjunctive	Form 1	Form 2
yo	viviera	viviese
tú	vivieras	vivieses
él	viviera	viviese
nosotros	viviéramos	viviésemos
vosotros	vivierais	vivieseis
ellos	vivieran	viviesen

	Command	Present Participle
(tú)	vive	viviendo
	no vivas	
(Ud.)	viva	
(nosotros)	vivamos	Past Participle
(vosotros)	vivid	vivido
	no viváis	
(Uds.)	vivan	

HABER ("TO HAVE" IN COMPOUND TENSES; THERE IS/ARE)
Irregular verb

	Present	Subjunctive
yo	he	haya
tú	has	hayas
él	ha	haya
nosotros	hemos	hayamos
vosotros	habéis	hayáis
ellos	han	hayan

	Preterite	Imperfect
yo	hube	había
tú	hubiste	habías
él	hubo	había
nosotros	hubimos	habíamos
vosotros	hubisteis	habíais
ellos	hubieron	habían

	Future	Conditional
yo	habré	habría
tú	habrás	habrías
él	habrá	habría
nosotros	habremos	habríamos
vosotros	habréis	habríais
ellos	habrán	habrían

Imperfect Subjunctive	Form 1	Form 2
yo	hubiera	hubiese
tú	hubieras	hubieses
él	hubiera	hubiese
nosotros	hubiéramos	hubiésemos
vosotros	hubierais	hubieseis
ellos	hubieran	hubiesen

	Command	Present Participle
(tú)	he	habiendo
	no hayas	
(Ud.)	haya	
(nosotros)	hayamos	Past Participle
(vosotros)	habed	habido
	no hayáis	
(Uds.)	hayan	

ALMORZAR (TO HAVE LUNCH)
Stem-changing (O > UE) and spelling-change (Z > C) –AR verb

	Present	Subjunctive
yo	almuerzo	almuerce
tú	almuerzas	almuerces
él	almuerza	almuerce
nosotros	almorzamos	almorcemos
vosotros	almorzáis	almorcéis
ellos	almuerzan	almuercen

	Preterite	Imperfect
yo	almorcé	almorzaba
tú	almorzaste	almorzabas
él	almorzó	almorzaba
nosotros	almorzamos	almorzábamos
vosotros	almorzasteis	almorzabais
ellos	almorzaron	almorzaban

	Future	Conditional
yo	almorzaré	almorzaría
tú	almorzarás	almorzarías
él	almorzará	almorzaría
nosotros	almorzaremos	almorzaríamos
vosotros	almorzaréis	almorzaríais
ellos	almorzarán	almorzarían

Imperfect Subjunctive	Form 1	Form 2
yo	almorzara	almorzase
tú	almorzaras	almorzases
él	almorzara	almorzase
nosotros	almorzáramos	almorzásemos
vosotros	almorzarais	almorzaseis
ellos	almorzaran	almorzasen

	Command	Present Participle
(tú)	almuerza	almorzando
	no almuerces	
(Ud.)	almuerce	
(nosotros)	almorcemos	Past Participle
(vosotros)	almorzad	almorzado
	no almorcéis	
(Uds.)	almuercen	

APARECER (TO APPEAR)
Spelling-change (C > ZC) –ER verb

	Present	Subjunctive
yo	aparezco	aparezca
tú	apareces	aparezcas
él	aparece	aparezca
nosotros	aparecemos	aparezcamos
vosotros	aparecéis	aparezcáis
ellos	aparecen	aparezcan

	Preterite	Imperfect
yo	aparecí	aparecía
tú	apareciste	aparecías
él	apareció	aparecía
nosotros	aparecimos	aparecíamos
vosotros	aparecisteis	aparecíais
ellos	aparecieron	aparecían

	Future	Conditional
yo	apareceré	aparecería
tú	aparecerás	aparecerías
él	aparecerá	aparecería
nosotros	apareceremos	apareceríamos
vosotros	apareceréis	apareceríais
ellos	aparecerán	aparecerían

Imperfect Subjunctive	Form 1	Form 2
yo	apareciera	apareciese
tú	aparecieras	aparecieses
él	apareciera	apareciese
nosotros	apareciéramos	apareciésemos
vosotros	aparecierais	aparecieseis
ellos	aparecieran	apareciesen

	Command	Present Participle
(tú)	aparece	apareciendo
	no aparezcas	
(Ud.)	aparezca	
(nosotros)	aparezcamos	Past Participle
(vosotros)	apareced	aparecido
	no aparezcáis	
(Uds.)	aparezcan	

CABER (TO FIT)
Irregular –ER verb

	Present	Subjunctive
yo	quepo	quepa
tú	cabes	quepas
él	cabe	quepa
nosotros	cabemos	quepamos
vosotros	cabéis	quepáis
ellos	caben	quepan

	Preterite	Imperfect
yo	cupe	cabía
tú	cupiste	cabías
él	cupo	cabía
nosotros	cupimos	cabíamos
vosotros	cupisteis	cabíais
ellos	cupieron	cabían

	Future	Conditional
yo	cabré	cabría
tú	cabrás	cabrías
él	cabrá	cabría
nosotros	cabremos	cabríamos
vosotros	cabréis	cabríais
ellos	cabrán	cabrían

Imperfect Subjunctive	Form 1	Form 2
yo	cupiera	cupiese
tú	cupieras	cupieses
él	cupiera	cupiese
nosotros	cupiéramos	cupiésemos
vosotros	cupierais	cupieseis
ellos	cupieran	cupiesen

	Present Command	Participle
(tú)	cabe	cabiendo
	no quepas	
(Ud.)	quepa	
(nosotros)	quepamos	Past Participle
(vosotros)	cabed	cabido
	no quepáis	
(Uds.)	quepan	

CERRAR (TO CLOSE)
Stem-changing (E > IE) –AR verb

	Present	Subjunctive
yo	cierro	cierre
tú	cierras	cierres
él	cierra	cierre
nosotros	cerramos	cerremos
vosotros	cerráis	cerréis
ellos	cierran	cierren

	Preterite	Imperfect
yo	cerré	cerraba
tú	cerraste	cerrabas
él	cerró	cerraba
nosotros	cerramos	cerrábamos
vosotros	cerrasteis	cerrabais
ellos	cerraron	cerraban

	Future	Conditional
yo	cerraré	cerraría
tú	cerrarás	cerrarías
él	cerrará	cerraría
nosotros	cerraremos	cerraríamos
vosotros	cerraréis	cerraríais
ellos	cerrarán	cerrarían

Imperfect Subjunctive	Form 1	Form 2
yo	cerrara	cerrase
tú	cerraras	cerrases
él	cerrara	cerrase
nosotros	cerráramos	cerrásemos
vosotros	cerrarais	cerraseis
ellos	cerraran	cerrasen

	Command	Present Participle
(tú)	cierra	cerrando
	no cierres	
(Ud.)	cierre	
(nosotros)	cerremos	Past Participle
(vosotros)	cerrad	cerrado
	no cerréis	
(Uds.)	cierren	

CONDUCIR (TO DRIVE)
Spelling-change (C > ZC) –IR verb; irregular preterite and imperfect subjunctive

	Present	Subjunctive
yo	conduzco	conduzca
tú	conduces	conduzcas
él	conduce	conduzca
nosotros	conducimos	conduzcamos
vosotros	conducís	conduzcáis
ellos	conducen	conduzcan

	Preterite	Imperfect
yo	conduje	conducía
tú	condujiste	conducías
él	condujo	conducía
nosotros	condujimos	conducíamos
vosotros	condujisteis	conducíais
ellos	condujeron	conducían

	Future	Conditional
yo	conduciré	conduciría
tú	conducirás	conducirías
él	conducirá	conduciría
nosotros	conduciremos	conduciríamos
vosotros	conduciréis	conduciríais
ellos	conducirán	conducirían

Imperfect Subjunctive	Form 1	Form 2
yo	condujera	condujese
tú	condujeras	condujeses
él	condujera	condujese
nosotros	condujéramos	condujésemos
vosotros	condujerais	condujeseis
ellos	condujeran	condujesen

	Command	Present Participle
(tú)	conduce	conduciendo
	no conduzcas	
(Ud.)	conduzca	
(nosotros)	conduzcamos	Past Participle
(vosotros)	conducid	conducido
	no conduzcáis	
(Uds.)	conduzcan	

CONOCER (TO KNOW)
Spelling-change (C > ZC) –ER verb

	Present	Subjunctive
yo	conozco	conozca
tú	conoces	conozcas
él	conoce	conozca
nosotros	conocemos	conozcamos
vosotros	conocéis	conozcáis
ellos	conocen	conozcan

	Preterite	Imperfect
yo	conocí	conocía
tú	conociste	conocías
él	conoció	conocía
nosotros	conocimos	conocíamos
vosotros	conocisteis	conocíais
ellos	conocieron	conocían

	Future	Conditional
yo	conoceré	conocería
tú	conocerás	conocerías
él	conocerá	conocería
nosotros	conoceremos	conoceríamos
vosotros	conoceréis	conoceríais
ellos	conocerán	conocerían

Imperfect Subjunctive	Form 1	Form 2
yo	conociera	conociese
tú	conocieras	conocieses
él	conociera	conociese
nosotros	conociéramos	conociésemos
vosotros	conocierais	conocieseis
ellos	conocieran	conociesen

	Command	Present Participle
(tú)	conoce no conozcas	conociendo
(Ud.)	conozca	
(nosotros)	conozcamos	Past Participle
(vosotros)	conoced no conozcáis	conocido
(Uds.)	conozcan	

CONTINUAR (TO CONTINUE)
Regular –AR verb, irregular accentuation

	Present	Subjunctive
yo	continúo	continúe
tú	continúas	continúes
él	continúa	continúe
nosotros	continuamos	continuemos
vosotros	continuáis	continuéis
ellos	continúan	continúen

	Preterite	Imperfect
yo	continué	continuaba
tú	continuaste	continuabas
él	continuó	continuaba
nosotros	continuamos	continuábamos
vosotros	continuasteis	continuabais
ellos	continuaron	continuaban

	Future	Conditional
yo	continuaré	continuaría
tú	continuarás	continuarías
él	continuará	continuaría
nosotros	continuaremos	continuaríamos
vosotros	continuaréis	continuaríais
ellos	continuarán	continuarían

Imperfect Subjunctive	Form 1	Form 2
yo	continuara	continuase
tú	continuaras	continuases
él	continuara	continuase
nosotros	continuáramos	continuásemos
vosotros	continuarais	continuaseis
ellos	continuaran	continuasen

	Command	Present Participle
(tú)	continúa no continúes	continuando
(Ud.)	continúe	
(nosotros)	continuemos	Past Participle
(vosotros)	continuad no continuéis	continuado
(Uds.)	continúen	

DAR (TO GIVE)
Irregular –AR verb

	Present	Subjunctive
yo	doy	dé
tú	das	des
él	da	dé
nosotros	damos	demos
vosotros	dais	deis
ellos	dan	den

	Preterite	Imperfect
yo	di	daba
tú	diste	dabas
él	dio	daba
nosotros	dimos	dábamos
vosotros	disteis	dabais
ellos	dieron	daban

	Future	Conditional
yo	daré	daría
tú	darás	darías
él	dará	daría
nosotros	daremos	daríamos
vosotros	daréis	daríais
ellos	darán	darían

Imperfect Subjunctive	Form 1	Form 2
yo	diera	diese
tú	dieras	dieses
él	diera	diese
nosotros	diéramos	diésemos
vosotros	dierais	dieseis
ellos	dieran	diesen

	Command	Present
Participle		
(tú)	da	dando
	no des	
(Ud.)	dé	
(nosotros)	demos	Past
Participle		
(vosotros)	dad	dado
	no deis	
(Uds.)	den	

DECIR (TO SAY)
Irregular –IR verb

	Present	Subjunctive
yo	digo	diga
tú	dices	digas
él	dice	diga
nosotros	decimos	digamos
vosotros	decís	digáis
ellos	dicen	digan

	Preterite	Imperfect
yo	dije	decía
tú	dijiste	decías
él	dijo	decía
nosotros	dijimos	decíamos
vosotros	dijisteis	decíais
ellos	dijeron	decían

	Future	Conditional
yo	diré	diría
tú	dirás	dirías
él	dirá	diría
nosotros	diremos	diríamos
vosotros	diréis	diríais
ellos	dirán	dirían

Imperfect Subjunctive	Form 1	Form 2
yo	dijera	dijese
tú	dijeras	dijeses
él	dijera	dijese
nosotros	dijéramos	dijésemos
vosotros	dijerais	dijeseis
ellos	dijeran	dijesen

	Command	Present Participle
(tú)	di	diciendo
	no digas	
(Ud.)	diga	
(nosotros)	digamos	Past
Participle		
(vosotros)	decid	dicho
	no digáis	
(Uds.)	digan	

DIRIGIR (TO DIRECT)
Spelling-change (G > J) –IR verb

	Present	Subjunctive
yo	dirijo	dirija
tú	diriges	dirijas
él	dirige	dirija
nosotros	dirigimos	dirijamos
vosotros	dirigís	dirijáis
ellos	dirigen	dirijan

	Preterite	Imperfect
yo	dirigí	dirigía
tú	dirigiste	dirigías
él	dirigió	dirigía
nosotros	dirigimos	dirigíamos
vosotros	dirigisteis	dirigíais
ellos	dirigieron	dirigían

	Future	Conditional
yo	dirigiré	dirigiría
tú	dirigirás	dirigirías
él	dirigirá	dirigiría
nosotros	dirigiremos	dirigiríamos
vosotros	dirigiréis	dirigiríais
ellos	dirigirán	dirigirían

Imperfect Subjunctive	Form 1	Form 2
yo	dirigiera	dirigiese
tú	dirigieras	dirigieses
él	dirigiera	dirigiese
nosotros	dirigiéramos	dirigiésemos
vosotros	dirigierais	dirigieseis
ellos	dirigieran	dirigiesen

	Command	Present Participle
(tú)	dirige no dirijas	dirigiendo
(Ud.)	dirija	
(nosotros)	dirijamos	Past Participle
(vosotros)	dirigid no dirijáis	dirigido
(Uds.)	dirijan	

DORMIR (TO SLEEP)
STEM-CHANGING (O > UE) –IR VERB

	Present	Subjunctive
yo	duermo	duerma
tú	duermes	duermas
él	duerme	duerma
nosotros	dormimos	durmamos
vosotros	dormís	durmáis
ellos	duermen	duerman

	Preterite	Imperfect
yo	dormí	dormía
tú	dormiste	dormías
él	durmió	dormía
nosotros	dormimos	dormíamos
vosotros	dormisteis	dormíais
ellos	durmieron	dormían

	Future	Conditional
yo	dormiré	dormiría
tú	dormirás	dormirías
él	dormirá	dormiría
nosotros	dormiremos	dormiríamos
vosotros	dormiréis	dormiríais
ellos	dormirán	dormirían

Imperfect Subjunctive	Form 1	Form 2
yo	durmiera	durmiese
tú	durmieras	durmieses
él	durmiera	durmiese
nosotros	durmiéramos	durmiésemos
vosotros	durmierais	durmieseis
ellos	durmieran	durmiesen

	Command	Present Participle
(tú)	duerme no duermas	durmiendo
(Ud.)	duerma	
(nosotros)	durmamos	Past Participle
(vosotros)	dormid no durmáis	dormido
(Uds.)	duerman	

ENVIAR (TO SEND)
Regular –AR verb with irregular accentuation

	Present	Subjunctive
yo	envío	envíe
tú	envías	envíes
él	envía	envíe
nosotros	enviamos	enviemos
vosotros	enviáis	enviéis
ellos	envían	envíen

	Preterite	Imperfect
yo	envié	enviaba
tú	enviaste	enviabas
él	envió	enviaba
nosotros	enviamos	enviábamos
vosotros	enviasteis	enviabais
ellos	enviaron	enviaban

	Future	Conditional
yo	enviaré	enviaría
tú	enviarás	enviarías
él	enviará	enviaría
nosotros	enviaremos	enviaríamos
vosotros	enviaréis	enviaríais
ellos	enviarán	enviarían

Imperfect Subjunctive	Form 1	Form 2
yo	enviara	enviase
tú	enviaras	enviases
él	enviara	enviase
nosotros	enviáramos	enviásemos
vosotros	enviarais	enviaseis
ellos	enviaran	enviasen

	Command	Present Participle
(tú)	envía no envíes	enviando
(Ud.)	envíe	
(nosotros)	enviemos	Past Participle
(vosotros)	enviad no enviéis	enviado
(Uds.)	envíen	

ESTAR (TO BE)
Irregular –AR verb

	Present	Subjunctive
yo	estoy	esté
tú	estás	estés
él	está	esté
nosotros	estamos	estemos
vosotros	estáis	estéis
ellos	están	estén

	Preterite	Imperfect
yo	estuve	estaba
tú	estuviste	estabas
él	estuvo	estaba
nosotros	estuvimos	estábamos
vosotros	estuvisteis	estabais
ellos	estuvieron	estaban

	Future	Conditional
yo	estaré	estaría
tú	estarás	estarías
él	estará	estaría
nosotros	estaremos	estaríamos
vosotros	estaréis	estaríais
ellos	estarán	estarían

Imperfect Subjunctive	Form 1	Form 2
yo	estuviera	estuviese
tú	estuvieras	estuvieses
él	estuviera	estuviese
nosotros	estuviéramos	estuviésemos
vosotros	estuvierais	estuvieseis
ellos	estuvieran	estuviesen

	Command	Present Participle
(tú)	está no estés	estando
(Ud.)	esté	
(nosotros)	estemos	Past Participle
(vosotros)	estad no estéis	estado
(Uds.)	estén	

HACER (TO DO, TO MAKE)
Irregular –ER verb

	Present	Subjunctive
yo	hago	haga
tú	haces	hagas
él	hace	haga
nosotros	hacemos	hagamos
vosotros	hacéis	hagáis
ellos	hacen	hagan

	Preterite	Imperfect
yo	hice	hacía
tú	hiciste	hacías
él	hizo	hacía
nosotros	hicimos	hacíamos
vosotros	hicisteis	hacíais
ellos	hicieron	hacían

	Future	Conditional
yo	haré	haría
tú	harás	harías
él	hará	haría
nosotros	haremos	haríamos
vosotros	haréis	haríais
ellos	harán	harían

Imperfect Subjunctive	Form 1	Form 2
yo	hiciera	hiciese
tú	hicieras	hicieses
él	hiciera	hiciese
nosotros	hiciéramos	hiciésemos
vosotros	hicierais	hicieseis
ellos	hicieran	hiciesen

	Command	Present Participle
(tú)	haz	haciendo
	no hagas	
(Ud.)	haga	
(nosotros)	hagamos	Past Participle
(vosotros)	haced	hecho
	no hagáis	
(Uds.)	hagan	

IR (TO GO)
Irregular –IR verb

	Present	Subjunctive
yo	voy	vaya
tú	vas	vayas
él	va	vaya
nosotros	vamos	vayamos
vosotros	vais	vayáis
ellos	van	vayan

	Preterite	Imperfect
yo	fui	iba
tú	fuiste	ibas
él	fue	iba
nosotros	fuimos	íbamos
vosotros	fuisteis	ibais
ellos	fueron	iban

	Future	Conditional
yo	iré	iría
tú	irás	irías
él	irá	iría
nosotros	iremos	iríamos
vosotros	iréis	iríais
ellos	irán	irían

Imperfect Subjunctive	Form 1	Form 2
yo	fuera	fuese
tú	fueras	fueses
él	fuera	fuese
nosotros	fuéramos	fuésemos
vosotros	fuerais	fueseis
ellos	fueran	fuesen

	Command	Present Participle
(tú)	ve	yendo
	no vayas	
(Ud.)	vaya	
(nosotros)	vamos	Past Participle
	no vayamos	ido
(vosotros)	id	
	no vayáis	
(Uds.)	vayan	

HUIR (TO FLEE)
Irregular –IR verb

	Present	Subjunctive
yo	huyo	huya
tú	huyes	huyas
él	huye	huya
nosotros	huimos	huyamos
vosotros	huís	huyáis
ellos	huyen	huyan

	Preterite	Imperfect
yo	huí	huía
tú	huiste	huías
él	huyó	huía
nosotros	huimos	huíamos
vosotros	huisteis	huíais
ellos	huyeron	huían

	Future	Conditional
yo	huiré	huiría
tú	huirás	huirías
él	huirá	huiría
nosotros	huiremos	huiríamos
vosotros	huiréis	huiríais
ellos	huirán	huirían

Imperfect Subjunctive	Form 1	Form 2
yo	huyera	huyese
tú	huyeras	huyeses
él	huyera	huyese
nosotros	huyéramos	huyésemos
vosotros	huyerais	huyeseis
ellos	huyeran	huyesen

	Command	Present
Participle		
(tú)	huye	huyendo
	no huyas	
(Ud.)	huya	
(nosotros)	huyamos	Past
Participle		
(vosotros)	huid	huido
	no huyáis	
(Uds.)	huyan	

OÍR (TO HEAR)
Irregular –IR verb

	Present	Subjunctive
yo	oigo	oiga
tú	oyes	oigas
él	oye	oiga
nosotros	oímos	oigamos
vosotros	oís	oigáis
ellos	oyen	oigan

	Preterite	Imperfect
yo	oí	oía
tú	oíste	oías
él	oyó	oía
nosotros	oímos	oíamos
vosotros	oísteis	oíais
ellos	oyeron	oían

	Future	Conditional
yo	oiré	oiría
tú	oirás	oirías
él	oirá	oiría
nosotros	oiremos	oiríamos
vosotros	oiréis	oiríais
ellos	oirán	oirían

Imperfect Subjunctive	Form 1	Form 2
yo	oyera	oyese
tú	oyeras	oyeses
él	oyera	oyese
nosotros	oyéramos	oyésemos
vosotros	oyerais	oyeseis
ellos	oyeran	oyesen

	Command	Present
Participle		
(tú)	oye	oyendo
	no oigas	
(Ud.)	oiga	
(nosotros)	oigamos	Past
Participle		
(vosotros)	oíd	oído
	no oigáis	
(Uds.)	oigan	

OLER (TO SMELL)
Irregular stem-changing (O > UE) –ER verb

	Present	Subjunctive
yo	huelo	huela
tú	hueles	huelas
él	huele	huela
nosotros	olemos	olamos
vosotros	oléis	oláis
ellos	huelen	huelan

	Preterite	Imperfect
yo	olí	olía
tú	oliste	olías
él	olió	olía
nosotros	olimos	olíamos
vosotros	olisteis	olíais
ellos	olieron	olían

	Future	Conditional
yo	oleré	olería
tú	olerás	olerías
él	olerá	olería
nosotros	oleremos	oleríamos
vosotros	oleréis	oleríais
ellos	olerán	olerían

Imperfect Subjunctive	Form 1	Form 2
yo	oliera	oliese
tú	olieras	olieses
él	oliera	oliese
nosotros	oliéramos	oliésemos
vosotros	olierais	olieseis
ellos	olieran	oliesen

	Command	Present Participle
(tú)	huele / no huelas	oliendo
(Ud.)	huela	
(nosotros)	olamos	Past Participle
(vosotros)	oled / no oláis	olido
(Uds.)	huelan	

REÍR (TO LAUGH)
Irregular –IR verb

	Present	Subjunctive
yo	río	ría
tú	ríes	rías
él	ríe	ría
nosotros	reímos	riamos
vosotros	reís	riáis
ellos	ríen	rían

	Preterite	Imperfect
yo	reí	reía
tú	reíste	reías
él	rió	reía
nosotros	reímos	reíamos
vosotros	reísteis	reíais
ellos	rieron	reían

	Future	Conditional
yo	reiré	reiría
tú	reirás	reirías
él	reirá	reiría
nosotros	reiremos	reiríamos
vosotros	reiréis	reiríais
ellos	reirán	reirían

Imperfect Subjunctive	Form 1	Form 2
yo	riera	riese
tú	rieras	rieses
él	riera	riese
nosotros	riéramos	riésemos
vosotros	rierais	rieseis
ellos	rieran	riesen

	Command	Present Participle
(tú)	ríe / no rías	riendo
(Ud.)	ría	
(nosotros)	riamos	Past Participle
(vosotros)	reíd / no riáis	reído
(Uds.)	rían	

SABER (TO KNOW)
Irregular –ER verb

	Present	Subjunctive
yo	sé	sepa
tú	sabes	sepas
él	sabe	sepa
nosotros	sabemos	sepamos
vosotros	sabéis	sepáis
ellos	saben	sepan

	Preterite	Imperfect
yo	supe	sabía
tú	supiste	sabías
él	supo	sabía
nosotros	supimos	sabíamos
vosotros	supisteis	sabíais
ellos	supieron	sabían

	Future	Conditional
yo	sabré	sabría
tú	sabrás	sabrías
él	sabrá	sabría
nosotros	sabremos	sabríamos
vosotros	sabréis	sabríais
ellos	sabrán	sabrían

Imperfect Subjunctive	Form 1	Form 2
yo	supiera	supiese
tú	supieras	supieses
él	supiera	supiese
nosotros	supiéramos	supiésemos
vosotros	supierais	supieseis
ellos	supieran	supiesen

	Command	Present
Participle		
(tú)	sabe	sabiendo
	no sepas	
(Ud.)	sepa	
(nosotros)	sepamos	Past
Participle		
(vosotros)	sabed	sabido
	no sepáis	
(Uds.)	sepan	

SEGUIR (TO FOLLOW, TO CONTINUE)
Stem-changing (E > I) and spelling-change (GU > G) –IR verb

	Present	Subjunctive
yo	sigo	siga
tú	sigues	sigas
él	sigue	siga
nosotros	seguimos	sigamos
vosotros	seguís	sigáis
ellos	siguen	sigan

	Preterite	Imperfect
yo	seguí	seguía
tú	seguiste	seguías
él	siguió	seguía
nosotros	seguimos	seguíamos
vosotros	seguisteis	seguíais
ellos	siguieron	seguían

	Future	Conditional
yo	seguiré	seguiría
tú	seguirás	seguirías
él	seguirá	seguiría
nosotros	seguiremos	seguiríamos
vosotros	seguiréis	seguiríais
ellos	seguirán	seguirían

Imperfect Subjunctive	Form 1	Form 2
yo	siguiera	siguiese
tú	siguieras	siguieses
él	siguiera	siguiese
nosotros	siguiéramos	siguiésemos
vosotros	siguierais	siguieseis
ellos	siguieran	siguiesen

	Command	Present
Participle		
(tú)	sigue	siguiendo
	no sigas	
(Ud.)	siga	
(nosotros)	sigamos	Past
Participle		
(vosotros)	seguid	seguido
	no sigáis	
(Uds.)	sigan	

SER (TO BE)
Irregular –ER verb

	Present	Subjunctive
yo	soy	sea
tú	eres	seas
él	es	sea
nosotros	somos	seamos
vosotros	sois	seáis
ellos	son	sean

	Preterite	Imperfect
yo	fui	era
tú	fuiste	eras
él	fue	era
nosotros	fuimos	éramos
vosotros	fuisteis	erais
ellos	fueron	eran

	Future	Conditional
yo	seré	sería
tú	serás	serías
él	será	sería
nosotros	seremos	seríamos
vosotros	seréis	seríais
ellos	serán	serían

Imperfect Subjunctive	Form 1	Form 2
yo	fuera	fuese
tú	fueras	fueses
él	fuera	fuese
nosotros	fuéramos	fuésemos
vosotros	fuerais	fueseis
ellos	fueran	fuesen

Participle	Command	Present
(tú)	sé	siendo
	no seas	
(Ud.)	sea	
(nosotros)	seamos	Past Participle
(vosotros)	sed	sido
	no seáis	
(Uds.)	sean	

TENER (TO HAVE)
Irregular –ER verb

	Present	Subjunctive
yo	tengo	tenga
tú	tienes	tengas
él	tiene	tenga
nosotros	tenemos	tengamos
vosotros	tenéis	tengáis
ellos	tienen	tengan

	Preterite	Imperfect
yo	tuve	tenía
tú	tuviste	tenías
él	tuvo	tenía
nosotros	tuvimos	teníamos
vosotros	tuvisteis	teníais
ellos	tuvieron	tenían

	Future	Conditional
yo	tendré	tendría
tú	tendrás	tendrías
él	tendrá	tendría
nosotros	tendremos	tendríamos
vosotros	tendréis	tendríais
ellos	tendrán	tendrían

Imperfect Subjunctive	Form 1	Form 2
yo	tuviera	tuviese
tú	tuvieras	tuvieses
él	tuviera	tuviese
nosotros	tuviéramos	tuviésemos
vosotros	tuvierais	tuvieseis
ellos	tuvieran	tuviesen

Participle	Command	Present
(tú)	ten	teniendo
	no tengas	
(Ud.)	tenga	
(nosotros)	tengamos	Past Participle
(vosotros)	tened	tenido
	no tengáis	
(Uds.)	tengan	

VENIR (TO COME)
Irregular stem-changing (E > IE) –IR verb

	Present	Subjunctive
yo	vengo	venga
tú	vienes	vengas
él	viene	venga
nosotros	venimos	vengamos
vosotros	venís	vengáis
ellos	vienen	vengan

	Preterite	Imperfect
yo	vine	venía
tú	viniste	venías
él	vino	venía
nosotros	vinimos	veníamos
vosotros	vinisteis	veníais
ellos	vinieron	venían

	Future	Conditional
yo	vendré	vendría
tú	vendrás	vendrías
él	vendrá	vendría
nosotros	vendremos	vendríamos
vosotros	vendréis	vendríais
ellos	vendrán	vendrían

Imperfect Subjunctive	Form 1	Form 2
yo	viniera	viniese
tú	vinieras	vinieses
él	viniera	viniese
nosotros	viniéramos	viniésemos
vosotros	vinierais	vinieseis
ellos	vinieran	viniesen

	Command	Present
Participle		
(tú)	ven	viniendo
	no vengas	
(Ud.)	venga	
(nosotros)	vengamos	Past
Participle		
(vosotros)	venid	venido
	no vengáis	
(Uds.)	vengan	

VER (TO SEE)
Irregular –ER verb

	Present	Subjunctive
yo	veo	vea
tú	ves	veas
él	ve	vea
nosotros	vemos	veamos
vosotros	veis	veáis
ellos	ven	vean

	Preterite	Imperfect
yo	vi	veía
tú	viste	veías
él	vio	veía
nosotros	vimos	veíamos
vosotros	visteis	veíais
ellos	vieron	veían

	Future	Conditional
yo	veré	vería
tú	verás	verías
él	verá	vería
nosotros	veremos	veríamos
vosotros	veréis	veríais
ellos	verán	verían

Imperfect Subjunctive	Form 1	Form 2
yo	viera	viese
tú	vieras	vieses
él	viera	viese
nosotros	viéramos	viésemos
vosotros	vierais	vieseis
ellos	vieran	viesen

	Command	Present
Participle		
(tú)	ve	viendo
	no veas	
(Ud.)	vea	
(nosotros)	veamos	Past
Participle		
(vosotros)	ved	visto
	no veáis	
(Uds.)	vean	

Appendix E

Answer Key

Chapter 5

Practicing Conjugations

1. *Yo abro la puerta para entrar.* (I open the door to come in.)
2. *Nosotros debemos estudiar mejor.* (We should study better.)
3. *Sandra y sus amigas caminan hacia la parada de autobús.* (Sandra and her friends are walking to the bus stop.)
4. *¿Ustedes asisten a las charlas del profesor Juárez?* (Do you attend the lectures of Professor Juarez?)
5. *Yo estudio los fines de semana.* (I study on weekends.)
6. *Carlos, ¿por qué (tú) acudes a las reuniones?* (Carlos, why do you do you go to the meetings?)
7. *Juan promete hacer sus tareas.* (Juan promises to do his chores.)
8. *Mañana (nosotros) caminamos al trabajo.* (Tomorrow we will walk to work.)
9. *Usted siempre cumple con sus promesas.* (You always keep your promises.)
10. *Yo aprendo la lección.* (I am learning the lesson.)
11. *Tú bebes demasiado.* (You drink too much.)
12. *Ellas buscan la calle Main.* (They are looking for Main Street.)
13. *¿Ustedes trabajan en la ciudad?* (Do you work in the city?)
14. *Él recibe cartas cada día.* (He receives letters every day.)
15. *Yo vivo feliz aquí.* (I live happily here.)

Chapter 6

Figure It Out

1. We are Italian. We live in Rome.
2. They are very interesting guys.
3. Three minus one is two.
4. I am a designer in a large company.
5. You are Elena's parents.

Chapter 7

Prepositions and Estar

1. I am here with a friend.
   Estoy aquí con un amigo.
2. We are returning with Rita.
   Regresamos con Rita.
3. Today I am not having luck.
   Hoy no estoy de suerte.

4. She is cold.
   Ella está con frío.
5. I am in a hurry.
   Estoy de prisa.

Ser or Estar?

1. We are sick.
   Nosotros estamos enfermos.
2. Miguel's friend is French.
   El amigo (La amiga) de Miguel es francés (francesa).
3. I am very tired.
   Estoy muy cansado (cansada).
4. I am a calm person.
   Soy una persona tranquila.
5. Venezuelans are friendly.
   Los venezolanos son amistosos.

Chapter 8

A Little Time Travel

1. *El señor Ochoa y su esposa hablaban con su vecino a menudo.*
   Mr. Ochoa and his wife talked (used to talk) to their neighbor often.
2. *En dos días, yo volveré a España.*
   In two days, I'll return to Spain.
3. *Si hiciera frío, tú te cubrirías con la manta.*
   If it were cold, you would cover yourself with a blanket.
4. *Cuando éramos pequeños, vivíamos en un apartamento y no en una casa, como ahora.*
   When we were little, we lived in an apartment and not in a house, like now.

5. *Marina contestó que nunca volvería a aquel lugar.*
   Marina answered that she would never return to that place.
6. *Si él abriera la puerta, tú entrarías adentro.*
   if he would open the door, you would enter inside.
7. *Yo pasé tres años en Nueva York.*
   I passed three years in New York.
8. *Nosotros nunca hemos tenido la oportunidad de hablar con él.*
   We have never had the opportunity to talk to him.

Chapter 9

Practice Counting

1.	*dieciocho*	18
2.	*veintidós*	22
3.	*cincuenta y cuatro*	54
4.	*noventa y tres*	93
5.	*ciento catorce*	114
6.	*doscientos setenta y nueve*	279
7.	*quinientos sesenta y dos*	562
8.	*setecientos treinta y cinco*	735

1.	18	*dieciocho*
2.	89	*ochenta y nueve*
3.	226	*doscientos veintiséis*
4.	345	*trescientos cuarenta y cinco*
5.	1,512	*mil quinientos doce*
6.	10,587	*diez mil quinientos ochenta y siete*
7.	22,713	*veintidós mil setecientos trece*
8.	3,080,000	*tres millones ochenta mil*

Days of the Week

1. Yesterday I was sick. (all day, but not today)
   Ayer estuve enfermo (enferma).
2. Saturday, I was with Elena
   El sábado estaba (or estuve) con Elena.
3. Sunday I will be in Florida.
   El domingo estaré en Florida.
4. I am better since last week.
   Estoy mejor desde la semana pasada.
5. I work Tuesdays.
   Trabajo los martes.
6. The birthday party is on the twenty-fifth.
   La fiesta de cumpleaños es el veinticinco.

¿Cuáles son los meses del año?

1. January is the first month of the year.
   Enero es el primer mes del año.
2. May is the fifth month of the year.
   Mayo es el quinto mes del año.
3. September is the ninth month of the year.
   Septiembre es el noveno mes del año.
4. I was in Europe for two years.
   Estuve en Europa dos años.
5. I am thinking about going to Mexico next December.
   Estoy pensando ir a México el diciembre próximo.
6. Each June I am ready to travel.
   Cada junio estoy listo (lista) para viajar.

What Time Is It?

1. It's a quarter to three in the afternoon.
   Son las tres menos cuarto de la tarde.
2. It's seven-thirty in the morning.
   Son las siete y media de la mañana.
3. It's midnight.
   Es (la) medianoche.
4. 14:36
   Son las tres menos veinticuatro de la tarde.
5. 8:23
   Son las ocho y veintitrés de la mañana.
6. 4:42
   Son las cinco menos dieciocho de la madrugada.

Chapter 10

Working with Tener

1. I have to drive the car.
   Tengo que conducir el coche.
2. You (formal) will have to go at four.
   Usted tendrá que ir a las cuatro.
3. They had to read the book (and did).
   Ellos tuvieron que leer el libro.
4. I have to dance with Fabian.
   Tengo que bailar con Fabián.
5. You (informal) have to attend the wedding.
   Tú tienes que asistir a la boda.

Working with Acabar

1. I finish work at three.
   Acabo el trabajo a las tres.
2. I have just finished eating.
   Acabo de comer.
3. They have just finished conversing.
   Acaban de conversar.
4. She has just lost her keys.
   Ella acaba de perder las llaves.
5. You (formal, plural) finished on time.
   Ustedes acabaron a tiempo.

Using Ir

1. We intend to wait for them in the store.
   Vamos a esperarles en la tienda.
2. I am going to listen to the music.
   Voy a escuchar la música.
3. She is going to go to the concert today.
   Ella va a ir al concierto hoy.
4. They were going to swim, but it did not happen.
   Iban a nadar, pero no ocurrió.
5. We are going to leave on vacation.
   Vamos a salir de vacaciones.

Using Saber and Conocer

1. I know how old Antonio is.
   Sé cuántos años tiene Antonio.
2. María knows how to drive well.
   María sabe conducir bien.
3. I don't know his brother.
   No conozco a su hermano.
4. We know that respect and communication are essential in a relationship.
   Sabemos que el respeto y la comunicación son esenciales en una relación.
5. He knows Acapulco well because he travels there a lot.
   Él conoce Acapulco bien porque viaja allí mucho.

Chapter 11

Verb Practice #1

1. I rent my dwelling.
   Arriendo mi vivienda.

2. What (are) you (informal, singular) think(ing)?
   ¿En qué piensas?
3. Today you (formal) start the new job.
   Hoy comienza el nuevo trabajo.
4. On Fridays we scrub the floors.
   Los viernes fregamos los pisos.
5. They want to go out to eat.
   Ellos quieren salir a comer.
6. We warn of the danger.
   Advertimos del peligro.

Verb Practice #2

1. I eat lunch at noon.
   Almuerzo al mediodía.
2. Tomorrow they fly to San Diego.
   Mañana ellos vuelan a San Diego.
3. I hang the shirts.
   Cuelgo las camisas.
4. You (informal, singular) show houses.
   Muestras casas.
5. She finds a coin on the floor.
   Ella encuentra una moneda en el piso.
6. I don't dream much.
   No sueño mucho.

Verb Practice #3

1. I (am) boil(ing) eggs.
   Hiervo huevos.
2. We elect the president.
   Elegimos al presidente.
3. You (formal, plural) always follow all the rules.
   Ustedes siempre siguen todas las reglas.
4. They follow the soaps.
   Ellos siguen las telenovelas.

5. You (informal, plural) are dressing a baby.
   Vestís a un bebé.
6. How tall are you (informal, singular)?
   (Literally: How much do you measure?)
   ¿Cuánto mides?

Chapter 12

Verb Practice #4

1. I take the small piece.
   Cojo el pedazo pequeño.
2. I choose the yellow apple.
   Escojo la manzana amarilla.
3. I protect the family.
   Protejo a la familia.
4. I gather the clothes from the floor.
   Recojo la ropa del piso.
5. I demand attention.
   Exijo atención.

Verb Practice #5

1. Intolerance destroys society.
   La intolerancia destruye la sociedad.
2. You (plural, formal) construct homes.
   Construyen casas.
3. We flee from the police.
   Huimos de la policía.
4. Michelle contributes to her church.
   Michelle contribuye a su iglesia.
5. You (informal, singular) flee from
   responsibility.
   Huyes de la responsabilidad.

Verb Practice #6

1. I give thanks for the help.
   Ofrezco gracias por la ayuda.
2. I do exercises in the morning.
   Hago ejercicios por la mañana.
3. I obey the rules.
   Obedezco las reglas.
4. The cow produces milk.
   La vaca produce leche.
5. The radio program introduces new singers.
   El programa de radio introduce a cantantes nuevos.

Verb Practice #7

1. I send Christmas cards.
   Envío tarjetas de Navidad.
2. Marcela adopts a kitten.
   Marcela ahíja a un gatito.
3. The story continues for another thirty pages.
   El cuento continúa otras treinta páginas.
4. Sandra pets the zoo animals.
   Sandra acaricia a los animales del zoológico.
5. Adam and Berta study medicine.
   Adán y Berta estudian medicina.

Verb Practice #8

1. I hear noises at night.
   Oigo ruidos por la noche.
2. Do you (formal, singular) hear her?
   ¿Usted la oye?
3. Ricardo does exercises at night.
   Ricardo hace ejercicios por la noche.
4. They come to visit.
   Ellos vienen de visita.
5. You (informal, plural) come to visit your parents.
   Venís para visitar a sus padres.

Chapter 13

Object Pronouns

1. You (formal, singular) have two cars.
   Usted tiene dos coches. Los tiene.
2. I am looking for the street.
   Busco la calle. La busco.
3. He makes the beds.
   Él hace las camas. Las hace.
4. I put the book on the shelf.
   Pongo el libro en la repisa. Lo pongo en la repisa.
5. Mr. Muñoz, I will see you tomorrow.
   Sr. Muñoz, lo veo a usted mañana. Lo veo.

Using the Personal A

1. I see Ignacio, Amanda, and Pedro.
   Yo veo a Ignacio, Amanda, y Pedro.
2. Who(m) do you (informal, singular) love?
   ¿A quién amas?
3. They have a daughter.
   Tienen una hija.
4. I am a citizen of the United States.
   Soy ciudadano de los Estados Unidos.
5. I love my cat.
   Amo a mi gato.

Indirect-Object Pronouns

1. I purchased him a beverage.
   Le compré una bebida. Se la compré.
2. I will send you kisses.
   Te mandaré besos. Te los mandaré.
3. I brought you (formal, plural) the book.
   Les traje el libro. Se los traje.
4. I show Berta the painting.
   Muestro la pintura a Berta. Se la muestro.

5. I told her all the news.
   Le dije todas la noticias. Se las dije todas.

Chapter 14

Ser in Possessive Constructions

1. It is my sweater.
   Es mi saco.
2. The telephone is his.
   El teléfono es suyo.
3. They're my trousers.
   Son mis pantalones.
4. They're (feminine) yours (informal).
   Son tuyas.
5. Good grades will be mine.
   Las buenas notas serán mías.
6. The eyeglasses are his.
   Los anteojos son suyos.

Members of the Family

1. The Garcías were my neighbors last year.
   Los García fueron mis vecinos el año pasado.
2. I (fem.) am your friend.
   Yo soy tu amiga.
3. He is my husband.
   Él es mi marido.
4. They are my children.
   Ellos son mis hijos.
5. I (masc.) am yours.
   Yo soy tuyo.

Working with Diminutives

1. *el padre* (the father)—*el padrecito*
2. *la piedra* (the rock)—*la piedrecita*
3. *el nieto* (the grandson)—*el nietecito*

4. *el caballo* (the horse)—*el caballito*
5. *pobre* (poor)—*pobrecito*

Chapter 15

Verb Practice #9

1. I searched for my book.
   Busqué mi libro.
2. He read the newspaper.
   Él leyó el periódico.
3. They believed the worst.
   Ellos creyeron lo peor.
4. I practiced all day.
   Yo practiqué todo el día.
5. You (formal) possessed courage.
   Usted poseyó valor.

Verb Practice #10

1. We drove to the party.
   Condujimos a la fiesta.
2. The salesman repeated the offer.
   El vendedor repitió la oferta.
3. Did you (informal, singular) translate the speech?
   ¿Tradujiste el discurso?
4. She introduced her friends.
   Ella introdujo a sus amigos.
5. They slept all day.
   Ellos durmieron toda el día.

Verb Practice #11

1. We gave Susy the gift.
   Dimos el regalo a Susy.
2. I placed the key on the table.
   Puse la llave sobre la mesa.

3. You (informal, plural) wanted a steak.
   Quisiste un bistec.
4. Julio came to Vita's birthday party.
   Julio vino a la fiesta de cumpleaños de Vita.
5. You (formal, singular) knew it.
   Usted lo supo.

Verb Practice #12

1. I abstracted the ideas from the book.
   Abstraje las ideas del libro.
2. We contracted the measles.
   Contrajimos el sarampión.
3. You (informal, plural) walked along the path that day.
   Vosotros anduvisteis por el camino aquel día.
4. You (informal, singular) distracted the driver.
   Distrajiste al conductor.
5. They heard the noise from far (away).
   Ellos oyeron el ruido desde lejos.

Verb Practice #13

1. I have opened an account.
   He abierto una cuenta.
2. She has put one hundred dollars in the account.
   Ella ha puesto cien dólares en la cuenta.
3. They have done the work.
   Ellos han hecho el trabajo.
4. You (formal, singular) have satisfied the requirements.
   Usted ha satisfecho los requisitos.
5. We have returned to university.
   Hemos vuelto a la universidad.

Verb Practice #14

1. Will you (informal, singular) make the bed?
   ¿Harás la cama?

2. My parents will come on Tuesday.
   Mis padres vendrán el martes.
3. We will not be able to walk more.
   No podremos caminar más.
4. You (informal, singular) will leave soon.
   Saldrás pronto.
5. They will want to wash their clothes.
   Ellos querrán lavar su ropa.

Chapter 16

Reviewing the Imperative

1. Listen (you, informal/singular) to the news!
   ¡Escucha las noticias!
2. Let's decide on a movie!
   ¡Decidamos qué película!
3. Wait (you, formal/singular) for me at the door!
   ¡Espéreme en la puerta!
4. Come (you, informal, singular) here!
   ¡Ven aquí!
5. Don't cry (you, informal/plural)!
   ¡No lloréis!
6. Look for (you, formal/singular) the key!
   ¡Busque la llave!
7. Don't put (you, informal/plural) it (masculine) here!
   ¡No lo pongáis aquí!
8. Let's travel to Mexico together!
   ¡Viajemos a México juntos!
9. Don't buy (you, formal/singular) it for her! *¡No se lo compre a ella!*
10. Bring (you, formal/plural) it to me!
    ¡Tráiganmelo!

A Subjunctive Matter

1. Dudo que este empleo pague mucho.
   I doubt this job pays much.
2. Es malo que nosotros no estemos listos.
   It's bad that we aren't ready.
3. *Es posible que el presidente no esté en la Casa Blanca, pero no lo creo.*
   It's possible the president isn't in the White House, but I don't believe it.
4. *Me gusta que ella viva en este vecindario.*
   I like that she lives in this neighborhood.
5. *Los estudiantes piden que el director de la escuela sustituya al nuevo profesor por otro.*

   The students ask that the principal substitute the new teacher with some other.
6. *Yo dudo que sea posible entrar por esta puerta sin ningún ruido.*
   I doubt that it's possible to enter through this door without any noise.
7. *No hay duda de que la película empiece en un momento.*
   There's no doubt that the movie will begin in a moment.
8. *Es interesante que vosotros pagueis tanto dinero por estos boletos.*
   It's interesting that you (would) pay so much money for those tickets.

Chapter 17

¿Qué te gusta?

1. You (informal, plural) like talking with your friends.
   Os gusta hablar con vuestros amigos.

2. They like to work.
   A ellos les gusta trabajar.
3. We like rice and chicken.
   A nosotros nos gustan el arroz y el pollo.
4. You (informal, singular) used to like the Johnsons.
   Te gustaban los Johnsons.
5. You (formal, plural) liked Spain.
   A ustedes les gustó España.

Yes or No?

1. I always eat vegetables.
   Siempre como vegetales.
2. I never eat vegetables.
   Nunca como vegetales.
3. Someone waits for you.
   Alguien te espera.
4. No one is here.
   Nadie está aquí.
5. At times, Fred and Ginger go out dancing.
   A veces, Fred y Ginger salen a bailar.

Practice What You've Learned

1. I was lacking courage.
   Me faltaba ánimo.
2. My head hurts.
   Me duele la cabeza.
3. Do you (informal, singular) miss your automobile?
   ¿Echas de menos tu automóvil?
4. We are interested in learning Spanish.
   Nos interesa aprender español.
5. Are you (informal, plural) pleased by romantic films?
   ¿Os agradan las películas románticas?

Listening to Music

1. We like to play CDs.
   Nos gusta tocar los CDs.
2. I listen to the news on the radio.
   Escucho las noticias en el/la radio.
3. They enjoy listening to Elvis Crespo and Carlos Vives.
   Ellos disfrutan escuchando a Elvis Crespo y Carlos Vives.
4. The CD player has headphones and two speakers.
   El tocadiscos CD tiene auriculares y dos altavoces.

Log On in Spanish

1. I turn on my computer every day
   . *Enciendo mi computadora cada día.*
2. She connects to the Web to read her e-mail.
   Ella se conecta a la Web para leer su correo electrónico.
3. Do you also search for interesting Web sites?
   ¿También busca usted sitios interesantes en la Web?
4. They chat with their brother on weekends.
   Ellos chatean con su hermano los fines de semana.
5. Humberto cannot start the computer because his brother changed the configuration.
   Humberto no puede encender el ordenador (la computadora) porque su hermano cambió la configuración.

Chapter 18

¡Qué fácil!

1. What a tall young man!
   ¡Qué joven tan alto!
2. What a sad story!
   ¡Qué cuento más triste!
3. How far she swims!
   ¡Qué lejos nada ella!
4. How lazy she is!
   ¡Qué perezosa es ella!
5. What a car!
   ¡Qué coche!

¡Cuánto sabes!

1. How much they ran!
   ¡Cuánto corrieron!
2. How I want to be tall!
   ¡Cuánto quiero ser alto!
3. How Marco and Lucía smoked!
   ¡Cuánto fumaron Marco y Lucía!
4. How much I wanted to eat!
   ¡Cuánto quería comer!
5. How many chores we have!
   ¡Cuántas tareas tenemos!

¡Cómo comparas!

1. You (informal, singular) sing as well as my sister.
   Tú cantas tan bien como mi hermana.
2. I have as many coins as you.
   Tengo tantas monedas como tú.
3. There is less work than people.
   Hay menos trabajo que gente.

4. Julio has more experience than Pedro.
   Julio tiene más experiencia que Pedro.
5. You (formal, singular) is older than Jenny.
   Usted es mayor que Jenny.

Chapter 19

The Daily Routine

1. I get up at ten at night.
   Me levanto a las diez de la noche.
2. We wash our hair every morning.
   Nos lavamos el pelo cada mañana.
3. Did you (informal, singular) shave your head?
   ¿Te afeitaste la cabeza?
4. I rinse my mouth after brushing my teeth.   *Me enjuago la boca después de lavarme los dientes.*
5. Leticia applies makeup on her eyes.
   Leticia se maquilla los ojos.

Reflecting on the Verb

1. He complained about the noise.
   Se quejó del ruido.
2. When are you (informal, plural) leaving to Florida?
   ¿Cuándo os vais a Florida?
3. She dares to steal.
   Ella se atreve a robar.
4. You (formal, singular) sit down.
   Usted se sienta.
5. She is called Nancy.
   Ella se llama Nancy.

What Color Is It?

Sample answers:

1. ¿De qué color es tu baño?
   Mi baño es blanco.
2. ¿De qué color son tus chanclas?
   Mis chanclas son anaranjadas.
3. ¿De qué color son tus sábanas?
   Mis sábanas son verdes oscuras.
4. ¿De qué color son tus cortinas?
   Las cortinas son pardas.
5. ¿De qué color es tu coche?
   Mi coche es azul.

A Sample Letter

Dear friend,

You don't know how happy I am to receive your new address. Too much time has passed since the last time that we talked. How is everybody? Your mother and father? I hope they are well. What's new? I hope that I see you all the next time that I travel over there.

I also remember all those times that we chatted. I hope to do it again, soon.

With all my affection,

Lisa

Index

Note: Verbs conjugated in the text are shown in Spanish.

The Everything® Language Series

YOU SHOULD CAREFULLY READ THE FOLLOWING TERMS AND CONDITIONS BEFORE USING THIS SOFTWARE PRODUCT. INSTALLING AND USING THIS PRODUCT INDICATES YOUR ACCEPTANCE OF THESE CONDITIONS. IF YOU DO NOT AGREE WITH THESE TERMS AND CONDITIONS, DO NOT INSTALL THE SOFTWARE AND RETURN THIS PACKAGE PROMPTLY FOR A FULL REFUND.

1. Grant of License
This software package is protected under United States copyright law and international treaty. You are hereby entitled to one copy of the enclosed software and are allowed by law to make one backup copy or to copy the contents of the disks onto a single hard disk and keep the originals as your backup or archival copy. United States copyright law prohibits you from making a copy of this software for use on any computer other than your own computer. United States copyright law also prohibits you from copying any written material included in this software package without first obtaining the permission of F+W Publications, Inc.

2. Restrictions
You, the end-user, are hereby prohibited from the following:
You may not rent or lease the Software or make copies to rent or lease for profit or for any other purpose.
You may not disassemble or reverse compile for the purposes of reverse engineering the Software.
You may not modify or adapt the Software or documentation in whole or in part, including, but not limited to, translating or creating derivative works.

3. Transfer
You may transfer the Software to another person, provided that (a) you transfer all of the Software and documentation to the same transferee; (b) you do not retain any copies; and (c) the transferee is informed of and agrees to the terms and conditions of this Agreement.

4. Termination
This Agreement and your license to use the Software can be terminated without notice if you fail to comply with any of the provisions set forth in this Agreement. Upon termination of this Agreement, you promise to destroy all copies of the software including backup or archival copies as well as any documentation associated with the Software. All disclaimers of warranties and limitation of liability set forth in this Agreement shall survive any termination of this Agreement.

5. Limited Warranty
F+W Publications, Inc. warrants that the Software will perform according to the manual and other written materials accompanying the Software for a period of 30 days from the date of receipt. F+W Publications, Inc. does not accept responsibility for any malfunctioning computer hardware or any incompatibilities with existing or new computer hardware technology.

6. Customer Remedies
F+W Publications, Inc.'s entire liability and your exclusive remedy shall be, at the option of F+W Publications, Inc., either refund of your purchase price or repair and/or replacement of Software that does not meet this Limited Warranty. Proof of purchase shall be required. This Limited Warranty will be voided if Software failure was caused by abuse, neglect, accident or misapplication. All replacement Software will be warranted based on the remainder of the warranty or the full 30 days, whichever is shorter and will be subject to the terms of the Agreement.

7. No Other Warranties
F+W PUBLICATIONS, INC., TO THE FULLEST EXTENT OF THE LAW, DISCLAIMS ALL OTHER WARRANTIES, OTHER THAN THE LIMITED WARRANTY IN PARAGRAPH 5, EITHER EXPRESS OR IMPLIED, ASSOCIATED WITH ITS SOFTWARE, INCLUDING BUT NOT LIMITED TO IMPLIED WARRANTIES OF MERCHANTABILITY AND FITNESS FOR A PARTICULAR PURPOSE, WITH REGARD TO THE SOFTWARE AND ITS ACCOMPANYING WRITTEN MATERIALS. THIS LIMITED WARRANTY GIVES YOU SPECIFIC LEGAL RIGHTS. DEPENDING UPON WHERE THIS SOFTWARE WAS PURCHASED, YOU MAY HAVE OTHER RIGHTS.

8. Limitations on Remedies
TO THE MAXIMUM EXTENT PERMITTED BY LAW, F+W PUBLICATIONS, INC. SHALL NOT BE HELD LIABLE FOR ANY DAMAGES WHATSOEVER, INCLUDING WITHOUT LIMITATION, ANY LOSS FROM PERSONAL INJURY, LOSS OF BUSINESS PROFITS, BUSINESS INTERRUPTION, BUSINESS INFORMATION OR ANY OTHER PECUNIARY LOSS ARISING OUT OF THE USE OF THIS SOFTWARE.
This applies even if F+W Publications, Inc. has been advised of the possibility of such damages. F+W Publications, Inc.'s entire liability under any provision of this agreement shall be limited to the amount actually paid by you for the Software. Because some states may not allow for this type of limitation of liability, the above limitation may not apply to you.
THE WARRANTY AND REMEDIES SET FORTH ABOVE ARE EXCLUSIVE AND IN LIEU OF ALL OTHERS, ORAL OR WRITTEN, EXPRESS OR IMPLIED. No F+W Publications, Inc. dealer, distributor, agent, or employee is authorized to make any modification or addition to the warranty.

9. General
This Agreement shall be governed by the laws of the United States of America and the Commonwealth of Massachusetts. If you have any questions concerning this Agreement, contact F+W Publications, Inc., via Adams Media at 508-427-7100. Or write to us at: Adams Media, an F+W Publications Company, 57 Littlefield Street, Avon, MA 02322.